Seeking God

Seeking God

A Mystic's Way

Michael H. Mitias

RESOURCE *Publications* · Eugene, Oregon

SEEKING GOD
A Mystic's Way

Copyright © 2012 Michael H. Mitias. All rights reserved. Except for brief quotations in critical publications or reviews, no part of this book may be reproduced in any manner without prior written permission from the publisher. Write: Permissions, Wipf and Stock Publishers, 199 W. 8th Ave., Suite 3, Eugene, OR 97401.

Resource Publications
An Imprint of Wipf and Stock Publishers
199 W. 8th Ave., Suite 3
Eugene, OR 97401
www.wipfandstock.com

ISBN 13: 978-1-62032-477-6
Manufactured in the U.S.A.

All scripture quotations, unless otherwise indicated, are taken from the Holy Bible, New International Version®, NIV®. Copyright ©1973, 1978, 1984 by Biblica, Inc.™ Used by permission of Zondervan. All rights reserved worldwide.

To Necip Fikri Alican

Contents

Acknowledgment ix

1. On the Way to Tadmur 1
2. Al Basiri Oasis 19
3. Supper at Saleem's House 46
4. Al Naseri Mountain 69
5. In Saada 102
6. On the Way to Amana Mountain 117
7. Amana Mountain 126
8. The Storm 191

   Bibliography 195

Acknowledgment

Dr. Necip Fikri Alican has meticulously read the manuscript and made many linguistic and conceptual changes, without which the text would have been severely defective; but I assume full responsibility for any mistake that might have slipped from his attention. To him I owe a handsome debt of gratitude, and to him, a man distinguished by a genuine love of truth, a refined sense of scholarship, and a warm human heart, I dedicate this book with a heartfelt satisfaction.

chapter 1

On the Way to Tadmur

IN ONE OF HIS most enigmatic but insightful lectures, my Aesthetics professor said that The Eternal reveals itself profoundly in the mystery of its infinite abundance, grace, and power in the Syrian Desert, and that you can feel the charm of its mystery when you allow your imagination to soar in the sky of its depth and glide on the waves of its yellow sand as it welcomes the dancing rays of the morning sun. Held gently within the arms of this charm, you can feel the harmony of its rhythm, the brilliance of its splendor, and the intensity of its depth; you can delve deep into the heart of that depth and gaze at the sun that glitters in the dark of Being; and you can sit on the edge, on that infinite edge, under the light of that glitter and listen to the song of The Eternal. And, yes, you can hear the silent song of The Master as he conducts the symphony of the divine realm during the act of cosmic creation. There, if you listen to the music with your heart, you will feel a surge of life streaming through your veins and a flood of light glowing in your mind. You become a ray of divine light, a pulse in the life of The Eternal, a fountain of being. You become joy without feeling the exhilaration of joy; you become understanding without knowing that you understand; and you become a lover without feeling the urge of love. In that state, the sting of desire, the ghost of fear, and the specter of loneliness vanish from your heart. A feeling of peace prevails, not the peace of ordinary silence, but of life, of fulfillment. This is your ultimate object of love and desire, and this is your destiny.

Frankly, I did not understand what my professor meant by this remark, which I still have in my files, even though I reflected on it several times in the past several years, to the extent that it remained alive in my memory and sat on the horizon of my consciousness as a kind of guard always reminding me, especially when I was studying physics and philosophy, of the supreme significance of the idea of The Eternal and the need to comprehend the world and the meaning of human life from its standpoint. The more I progressed in my study of the nature of physical reality and humanity, the more I became aware of the urgent need to expand my understanding of The Eternal. My mind was always moving from one horizon of reflection to another, from one horizon of being to another. Every time I tried to see what lay beyond the existing horizon of consciousness another was waiting for me! I found myself driven to a search for the final horizon which embraces every imaginable, or possible, horizon, as if this final horizon contained the secret of the world as we know it. I confess that in time I became a captive to this search, because I developed, without knowing how or why, an insatiable appetite to know what lies beyond, or inside, this world of ours. I felt that such knowledge would shed some light on what I am and why I exist, especially why my life is short, indeed a flicker in some kind of everlasting fire.

Now, having devoted many years of theoretical and existential reflection on the nature and meaning of my life, on whether the kind of life I led is in any way justifiable, I came to the conclusion that I am a flicker of light that is at once infinitely luminous and a twinkle that will soon fade into nothingness. Yes, I stand before myself as a paradox in the mirror of my own life. How can I explain this paradox? Well, how can I answer this question if I do not pay a visit to that final horizon in whose bosom the answer to my question must necessarily lie? But how? I have read the theories of the major philosophers and physicists with an eye on a possible answer, or maybe on a clue, but I could not find any! What I found were views, descriptions, and explanations of this or that phenomenon of nature or human life, but not of their ultimate source. Some thinkers dared to raise the question of the source of the world as a whole; they devised impressive logical, methodological, and conceptual tools to analyze and answer the question, but the answers they advanced were mostly naïve and at best hypothetical. How can we hypothesize on the nature of the final horizon if we do not stand on the edge that overlooks its realm, if we do not have some kind of encounter with it? This realization, which was gradually unfolding in my mind, kept my professor's remark forcefully active in the sphere of my consciousness. It stood there staring at me with its wide open, wild eyes every time my mind gravitated toward the question of the meaning and destiny of the world, especially my own life.

I have always thought that my desire to know this two-fold destiny was not an end in itself but a means to an end, and the end was simply to know why and how I should live as long as this flicker should shine. It is really pathetic, indeed tragic, for a human being to live and die without knowing why she lived and died, regardless of how she felt during her lifetime. I do not mind the fact that all I am is a flicker, but I have an irresistible desire to know why I am a flicker. I really want to shine as luminously as I can before I fade into nothingness, and I want to be as true as I can to the light that glows from my heart. I have reached this conviction, which became firmly established in my mind, after a long and critical examination of the importance and meaning of human life. The majority of people around me do not even raise the question of their destiny; they seek pleasure, power, health, wealth, knowledge, and fame without wondering whether the life they lead is justifiable. They simply immerse themselves in the river of social existence without questioning the source and destiny of this river. It may well be the case that I am the one who is wrong in my way of thinking and they are the ones who are right. This possibility did not escape my attention, and I think there is a good reason to entertain it; for, after all, this is how the majority of human beings have been living since the dawn of civilization. Honestly, I thought about this fact for a long time and was tempted to follow in their footsteps, but I could not, not only because I kept reverting to my professor's enigmatic advice, which became, as time marched on, a kind of warning; it acquired this character because its logic seemed to me unquestionable. It is quite possible that the logic I rely on in my thinking is at bottom faulty and that there is another, superior logic that surpasses mine in delivering the truth of our experience of ourselves and the world.

Let me explain to you how I felt last night when I was in the heat of scrutinizing my professor's advice to pay a visit to the Syrian Desert in the hope of discovering an answer to my questions. I want you, please, to imagine a rose bud in the early period of its inception and later on growth. In late winter and early spring it begins to swell. At first it is a bit timid, because the conditions under which it can grow—temperature, soil, light, chemicals—are not quite conducive to its development. But when spring advances, when these and other conditions become appropriate, then it begins to bulge and in time to unsheathe itself and burst into a rose: It blossoms! The course of development proceeds according to a logic implicit in its genetic make-up and the laws that govern the mechanism of its growth. Its identity as a rose exists at first as a potentiality in the embryo and comes into being when the conditions of its fulfillment are fulfilled, when this potentiality is actualized. Let me tell you that I feel like this rose! Let me tell you that my life story is similar to the life story of this rose. Ever since I opened my eyes to the world at the peak of my adolescence, I felt a strong desire to be myself without yet knowing what it means to be a self and what kind of self I should be. When, for reasons I still cannot comprehend, I proceeded into the process of growing up as a human being, this desire increased in its strength and determination; it generated a subterranean feeling of restlessness. At first, I could not explain its source or goal. But then, when I began my study of the humanities, and, later on, when I devoted much time to philosophical inquiry, I paid serious attention to this feeling. It was kindled by my professor's lectures on metaphysics and aesthetics and especially his remarks on The Eternal. He did not mean that The Eternal reveals itself only in the Syrian Desert; no, for him, it reveals itself in every element of reality, be it natural or human. I think he chose the Syrian Desert for emphasis, as I surmised later on, because he himself felt its presence acutely when he paid a visit to the historical sites of that part of the world. In fact, I took what my professor said about The Eternal seriously. Accordingly I decided at that early stage in my life to devote myself to the study of philosophy and physics, because I discovered that these two academic disciplines inquire into the nature and ground of the universe.

Well, here I am, almost close to the end of the road I have chosen for my life. My body is wrinkled up, my hair is white, and, though I am still strong, my physical health is waning. To my sad surprise, I can report that the extensive inquiry I have undertaken into these two disciplines, not to mention my personal adventures in the course of my daily living, did not deliver any answers to my questions. The restlessness with which I began my life as a young man did not leave me; on the contrary, it increased as I charged into my fifties and especially as I look with some anxiety at the prospect of my retirement in the not too distant future. But now having exhausted the fund of my theoretical and practical wisdom I have so far accumulated, I made a decision to heed my professor's advice, to pay a visit to the Syrian Desert and explore the possibility of having an encounter with The Eternal there. I did not, in making this decision, intend to act the way the early Greeks did in seeking answers to recalcitrant questions by going to the Oracle at Delphi, for there are no oracles, experts, or clinics for answering such questions.

I made my decision without knowing or planning my adventure. How can we have an adventure of any kind if we proceed into it from a rigid plan? The only idea that loomed vividly in my mind was this: If my professor did have an experience of The Eternal in the desert, I should be able to have one. But then, would this kind of experience deliver answers to the questions I had? I could not answer this question, but I felt deep in my heart that, regardless of the outcome, it would be a worthwhile experience: What would I lose even if I did not experience The Eternal in the desert? In fact the voice of reason clearly said that it would be a most valuable experience, because growth in knowledge is always beneficial in trying to realize the projects of our lives. Another question forced itself upon my mind in the midst of my deliberations: What if your questions are finally answered, what if the answers you will discover, or perhaps stumble on, show that the life you have so far lived is not the right kind of life, what then? To tell the truth, I was gravely perturbed when I reflected on this question, and yet I was not discouraged by the possibility that the life I have so far led was not the right kind of life, because I always believed that it is never too late to do what is good and right and to avoid what bad and wrong! Implicit in this belief is the conviction, from which I never wavered, that human life is an adventure, an adventure of creation, and that I should never shrink from the challenge of creation, especially the creation of my life, regardless of the consequences. Moreover, I have always acted on the principle that we should not judge a person on the basis of the "mistakes" she has made but on the basis of her attempt to grow as a human being, and to produce the greatest amount of good in her life and in the lives of others. Most of the time, mistakes are defined by society, whose judgment is frequently vague, subjective, limited, one-sided, and lacks objective verification. However, human growth is defined by reason, by the inner demands of human nature to grow from within, to become the human beings we should be. The more we succeed in meeting these demands, the more we grow as human individuals. Success in human growth should in the end be the criterion we rely on in doing what is good and right.

Encouraged by the understanding these reflections prompted in my mind, I decided, shortly after we concluded the spring semester last year, to make my eastward journey toward the Syrian Desert. I chose to travel by ship, mainly because a trip of this nature would give me an urgently needed respite from my daily concerns and an opportunity to enjoy the beauty of the sea, especially the Mediterranean Sea, which I had never seen before. Having stopped first in Marseilles, France, and then in Napoli, Italy, my ship cast anchor at Latakia, an ancient Phoenician city. There I visited Ugarit, the cradle of Phoenician civilization, and a number of Greek, Roman, and early Arab historical sites. I still remember how I walked in the narrow streets of that city exploring its houses, shops, cemeteries, and public buildings. It was a ghost town, but I could breathe the air of Phoenician culture and feel the spirit of its people everywhere I walked. More than once, I touched the stones of its walls and felt the wild flowers that grew in the crevices that time carved between them. I felt the presence of the past in these stones; I felt the life of a people pulsating in their grain! Alas! The human spirit lingers in what it creates!

My short visit to that old historical landmark was, without being directly aware of its cultural significance, critically valuable for the achievement of my purpose; it enabled me to assume a sympathetic, objective attitude to this part of the world and to see and feel things as they are in themselves. You see, when you assume this kind of attitude, you can see with innocent eyes, feel with a pure heart, and appreciate what you experience without the influence of individual biases and prejudices. Innocent human beings live according to the laws of nature, spontaneously, modestly, and passionately. They love life in all its seasons, in good and bad times, as a gift to be appreciated and cherished. I gradually discovered that this kind of attitude is a necessary condition for experiencing the beauty and mystery of nature and humanity.

The manager of Meridian Hotel, where I stayed during my visit to Latakia, helped me secure a bus ticket to Tadmur, formerly known as Palmyra. The bus stopped for about an hour in the city of Homs. There, I learned that Syria was home to a number of civilizations: Aramean, Phoenician, Assyrian, Greek, Roman, Byzantine, and Arab civilizations. No wonder the people in that country were predominantly cosmopolitan in their social outlook and behavior. I wish I could have spent more time exploring and feeling the spirit of the different cultures that thrived in that country, but I could not, because I was preoccupied with the desert and the gift it had waiting for me. As the bus left the Alawite Mountain, which extends from southern Turkey to central Syria, and slowly moved into the heart of the desert, I began to see why my professor recommended the Syrian Desert as an appropriate place for having an encounter with The Eternal. The terrain that stretched between Homs and Tadmur is rugged, flat, and barren, except for some dry riverbeds and hilly patches scattered on both sides of the road. The azure sky, which arched over the desert as a beautiful summer umbrella, joined hands in harmonious oneness with the distant horizon. It seemed to me that the bus had a rendezvous with the horizon, because it was the only object I could see around me and in front of me, no matter where I looked.

It occurred to me, as I contemplated this scene, that this rendezvous was not with the horizon but with the infinite itself, and, further, that participation required an existential change of attitude, of attention, a change away from the concerns of quotidian life, in which people usually hop from one demand to another, and away from the urban environment, in which they move from one built structure to another, to an open world, to a world of pure being; in which our minds, hearts, and bodies experience the pulse of life freely; in which we are able to feel ourselves, to be in touch with ourselves, and to feel the natural elements that buzz on every side of our being; and in which we are able to glean that we are the ones who feel, think, wonder, ask questions, and care about the meaning of our lives.

As the bus drove deeper into the desert and turned its back to the social existence that filled my consciousness, I felt a gush of life, perhaps of fire, gliding in my veins. I felt its warmth, and I felt its exuberance. It seemed as though it was energizing every cell of my blood. It reached my temples, which began to throb forcefully, and then my cheeks, which began to burn with passion. My heart felt its impact: I felt thirsty! A gentle warm breeze playfully caressed my eyes. My mind was aflame with a desire to feel and to know! What stretched around me as a limitless expanse of barren land was suddenly transformed into a vibrant vista of loveliness. Yes, space! Have you ever experienced space in its purity and simplicity? An indefinable feeling of longing crept into my consciousness. It did not have a recognizable object but appeared as a force in need of guidance, and yet it was a feeling of longing, of reaching out for something I urgently needed. It appeared as if it came from the depth of my being, from a box hidden somewhere in its treasure chest. Its appearance was similar to the appearance of a significant idea that was buried in memory or to an important desire that was dormant in the subconscious. I tried my best to take hold of this feeling with the intention of discovering its aim or source, but I could not. My mind felt restless and my heart anxious. For a second, it seemed that I was swept by a quiet storm of passion, because every part of my being was feeling the pangs of longing, as if it were crying for something vitally important, for something indispensable for my survival.

Tremors of change, novel to my consciousness, reverberated through my psychological constitution. I felt them in the way my mind was thinking; in its alacrity, sense of direction, and sharpness of perception; in the way my senses were reacting to the changing spectacle around me; in their ability to grasp the color, shape, and magnitude of the objects of this spectacle; and in the way I was feeling, in the fact that this spectacle was not a configuration of dead matter but a living scene radiating a peculiar kind of importance: Meaning! In the middle of this state of exhilaration a subtle feeling of guilt surfaced in my mind, yes, guilt, because I instantly recognized that I had, until that moment, expelled from the sphere of my growth and development as a human being, a supremely important dimension of human experience: Nature. For the first time I began to notice that nature is a world, a distinctive domain of being, and that the book of this domain is a treasure of beauty, mystery, and life. Getting acquainted with this treasure, trying to understand it and feel the variety of truths and values implicit in it, should be a source of deep satisfaction, not the kind we derive from pleasure or from short-lived titillations, but the kind that intensifies our inner being, that expands the horizon of the mind, magnifies the capacities of feeling, and enhances the sense of appreciating beauty, truth, and goodness. I have always thought that we grow as human beings only when we seek and realize this kind of satisfaction. I was not aware of it at first; I was in a state of reverie. The power of this revelation opened my eyes to the being of nature and the treasure hidden within its womb. A strong interest began to emerge in my mind; it dragged with it a load of desire to explore this treasure. I did not merely think, infer, or speculate about the existence and nature of this being; I saw it, I felt it. The feeling that was generated by my experience of it suffused my mind. How could I, or anyone, remain indifferent to it after having this kind of experience? I have always believed that perception entails a recognition, an admission, or a kind of assertion that something is the case. How could I ignore what I saw and felt? I resolved there and then to experience nature and try to understand it in all its aspects, not with the mind of the physicist or the geologist but with the mind of the lover who is inflamed with desire to feel, to know, to appreciate his beloved for what she is. How else can anyone be or love his beloved? Most people, even some scientists, tend to think that the spectacle of nature is an appearance without an internal being, or a soul. Frankly, I have been, until this moment, one of those people. No, nature has a life of its own, not in the sense that it gives rise to botanical and animal life, but in the sense that it throbs with life! And, yes, I can say that the whole cosmic process is a living organism. The cosmic panorama that has fascinated the mind of the scientist, the philosopher, the artist, and the theologian, and inspired many a thinker to discover its laws and transform it into a human dwelling, was not the result of a passing fantasy. This panorama is an order; it is an intelligible, beautiful order. Could it be that this panorama is the halo, the effulgence that glows from the power that underlies it? I am neither a philosopher nor a scientist; I am a restless soul in search of the source of this panorama. I feel a very sharp itch, the itch of longing, for this source. I want to feel it, and I want to be baptized by its radiant presence. I want to sit at the fountain from which flows the wealth of values—love, beauty, and truth—and I want to drink from its holy water! I want to be smitten by its sweetness, enveloped by its warmth, and held tight within its arms!

The bus was approaching Tadmur when I stepped down from the wings of my reverie. The first gift my eyes received when we arrived was a pleasant smile from an opaque, indefinable horizon pointing upward to the golden disc of the sun and downward to a boundless ocean of sand. Its opaqueness was produced by the golden rays of the sun as it was descending from the sky. This disc was adorned with an amazing spectrum of purple waves gently thinning into mild ripples of orange and then of soft, dreamy pink. The horizon ceased to be a line where sky and land connect and in some cases intersect, and it ceased to be a limit that checked the sweeping advance of infinity. How could it, when the infinite reveals itself in the finite, when the two blend into magical oneness? The golden disc had, with a magical touch, transformed it into a zone of being in which sky and land fused and formed a transparent sheath of light through which one could have a peek into The Dark that made this whole spectacle possible. I stood next to the bus for a few minutes contemplating this sublime spectacle. How could this exquisite, this magical, this enchanting spectacle be caused by a freaky accident? How could I, this speck of consciousness, delight in its beauty and wonder about its mystery? How could his speck stand in the midst of the infinite and challenge it with its gaze? Well, I did not allow the temptation of this kind of wonder to steal me away from this magical scene, from its seductive bosom, from the delight that was joyfully dancing in my heart. Has it occurred to you that the experience of the magical transcends the aesthetic as such, be it the experience of the beautiful or the sublime; the religious as such, be it the experience of the holy or the mighty; the good as such, be it the experience of love or justice; and the experience of the true as such, be it the experience of knowledge or wisdom? Has it occurred to you that in the lap of the magical, the fountain of your heart, mind, and body fuse into one cry of life, one pulse of life? Yes, I became this pulse on the stage of this exquisite panorama: I became an actor on this stage! How can you seek the beautiful, the sublime, the true, or the good when they flow in your veins harmoniously? How can you seek love when you are within the arms of your beloved? All seeking comes to an end when you are within the arms of The Magical!

But this excursion into the magical did not last. The vista that stretched before my eyes as a calm ocean was undergoing a gradual transformation of identity, not only because the golden disc that was hanging over it as a divine lamp began to glide over the magical edge, as if to hug our earth one more time before the Owl of Minerva spread its wings over the dusk, but also because a rather dark spot began to rise from its midst. This spot, which was at first indistinct, soon acquired a familiar contour, that of a town sitting coyly at the foot of a rather lonely mountain: Tadmur.

I spent two days at this historical legend. I was not interested merely in the historical significance of its remains, which revealed the cosmopolitan orientation of Hellenism, but especially in what they stood for, in the meaning embodied in them: in the spirit of the various cultures that flourished within its walls from the days of the Amorites and Arameans to the present; in having a glimpse into the soul that shone in its sky for so long; and in having a cultural dialogue, albeit silent, with that soul. Is there anything more delightful, more uplifting, and more invigorating than to communicate with the soul of the human as such?

On the second day of my arrival in Tadmur, after having a very relaxing sleep and a wholesome breakfast at the Phoenicia Hotel, I joined a tour group in a bus that accommodated about fifty tourists. Soon after we arrived at the main site of the ruins I decided to leave the group and go my separate way, mainly because my interest in the ruins was quite different from that of the tour guide and the rest of the tourists. I did not need to be informed about the history of the ruins or about their historical significance, because I possessed extensive knowledge of the history of the ancient and medieval world; I needed an opportunity to feel the spirit that dwells within the stones, walls, columns, streets, and different types of buildings, yes, the spirit that celebrated the power and wisdom of the divine in the desert. What is the use of visiting the remains of a past culture if the visit does not enhance our appreciation of the values they embody, expand our understanding of that culture, and animate our sense of well-being? I wanted to take my time in visiting every important architectural structure: the colonnade, the streets, the temples, the amphitheater, the funerary, the arch of triumph, and the commercial and residential sections that were obliterated by the hand of time.

I remember lingering in the Temple of Nabu and the Temple of Bel Shemin, King of Eternity, where I tried to form an idea in my mind of how they expressed their religious feeling; in the funerary, where I tried to capture their view of death and the afterlife; in the theatre, where I wanted to capture the aesthetic feeling they might have had when they watched a Greek or Roman drama; in the streets, where I imagined myself walking with the people as they were trying to conduct the activity of daily living; and under the arch of triumph, where I imagined Queen Zenobia returning from a gloriously won battle. I tried to feel the beat that throbbed in the heart of the city that was a theatre on whose stage the Amorites, the Arameans, the Assyrians, the Romans, the Byzantines, the Arabs, and the Ottomans played vital roles in the development and preservation of the civilization of that part of the world. I even sat one afternoon at the base of a tall, beautiful column and watched the sun as it was setting and listened to the wind singing the song of the desert. It was a sad song. It was lamenting, in a most sorrowful, hopeless, and dejected voice, the ruthlessness of the most striking aspect of nature and human life: Perishing. And it lamented in a striking refrain the fact that everything that exists, human or natural, perishes and that it begins to perish the moment it comes into being, as if to mock the mighty and the arrogant by reminding them that all their pursuits, all their ambitions, and all their glories are nothing but a puff of air, a strike of vanity!

I have read extensive analyses of this fact and lectured on it several times in the course of my professional life, but I confess to you that I had never experienced it in the fullness of its actuality, what it is like to confront it existentially and feel it personally, until that moment. I took the needed time to consider the depth and implications of its significance. I had been stuck and became almost immobile in the ever turning wheel of daily living. Well, there I sat that afternoon and watched the sun setting as the wind was still singing its song. I was alone with myself, alone with the ruins, alone with the sun, and alone with the moon, enveloped with the soothing peace of the desert. I did not shrink from the demand of that moment; on the contrary, I felt an urge to reflect on the significance of the song I was hearing. Can a rational human being, a being with a living moral sense, afford to neglect the implications of this song in planning and living his life? Is there a question more important than that of being and nothingness—my own being and nothingness?

In this reflective mood, I turned my attention to the ruins in whose center I was ruminating on the supremacy of change as a law that seems to govern the operations of nature and human life. Here in this spot, one kingdom after another rose and fell, one culture after another flourished and passed away. Here in this solitary spot, as in many other spots on the face of our earth, the human spirit struggled to survive and to build an environment in which human beings can breathe the air of freedom, beauty, and love. Why? More than once I tried to imagine what it would be like to live in this city at the height of its glory and be a part of its life and witness the way its people strove to cultivate their culture, the way this culture reached a high peak of development, and the way it crumbled into the belly of a merciless, greedy past! I also tried to imagine how, again and again, the human spirit tried to rise from the ashes of destruction and cultivate a new culture, a new lighthouse for the human spirit. How adventurous, how resilient, how intriguing is this spirit! I was haunted by the painful consciousness that this city was, like its builders, a passing show on the theatre of eternity. Every stone I touched, every architectural formation I perceived, and every whisper I heard as I moved from one street to another echoed the song of the wind. And yet, in spite of this realization, I felt in the depth of my being that the enactment of this show was not a vain, freaky, or accidental phenomenon. How can this or any kind of show be enacted on the stage of cosmic creation?

A sparrow fluttered and chirped on a decapitated capital half sunk in the sand a few feet away from me. I watched it for a few seconds. What role does this innocent, beautiful creature play on this cosmic stage? My train of reflection was interrupted by the tour guide as he was making his final call for returning to the hotel. On the way back, he reminded the group that it would be a grave mistake to leave Tadmur without visiting Ibin Maan Castle. He also recommended that we pay a visit to the Tadmur Oasis: "It is a geological wonder," he said. His recommendation was, I think, genuine and important for cultural and historical reasons. But I was not a tourist, and I was not in quest of interesting places, nor was I looking for a diversion from a dull life! I was in quest of The Eternal.

For some reason, I was inclined to visit the castle on the following day. I asked the hotel manager to help me find a guide who was knowledgeable in the ways of the Syrian Desert and who would be willing to be a companion on a somewhat personal and extended tour of the desert. He was at first surprised to hear my request and for a moment he was thoughtful. He cast a questioning, interested look at me, as if he were examining a hidden closet in the back of his mind. Then his face changed into an expression of kindness, of understanding. "Not many people are interested in the ways of the Syrian Desert!" he said with a gentle, friendly voice. "They are usually interested in Tadmurite ruins and especially in the entertainment the office of tourism offers at the end of the day. They just like to have a nice, culturally colorful vacation! When I was a tour guide some fifteen years ago, I recall accompanying an American gentleman on a tour into the heart of the Syrian Desert. He was not a typical tourist, for he was not interested in any ruins, even though he spent much time looking at them with serious interest; he would examine what seems to ordinary people secondary, or unimportant, aspects of the ancient city. Every time he visited an architectural site or a part of a site he would take a break, sit on a stone nearby, and lose himself in a long meditation. It seemed to me that he was conversing with the ruins, because he would walk around them, touch them, and with passionate eyes scrutinize every part of the ruins. It was clear that he understood them; he even loved them more than anyone who walked in this old city. And let me tell you that he was the kindest, friendliest human being I have ever met!"

My heart leaped within my chest, but I was able to remain calm, self-possessed. I simply asked if he could secure a guide who was trained in the ways of the Syrian Desert and interested in being my guide for a week or two. "Of course, I know a veteran guide who is fluent in English and would welcome the opportunity to be your guide for as long as you need. I shall be happy to explain to him the nature of your trip. He shall meet you here early tomorrow morning."

A feeling of quiet exultation coursed through my heart. Looking at the manager with grateful eyes, I thought to myself: "The same place! The same guide! Does he know my professor's secret, and perhaps mine? I wonder!" The manager must have sensed the kind of thoughts and emotions that were dancing in my mind, for he responded to my look with the most compassionate, most poignant smile I had ever felt, as if he understood the kind of adventure I was embarking on. "This man must have been initiated into the mysteries of Time," I thought. He wished me a good night and a good journey. I went to bed early that evening, since we were scheduled to leave the city before sunrise, first paying a visit to the castle and then moving southward into the heart of the desert.

Exactly at 5 a.m. I heard a soft knock at my door. I was already dressed and ready for the trip. The guide, who was about fifty-five years old, greeted me with a cheerful smile and expressed a sincere feeling of pleasure at meeting me and being my guide on this interesting "expedition." Why did he say "expedition" and not "journey," or "trip," or "adventure"? I wondered whether the manager briefed him on the nature of my quest! Very soon I discovered that he did. He exuded amiability and trustworthiness. Without knowing why, I felt that I was in competent hands and that this gentleman was the right guide. He helped me move my luggage to a van that was parked at the main entrance of the hotel. Before starting the engine, he told me that his name was Kamal and insisted that I should feel free to ask him any question I might have. Then, I introduced myself: "My name is Dimitri Christophides."

"Greek?" He asked.

"No, American, but the background is Greek."

"The Greeks are our neighbors and friends. We share a long history, and we practically share a similar worldview. Do you speak Greek?"

"No, I wish I did."

"The spirit of ancient Greek culture still pulsates in the heart of my country."

The road to the castle, which sat at the peak of a high mountain, was very steep, narrow, and winding, but Kamal slithered through it with impressive skill. It was almost dawn when we were making our ascent, but not quite. A soft, fresh breeze was blowing in the parking lot when Kamal parked the van close to the gate that led directly to the castle. Its freshness suggested a feeling of beginning, of renewal. It enlivened every cell of my body. A surge of life streamed through my veins and a feeling of rapture permeated my heart. I walked toward the rail that girded the parking lot. There, at that limit, I stood and tried to contemplate the infinity that embraced me and the mountaintop on which I was standing. I was at first attracted to the amazing tapestry of jewels that glittered over my head. These jewels were dancing between the beams of the soft light the sun had already sent to the desert as a herald. I was absorbed in this dance, in its playfulness, in the way the beams of light weaved their way through the jewels, and especially in the way they illuminated the beauty of the smiling moon. But this moment of aesthetic absorption did not last long, because I could not help succumbing to the call of a thought that was knocking at the door of my consciousness: "Nature is not a work of art; no, nature is an artist. Why do human beings dismiss the domain of artworks created by nature from their aesthetic interest? We ordinarily appreciate works of art because they are human creations and because they are expressive objects. They express human feeling, the kind that communicates the truth, goodness, and beauty of the human spirit. But alas! Nature has its own depth: its own truth, goodness, and beauty. Why do we ignore this depth? Could it be that the whole scheme of nature is no more than a radiant expression of an ultimate creative, wise, and good power? Why do we install ourselves as the standard by which we evaluate the truth and meaning of what happens around us and to us? What makes us certain that the human mind is the final measure of our knowledge of what exists and does not exist?" Although somewhat provocative, I was unable to pursue this train of thought, because of the sudden recession of the celestial dancers and the gradual advance of the golden rays of dawn, as if light were triumphantly advancing from the depth of darkness, crushing it with the power of its light. My eyes were enamored by this spectacle. It seemed to me that the glowing light was giving birth to the scene I was about to witness. Could it be that light is the source of being? Frankly, I could not take my eyes off the rising sun until it finally sat majestically on the edge of the infinite horizon. Please, try to imagine this glorious posture of the sun; then cast a contemplative look at its creation: the desert. Allow your eyes to look upward into the blue sky and try to comprehend the infinity of its being. Slide your vision downward into the infinity of the desert, and then look around into the infinity of the horizon. Then allow yourself a contemplative moment of self-consciousness as you stand on the peak of a mountain, as if you were standing on the tip of a pin, in the belly of infinity. You, who are less than a speck, confront the infinite and in a mysterious way comprehend its spirit, at least what it means for something to be infinite, not mathematically but existentially, cosmically. What a paradox! How is this possible? By what power can the human mind make this leap of transcendence, of being absorbed by the infinite, of comprehending it yet at the same time vanishing in its belly? The more I reflected on this existential consciousness, the more I felt the grip of the same mystery that has been haunting me ever since I dipped my mind into the cosmological speculations of the physicists and philosophers.

In the awe-inspiring silence of this meditative mood, I heard a whisper coming from my inner being: "Can the infinite that confronts you as a defiant challenge, as an antagonist, even as an enchanter, stand before you as an infinite if your mind itself were not a possible infinite? How can it be that the finite, the limited that cannot transcend its own boundaries, because this is what it means to be finite, grasp, much less comprehend, the infinite? Could it be that the infinite, The Eternal you are seeking, lies in you as much as it lies in the depth of nature?" I was about to begin a dialogue with this voice, but I could not, not because I did not want to, indeed, I have always desired such a dialogue, but because I heard Kamal's voice calling me to breakfast. He had already arranged with the Castle's superintendent an informal breakfast for the three of us in his office. The food we ate was simple but delicious. Soon after we ate our meal, the superintendent, who spoke English with a heavy accent, inquired about my nationality and professional background. I told him somewhat briefly that I was a student of philosophy and that I dabbled in teaching and insisted that my main interest lay in the area of culture.

"Human culture?" He asked with emphasis on the word "human."

"Kamal told me that you are interested in the ways of the Syrian Desert. Your interest excites my curiosity. I hope you would be kind enough to explain to me how, or why, a student of philosophy, who is devoted to an inquiry into the nature of wisdom, wants to explore a cultural wasteland, a desert?" The expression on the superintendent's face was serious but amiable. He seemed to be an educated and well read person. My immediate impulse was to give him a detailed account of the nature of my interest, hoping that this would lead to a fruitful discussion, one that would increase my own understanding of the purpose of my trip, but I refrained from taking this step, because I was convinced that the kind of mission I was embarking on should be achieved in the privacy of my soul. It was extremely difficult for me to give an adequate explanation of the dynamics of my mission. But I thought it would be appropriate to give him a brief, albeit a meaningful, answer.

"Is the Syrian Desert a cultural wasteland?" I asked. He looked at me with baffled eyes for a few moments, and then he said: "Hardly any human settlement thrives in this godforsaken land. All you will be able to find is, at best, a few oases, some trading posts, and a number of camel caravan stations here and there. The desert is barren, really barren."

"I am not a student of anthropology, but of philosophy. I am interested not only in what flourishes in the desert, but also in the desert itself, in its ground, in what makes it a desert." I said with a kind, but subdued spirit. He drew in a long and heavy breath and fixed his puzzled eyes on me: "How can you observe anything related to our humanity in a desert? How can you seek the ground of the desert in the desert?" I did not answer his questions only because I could not, at least not adequately, and not easily. I simply conveyed to his questioning eyes a look of sympathy and compassion. He responded in kind and then said: "You have a long and arduous trip ahead of you," and, turning to Kamal, he added, "Please, call me if you need any help. Do you have my phone number?"

"Yes, thank you, Mr. Fadel!" I too thanked the superintendent for his hospitality and gladly went into the castle with Kamal.

Kamal was silent during the short interchange I had with Mr. Fadel after we had our breakfast, but he was neither indifferent nor inattentive to our conversation. His silence was not passive, for he seemed to be very involved in what was said by both of us. It seemed to me that he was an introvert; he spoke more with his body than with his words. His eyes were aflame with a desire to know my view of the relation between humanity and the desert, especially the Syrian Desert. There are, in the world, many, perhaps more important, deserts. Why did I choose to visit this particular desert? Kamal graciously gave me a most interesting and informative tour of Bin Maan Castle, from which I emerged a more enlightened person, not only about the cultural history of Tadmur but also about a possible relation between this history and my quest for The Eternal. The sun was already on its way to its throne when we began to descend the mountain. Kamal explained to me the plan of our trip and the general location of our destination. He noted that we should be there in about three or four days and that our first stop would be the Basiri Oasis, a rather small but attractive oasis. It would be a good place to rest and have a quick lunch.

chapter 2

Al Basiri Oasis

On our way to this oasis, Kamal gave me a detailed account of the terrain we were traversing, the various settlements that were scattered on both sides of the road, and the customs and values of the Bedouins who claim the desert as their home. In fact, his remarks, informal but sophisticated, deepened my knowledge and appreciation of that part of the world. I expected the desert I was visiting to be a flat expanse covered with sand and sand dunes. A smile surfaced on his lips, exposing this preconceived and apparently mistaken idea. "Yes, some parts are, as you shall see, flat and sandy and sometimes a theatre for sand dune formations, not to mention other types of formation, but this is not characteristic of deserts in the Middle East. It is more accurate to say that they are barren, rugged, inhospitable lands for both zoological and botanical life in general." He also reminded me that this whole area was, not long ago, covered with dense forests and many rivers. A few minutes after he made this remark, a mountain called "Al Khumayzer" appeared on our right. "It might be a good idea to visit this mountain, because standing on the top might give you a general view of the desert. Would you like to have such a view?"

"Of course, I welcome the opportunity!" I said without a moment's hesitation. Within a few minutes Kamal stopped on the side of the road and asked me to follow him. I did. This mountain was rather high; its peak was, according to Kamal's estimate, more than fifteen hundred meters high. He led me through a narrow pass and then to a steep hill, where we rested a little, and then we climbed all the way to the top, which we both climbed with some difficulty. The peak was not pointed; it was rather flat. I sat on a small rock for a few minutes and then walked around surveying the desert on all sides. I cannot explain why, but I have always had a strong desire to climb mountains. As a matter of fact I enjoyed the activity of climbing. Could it be because when we stand at the peak, be it physical or intellectual, we can have a synoptic vision of what we see or seek; because we have a feeling of freedom, not only from gravity but also from the murky details of practical life; because the higher we climb, the closer we get to the gods? I wonder! Well, as I stood there almost in the silence of the desert, Kamal was examining a dry plant protruding from a crack in a huge rock. Apparently he was interested in plants. "This plant," he pointed out, "which gives beautiful flowers in springtime, remains dormant in summertime, because it cannot withstand the heat of the sun and the lack of water." He unearthed the plant and planned to take it with him to the van. As we were descending the mountain he pointed out to me some black and red stones. "These stones," he said, "were spouted by a nearby volcano five centuries ago. Some volcanoes in the desert are still active."

We arrived at the oasis after the sun left its zenith and was on its way westward toward the horizon. This oasis, which was an important trading center and a rest area for travelers, is a center point that connects Damascus and Homs in Syria with Rutba in Iraq. Apparently, Kamal knew the different parts of the oasis, for he parked the car close to a grocery store, which also served freshly cooked meals. Next to the store there was a "tannour," a well-like formation over the ground for baking bread, and a tent made from palm leaves. The owner of the store extended a warm welcome to us; he was especially glad when he discovered that I was an American. He had a short conversation with Kamal and then vanished from our presence. He returned an hour later with what he called Taglib dishes. He told us that all the ingredients used in cooking the meal, including the recipe, were indigenous. Let me here confess that that was one of the most delicious meals I have ever eaten.

I asked Kamal if I could pay a short visit to the Basiri Oasis before continuing our journey southward. "Of course!" he said. "Although small, this oasis is as old as the Tadmur Oasis. The Basiri community is very proud of its dates and camels." Having paid Adnan, the owner of the store, for the meal and for the supplies he purchased for our trip, Kamal drove to the oasis. A herd of camels were resting on the edge.

As soon as I left the van, I moved in their direction and cast a quiet yet reflective look at them. I say "reflective" because I was not interested merely in their physiognomy but mainly in their significance to that part of the world—in their capacity of endurance, of being the most loyal ally to human beings in the harshest possible conditions of life, in the pivotal role they played in the development of the different civilizations of the whole Fertile Crescent.

I felt an urge to move closer to one of them, close enough to stroke his forehead. I did. I contemplated his body and his posture. He must have understood and appreciated my stroke, but he did not make a stir; he was not interested in me or in anything around him. Then I looked into his eyes. Alas! They were peaceful but shining with life. I had a feeling that he was not interested in my presence, because his eyes were indifferent to me; they were focused on the distance that lay in front of him as an ocean of space, as if this ocean was his home, and his destiny. He must have been communing with The Infinite!

I wished I were able to see The Infinite from the standpoint of those eyes! "Was he born of the desert, and for the desert?" I wondered to myself. I knew that the camel has always been the most reliable means of transportation in the desert, and one of the most suitable animals for desert life. But as I stood there lost in the world of those peaceful eyes, it became clear to me that he was born of the desert, being most suitable for its life. He was practically its concrete reflection: the infinity and sublimity of the Syrian Desert shone in his eyes as a splendid spectacle of peace. Could it be that the camel is a living microcosm of the desert? If only I spoke his language, I would have listened to the story of his life in the desert, nay, with the desert. Oh, how I wish I spoke his language! As far as I know, he can, better than anyone else, tell its story. Its ways and secrets are hidden in those eyes. How many a day did he walk onward, unperturbed by the loneliness of the infinite space around him as he carried his master into the unknown? How many a century did he give his flesh to the people of the desert? How many tons of goods did he carry on his back from one side of the desert to the other? How many a time did he carry the Hawdage (canopy) of the bride from her parent's tent to that of the groom? How many a time did he lead the Bedouin against the invading armies? And yet, he sits there with the utmost of peace and contentment in the shade of the palm trees gazing into the infinity of the space around him. Where does he derive his strength, patience, and wisdom?

I was not aware of his presence, but Kamal was standing in my proximity almost behind me, gazing like me, into the eyes of the same camel; and like me, he seemed to be caught in the mystery of the infinity of their depth, in the wonder of their contentment. Was he, too, enamored by the mystery of those eyes? "I am a son of the desert," he had mentioned, when we were descending the Khumayzer Mountain. Is it possible for a person to be a son of the desert without being a son of its secrets? He wafted into my eyes a tender, understanding smile. He was neither impatient nor irritated by the fact that I was having a silent dialogue with that camel; on the contrary, he seemed curious and amused. Indeed, I am certain that he, too, was having a similar dialogue. I wanted to inquire whether his interest in those eyes was similar to mine, but I refrained from such inquiry, because this would have been an infringement on his privacy. Secrets of the desert are sacred and cannot be desecrated by the intrusion of human convention. But I could not say, in retrospect, that at that time he was truly a son of the desert.

"Would you like to take a look at the lake?" he asked. "It is not as large as the Tadmur Lake, but it is very beautiful. Its beauty expresses, unlike any other oasis I have seen, an alluring quality of intimacy. It is seductive in its charm. It is not an accident that most travelers and tribes frequent this oasis. I sometimes feel that God has favored it with his presence. I do not think that it is wise to leave this region without a communion with it." Communion? Why did he not speak of beauty or aesthetic depth or some other type of experience? I had already begun to recognize that Kamal was a very insightful person. When the dominant aspect of any significant form is divine presence, not merely some divine quality, it would be a mistake to say that the experience of such a form is an aesthetic experience, mainly because divine presence is not a quality or an aesthetic content of some kind, but a reality that transcends any category of intellectual or logical discourse. Divine presence may, as a reality, have an aesthetic quality. It shines with divine qualities the way a work of art or a natural object or scene can shine with aesthetic qualities.

"Communion?" I asked, puzzled by the way he expressed himself.

"Yes, communion. This oasis is not an ordinary garden. It is the kind of landscape that speaks, that reaches out to you, that leaps into your heart. And if you are not careful, you might be enchanted out of your wits. When I was still a teenager, I heard my grandfather say more than once (and, by the way, my grandparents used to live near this lake) that there is magic in this place. I have a vivid memory of him spending many an hour in the evening sitting on the edge of the palm orchard gaping, almost abstractly, into this modest spectacle. One day, when I came to announce to him that supper was ready and that everybody was waiting for him, I heard him mumble to himself: "What an icon! Blessed be The Divine!" On our way back to the tent, he never looked at me or even in my direction. When he approached the door of the tent, I saw him wiping tears from the corners of his eyes. I did not take him seriously then, thinking that he was an old, senile man. But now, after growing up intellectually, emotionally, and in the ways of human life in general and the ways of the desert in particular, I began to think differently, not only about my grandfather's unusual interests but also about the meaning and destiny of human life. I now understand a little, a little, mind you, why my grandfather was attached to this oasis. I have a good feeling that you would not regret having a visit with it."

"With it"! Not "to it" or "in it?" Kamal seemed to choose simple but profoundly meaningful expressions when he described his ideas and feelings. "I ought to be attentive to this man," I thought to myself as I walked with him to the lake. We went through a dense maze of palm trees. Jointly, they formed a canopy over the periphery of the oasis. Families as well as travelers were sitting in groups under this canopy on what seemed to be hand-woven rugs, conversing while eating food they had already prepared, while children were running here and there playing hide-and-seek or building castles out of the sand that covered the ground everywhere. I asked Kamal if it would be alright to linger a little under that canopy. I was really interested in taking a good look at that amazing human scene. "Of course!" was his immediate and gracious response. He must have understood the purpose of my request. He remarked that most of the people who were enjoying a rest there were travelers native to that region. "They are decent human beings. They are proud of their traditions, and they view themselves as children of the Syrian Desert. Many of them shy away from city life."

Kamal was right, I thought, because what I saw when I stole an examining but respectful look was cheerful, contented people. I saw happy people. They seemed to enjoy the food they were eating and the conversations they were conducting. They were not sitting on chairs or sofas under metal or concrete or plastic roofs or within decorated walls but on the sand under the palm trees. They were in touch with nature, and they seemed to be one with it. "What does it take to be and to live in harmony with nature? Can we be in tune with ourselves if we are not in tune with nature?" I do not mean, in allowing these ideas to cross my mind, to reject or underestimate the world of technology, in which contemporary society lives, in which it seems to be increasingly tethered, to which it is abandoned, and which seems to have a final authority in shaping the lives of contemporary people and consequently their being, but I do mean to question whether adopting this new kind of world should necessarily imply alienating ourselves from the world of nature. Do I need all the new technological innovations in order to be a fulfilled human being? I am the staunchest advocate of technology as a means of expanding the possibilities of scientific discoveries, technological advances, artistic creation, and making our practical life easier, but I am equally the staunchest advocate of the natural way of life, the sort that keeps us in sync with the laws that govern our inner being, and especially with the ultimate source of these laws. I was unable to continue this process of thinking, because a man who was enjoying a meal with his family, who apparently noticed that we were strangers, hailed us, saying in Arabic:

"Welcome, join us! Please, come, have a bite with us!"

"We have just eaten. Thank you very much!" Kamal answered him in Arabic. Having exchanged a few more words in Arabic with him, the same man continued:

"Well, then you must have some sweets. My wife makes the best sweets in this part of the desert. You cannot say no to her." Kamal suggested that it would be a good idea to visit with them and try his wife's sweets. He told us that sharing this modest meal with them would bestow a great honor upon him and his wife. "You must try her marceban (a kind of almond pastry)," he insisted. Our host was right; the marceban was truly delicious. I sent a thankful smile from my lips to the lady's eyes, accompanied with a felicitous nod. She understood what I meant. The language we spoke was human, for she did not speak English and I did not speak Arabic. It was the sort of language that should be the vehicle of verbal language people use in ordinary life, I thought. The husband participated in this kind of communication with me. He was gratified that I enjoyed and appreciated his wife's handiwork. He was proud of his wife! He introduced me to his children: two teenage daughters, and two sons in their early twenties. They seemed to be curious about me. Like their parents, they exuded friendliness and a sense of contentment. I wished I were able to converse with them, to discover how they understood themselves and their future expectations. In general, they were excited when they discovered that I was American. Fareed, the husband, asked Kamal a number of questions about the U.S.A. He was interested in knowing why I was roaming the Syrian Desert. Kamal told him that I was interested in its ways. He did not know what that expression meant, but he was elated when he heard the last part of my answer. The wife, who disappeared for a few minutes, reappeared with a tray of demitasse coffee cups. Our host looked at Kamal and told him that we could not leave without drinking a cup of real Arabic coffee. We did. It was not as dark as the coffee we ordinarily drink in the U.S.A., and, though mild, it had a distinct, enjoyable flavor.

It was a short but very pleasant visit. Although I did not speak Arabic, I nevertheless conveyed to this gracious family the deepest of my appreciation for their warm welcome and concluded my speech with "shukran gazeelan" ("thank you very much," which Kamal had already taught me). Then, they all stood up and shook hands with me, expressing gestures of deep satisfaction at making my acquaintance, and wishing me a safe and successful journey.

Kamal and I weaved our way slowly through the palm trees, leaving behind an oasis of human presence, the kind that does not actually leave you but lingers in your heart forever. We undergo myriads of experiences in the course of our lives: social, intellectual, biological, cultural, religious, professional, and aesthetic experiences. Most of them fade into oblivion as we proceed from one day to the next, one week to the next, and sometimes from one year to the next. They do not play a significant role in the way we think, feel, and act. Only those that are transmitted on the wings of our humanity linger in our hearts and make a difference in how we understand ourselves and the world, in how we grow in self-fulfillment. Acts of love, those that originate from the heart, have the power to sting us, to open our minds to the vision and appreciation of truth, goodness, beauty, and holiness. We believe our teachers, parents, priests, politicians, friends, and social leaders, and we take them seriously and feel inclined to learn from them, when we know in the depth of our hearts that they are honest, genuine. What comes from the human heart, the heart that is cultivated by reason and love, reaches us as a flame of passion, of fire. I felt the warmth of this fire

Seeking God

as I walked with Kamal in the silence of the palm trees. Although I cannot verify it, I felt that Kamal was the beneficiary of the same feeling.

It was late in the afternoon when we emerged from the palm orchard. Although the sun had already left its zenith and was moving toward the western horizon, its rays were still vibrating in the space that floated over that circular lake gently, ever so gently. It seemed to me, at first sight, that the palm trees were gliding hand in hand around this lake in the most elegant dance I could imagine. "What are they celebrating?" I thought to myself. I had learned when I was a college student that the circle symbolizes infinity. A straight line must necessarily reach an endpoint, but the line of the circle moves on endlessly. Is this why so many western artists frequently crowned their religious figures with a halo? Is this why the sun has always been used in the works of the major philosophers of antiquity to symbolize the ultimate? Could it be that this line, unlike any other, captures in its simplicity the transcendence of the ultimate that defies any kind of conceptual or pictorial representation? Alas! I was watching with my two eyes a dance of infinity. Goosebumps spread over my skin. I felt an irresistible desire to watch this dance.

Kamal must have been moved by this dance the way I was, for he hesitated a little and then asked: "Would you like to. . .?" I did not wait for the rest of the question, because I involuntarily nodded with my eyes and head approvingly. Can you resist the god of magic when he winks at you with a seductive look, when he favors you with a beguiling smile, when he draws you into his world with the elegance of his enchantment, when he sends you a warm welcome with open arms? Yes, when you stand within the warmth of his arms, when you feel the sweetness of his magic, of its enchanting smile, you certainly feel that you are called upon, that you are invited to a feast incomparable to any other you have attended. What is curious, perhaps baffling, is that you proceed into this invitation confidently, you surrender your heart and soul to it without fear or hesitation; you know in the depth of your being that you are a favored guest and that the musicians have been waiting for your arrival. In the arms of such magic, you do not ask why or how or what. You do not feel a need to ask any type of question. You accept the invitation as a favored son or daughter.

It was a solemn moment, and it was a moment of serene joy, the kind that lifts you from the mundane, from the mediocre, from the transient, to a serene, imperturbable, noble state of mind that holds every pulse in your being in check, as if your mind were captivated by a vision of The Beautiful in the richness of its splendor. Yes, who can resist the beguiling eyes of this bewitching god?

This small lake, which sat in the middle of the oasis as a shining disc, was surrounded by a narrow line of yellow sand except in one spot on its eastern shore, where I noticed, as Kamal was leading me in that direction, a rocky elevation. Both of us walked on the narrow shore for a few minutes. When we reached this spot Kamal pointed out that the source lay under that elevation. By "source" he meant the spring that flowed into the lake. Then he directed my attention to the unusual configuration of this rock elevation. It was composed of a symphonic structure of large, wavy holes. No one but the skillful and patient hands of Time could have carved it: "One can spend the night in any one of these hollow volumes," Kamal said. "My grandfather spent many a night here in this spot. My grandmother tolerated his absence," he added, "because he used to return to our tent the next morning rejuvenated, full of smiles. But she never understood why he was passionately attached to this spot. I am inclined to think that she viewed this attachment as a harmless idiosyncrasy. Every member of the family, and the whole tribe, was in love with him. He was a model father, husband, and friend. People came to him for advice all the time, and they revered him as a kind of elder, maybe as a sage."

Kamal's reminiscence about his grandfather was interrupted by a young man who must have been running after us. He was shouting from a distance, asking Kamal to slow down for a moment, thinking that our destination was the other side of the lake. Kamal immediately stopped and turned his face toward him. He walked back to meet him halfway. I was left alone motionless with the rock formation—yes, alone. A strange feeling pulsated in my heart; it created a desire in me to move closer to the rock and explore it. The strange, the exotic, the unfamiliar always excites our curiosity. Frankly, I was inflamed with curiosity, not only because it stood in front of me as a rock formation but also because there was something peculiar about it. Why would wise people like Kamal's grandfather frequent this rock and even spend nights in its mini-caves? Why would Kamal himself favor it with distinctive attention? So, while Kamal was having a conversation with that young man I took the liberty of paying a visit to the rock. Yes, there was something special about it, a kind of inexplicable aura. As I moved around it, contemplating its lines and tactile qualities with my two hands, and then as I approached the hollow volumes that looked like grottos, even shrines, I felt a burning desire to climb that rock and crawl into them. Perhaps what I felt was the desire of a child, but it was more appropriate to say that it was the desire of an adventurer, a person who wants to know the secret of things: that which makes them tick! Within seconds, I was in one of them. It was really accommodating, for I was able to sit and even move around it rather comfortably. The walls of the first cave I visited were smooth. I saw some writing in Arabic, which I could not read, and signs, which I could not decipher. At its end, there was a door-like opening that led to another cave. "This is exciting! Am I in a labyrinth?" I asked rhetorically. Well, I proceeded into my small adventure. I moved through that opening very carefully, because it was rather narrow. Lo and behold! The moment I walked into the second grotto, on my way to the second opening, the light of the afternoon sun almost overwhelmed my eyes with its brightness. It took me a few moments to get adjusted to this flood of illumination. As I reached the opening of the grotto that overlooked the lake I found myself standing before the most exquisite natural scene I had ever experienced in my life. The golden rays of the late afternoon sun were gliding softly, almost effortlessly, on the ripples of the lake in a supremely elegant dance. At first I was unable to focus my perception on the totality of the scene that stretched before my eyes as a round theatre surrounded by rows of palm trees, as if those trees were celebrating a special event prepared by the desert. "What a marvel!" I cried in the midst of this excitement. And before I allowed myself to become a participant in this celebration I heard Kamal calling my name. Painfully and reluctantly, I could not help thinking: "Oh, no, not now!" I felt the way a human being dying from thirst feels when you take away a glass of water from his lips. I felt as if I was allowed to take a peek into the most beautiful garden of the world without being allowed to relish it in the fullness of its beauty. I stood at the door of my grotto and waved to him, and then, when he did not notice me, I called him back. He climbed the rock and in a few seconds he joined me with a small package on his shoulder.

"I missed you! I was really worried. I never thought you would find your way into what I usually call desert grottoes. I am very glad to see you in this cavern. This used to be my grandfather's hideaway. The family found him here whenever they missed him at the village," he said with a panting heart.

"I am sorry; I did not mean to scare you," I rejoined apologetically. "I was simply intrigued by this rock formation; its structure is really provocative. One cannot resist its appeal."

"Oh, no, it is quite alright. I am very glad you took the initiative to explore this place. I was detained a little by Jamal, the oldest son of Adnan and Fareeda, the couple we have just visited. Adnan has sent you this prayer rug. He wants you to have it as a souvenir from the Syrian Desert. His wife weaved it. They would feel much honored if you accept it as a gift from them. They only hope that you like it. By the way, it is made of sheep wool. They were really very happy to meet you. I could not decline his offer, because this would have been an insult to them. They wished that you could have spent more time with them, especially the young people, because they wanted to ask you a few questions about America. Their interest was intensified when they heard that you are a university professor." With this retort, Kamal unrolled the rug for me to look at. It was a beautiful piece. One could easily classify its form as an arabesque. It was composed of an interesting interplay of black and red color formations. Kamal pointed out that the red symbolized the passion of the human heart, while the black symbolized the infinity and mystery of the desert. To confess, I was speechless before the generosity of these people. Is it possible that the spiritual temper of a people reflects, perhaps modestly, the temper of the natural environment they inhabit: the air they breathe, the water they drink, the food they eat, the ground they walk on, the sun that warms their heart, the sky they gaze at, the moon that gives them romantic inspiration, and the natural disasters they fear and struggle with?

After I expressed my deep appreciation for the gift Adnan and his wife sent, Kamal took the opportunity to suggest that it would be wise to spend the night at the oasis, since the sun would be leaving the desert shortly. He also suggested a place where we could spend the night. But I hesitated a little before acquiescing to his suggestion, because a desire was brewing in my mind.

"Would it be alright," I asked, "if I, and hopefully both of us, spend the night here in this grotto? This oasis is growing on me in a strange way. I would like to experience it, to feel the pulse of its spirit in the evening when the sun sets and in the morning when it rises." Kamal's eyes sparkled with gladness when he heard me speak of the spiritual pulse of the oasis; his lips were about to quiver with a smile had he not suppressed it, most likely out of shyness. He impulsively responded with a nod of approval. "Allow me, then," he added, "to bring some blankets, sleeping bags, food, and your briefcase from the van."

"Can I stay here while you run this errand?" I asked.

"Of course! I shall be back shortly," he answered contentedly. Kamal was always careful to respect my privacy. He never imposed his will or desire on me; on the contrary, he always tried to glean my wishes, desires, or needs, and then acted accordingly. Although he was an introvert, he never pretended to be what he was not. He was a genuine human being.

His errand gave me an opportunity to be with myself, alone with the dramatic performance that was unfolding before my two eyes. Yes, I was by myself, but neither lonely nor alone. How can anyone be alone in the presence of a thrilling dramatic performance? No, in such a moment, it is more appropriate to say that I was held snugly within the warmth of solitude, a most desirable refuge from the empty noise of social existence, from its empty talk, empty thoughts, empty pursuits, and empty pleasures. At that moment, I was alone in my grotto watching the regal descent of the sun into the horizon of the desert, into the infinite ocean of being. It was a quiet, peaceful moment, free from every possible stir or disturbance that might burden or distract one's attention. You see, when you are in this intellectual mood, yes, intellectual mood, you can see, hear, and feel innocently: You can see and feel your inner self, even the world around you, in the fullness of its being, of its truth. The object of your perception rises to your field of consciousness as it is in itself: Its essence becomes the crown of its existence; it becomes one with its existence. The object ceases to be an "it," an alien or external object; it becomes a quasi-subject. It becomes an object that speaks to you, that communicates something to you, that can have a dialogue with you. Without this kind of communication the very act of thinking, or understanding, is not possible. How can I be said to understand something if what I understand does not come into my mind and become an integral part of it? And how can this happen if it does not assume, or become, a nature similar to that of my mind: spirit? Once more, how can it come into my mind if it does not offer itself to my mind? And how can it offer itself if it does not speak the language of my mind? I discovered some time ago that any meaningful experience, be it natural, social, intellectual, emotional, political, aesthetic, or religious, is dialogical in nature. It involves an active, interactive, and productive synthesis between what is experienced and the mind of the person who undergoes the experience. I am inclined to think that this kind of synthesis represents an essential dimension of human growth.

A festive spirit was floating in the air of the oasis. One could breathe it like breathing in the fragrance of a beautiful rose on a sunny spring day. The birds were twittering and fluttering their way from one palm tree to another, as if they were looking for the best seat in the auditorium of that grand theatre. Even the trees must have felt the solemnity of the occasion, for they were still as the stillness of silence. The whole theatre around me expressed a mood of anxious expectation. Strange enough, a wild thought forced its way into my consciousness in the midst of that mood: "Is this performance prepared for me, for me alone, or is it an unfolding cosmic performance available for anyone who is interested and willing to participate in the splendor of its creation?" I was unable to dwell on the meaning and implications of this thought, because something extraordinary happened as I sat on the ledge of the grotto waiting for the performance the oasis was about to present on its luxurious stage. The rays of the sun that gradually changed into a deep golden beam, permeated by a shade of soft red in some waves by light purple motifs, creating a living mosaic of divine colors, approached the glittering ripples of the lake with a seductive touch. They produced the most enchanting, the most exuberant dance the human eye could possibly witness. This beam glided over the ripples, and, I should say, with them, with delicate nimbleness and amazing grace. The glitter of those waves gave rise, as they floated between and over the ripples, to a most fascinating kaleidoscopic display of vibrant colors. The ripples ceased to be ripples, the light ceased to be light, and the stage ceased to be a stage. The whole scene was transformed into a remarkable dance, into an icon of beauty that surpassed in dignity and nobility any beauty I have ever witnessed or read about in the books of the poets and novelists. It seemed to me that I was swept by that scene, by the magic of its charm, the elegance of its effulgence, and the power of its seductive appeal. I was no longer conscious of my body, the grotto, the desert, or even the fact that I was breathing. I became a ray in that beam; a flare of joy dancing the dance of the divine on those ripples; a flicker of light reflecting the light of the sun; a flame of fire dancing in the heaven of being. It was inconceivable for me during that moment to feel the process of time or the limits of space, or what it means to desire, or even feel happy, or what it means to be one or many, finite or infinite. How could I when I was an infinite drop of being? Frankly, I was not even aware that I was such a drop! When a drop of being blends with The Infinite it becomes one with it: In a mysterious, inexplicable sense, it becomes The Infinite. It was difficult, indeed impossible, for me, during that moment, to realize that I was in this mode of consciousness: My capacity to be aware, of myself or anything else, had come to a standstill. And it reached this point not because my consciousness was annihilated but because it expanded to its infinite limits, because, as I was able to define it later on, I was overwhelmed by a deluge of ecstasy. Within the folds of this kind of deluge, you do not undergo a feeling of pleasure, happiness, or satisfaction of any kind, because you are fulfilled, and you are fulfilled in and through the being of The Infinite. Yes, this kind of fulfillment is our true destiny; and seeking it is our true vocation in this short life of ours.

I do not, to this day, remember how long I remained dancing with the divine on that stage, because it was almost dusk when I noticed Kamal climbing the rock with a big bundle on his shoulder and a big bag in his hand. With a special effort, the kind you need when you wake up from a very deep sleep, I rushed toward him in an attempt to relieve him from his load. He was apologetic about being late. "The owner of the store, where we ate our lunch and replenished some of our supplies," he explained, "insisted that we should have a hot meal. It should be ready in about one hour. I hope you were not bored in my absence?" A little confused and unable to speak as coherently as I should have, for I had not yet fully recovered from my most recent adventure, I evaded the question of food or hunger and told him that I was enjoying the beauty of the lake and that it was a worthwhile experience! "Are you hungry?" he asked, after he placed the bundles he was carrying on the floor of the grotto.

"Not really!" I replied. I assured him that I could wait and that he should not worry about this matter. How could I feel hungry or thirsty or lonely or upset about anything after such an adventure? I do not exaggerate if I say that I was still intoxicated by the profound feeling of ecstasy that adventure left in my heart, the echoes of whose throbs were still pounding delightfully on the walls of my chest, temples, and eyelids. The only word I can use to describe the state I was in is "catharsis," and I do not mean here to invoke images of the fallen hero in ancient Greek tragedy; I rather mean a state of enlightenment, of tranquility, of self-possession, in which we are not encumbered by the nagging awareness of ignorance, mystery, doubt, fear, or even desire. In this state our consciousness is completely drowned in the bright light of The Sun. You no longer see the truth of yourself or of anything around you as through a dark or misty glass but directly. In this state, your eyes are not covered by any kind of veil; you see, feel, and act from the heart of the child that resides in you. You feel in touch with yourself, not merely with the ideas, images, emotions, or sensations that throng your mind, but with what lies behind them; you see the spark that illumines them. You are privy to what you see, and you alone are the custodian of what you see.

And what I saw when I was sitting on the ledge of my grotto was not merely the descent of the sun behind the western horizon of the desert, which the ordinary person normally sees, no, I was not even in the presence of a natural scene, although it was beautiful: I was in, and with, the radiance of divine presence. The dance I was absorbed in was a manifestation of this presence, a reverberation of its grandeur, of its excellence, of the marvel that underlies the creative power of this presence. Before this marvel, you are not and you cannot remain a passive spectator. You are prompted to participate in it, not because it is pleasant or exciting, but because you feel invited, welcomed to share in it, because you feel from the center of your heart that this is what you should do now and always. I am compelled to use superlatives to communicate aspects of my experience of the divine dance only because human language is a poor, painfully poor, instrument for communicating that which transcends linguistic communication. When you feel the touch of the divine, when you fly on the wings of its brilliance, you do not need the theodicy of the philosopher, the ritual of the priest, or the exhortation of public opinion, or the command of your parents to believe, because in this kind of divine disclosure you see with your own eyes the truth which neither the philosopher, the priest, society, nor your parents can even utter, much less comprehend.

Then Kamal walked with me toward the door of the grotto that overlooked the divine theatre of the oasis. Both of us sat on the ledge and watched the sun hugging the ripples as they leisurely floated on the water.

Kamal broke the silence: "My grandfather used to favor this spot, especially at dusk. He was enamored by the sunset. He remarked, whenever he was in a serious mood, that sunset is the womb that gives birth to sunrise. I have a feeling he was attached to the dark, to its depth, to its mystery, to its abyss! Sunrise is the harbinger of the night. Many people are afraid of the dark, but not my grandfather. On a number of occasions I tried to understand why. At first, I thought that most people have eyes but do not see well, because they are not trained in the art of seeing. When they are ignorant of their surroundings, or of the perspective that surrounds them, they feel at a loss. Ignorance arouses a feeling of doubt and, in most cases, of fear. But then, as I grew older and became more skilled in thinking and meditation, as I found myself contemplating the infinite network of relations that weave this whole universe into a remarkable work of art, as I found my mind moving onward to explore what lies beyond this network, I found myself standing face to face before The Dark."

"The Dark? What do you mean?" I broke in.

"Yes, The Dark, not the dark which follows daylight and which is caused by the absence of the sunlight in nature, but the abyss that stretches everywhere as the infinite before our own eyes and which the human intellect can neither think nor comprehend. When I stand at the edge that overlooks that abyss, when I try to penetrate its immense structure, seeking its ultimate ground, I go nowhere; I remain on the edge. The abyss that confronts me as The Dark remains a mystery to me."

Suddenly Kamal fell silent and his eyes were closed for a few seconds, as if he were scrutinizing something serious, as if he were trying to harness some stubborn ideas. Having regained his earlier state of mind, he continued: "But you see, I felt safe standing on the edge. You cannot imagine how frightful, how terrifying it is to stand on that edge, because when you first stand on it you feel like you are about to fall from the highest mountain into the deepest valley in the world. You feel like you are about to perish and that your end has arrived. And let me tell you that the moment you are conscious of this possibility the armies of dread swarm around you with their ugliest teeth. But I did not feel any kind of fright, and I did not feel the pangs of dread the way a child feels when she stands on the edge of a fifth-storey building indifferent to the depth that lies beneath her. It takes courage to stand on such an edge, not the courage of the soldier or the seeker of wealth but the courage of innocent human beings. I confess to you that the innocent child I was some years ago never left my breast. I have been living with this secret all my life. Ah, it is not easy for a child to live among adults, among so-called adults.

"Yes, I stood on the edge, on the last stop of my contemplative adventure and directed all my powers toward The Dark. I was unable to move one step into its domain, and although I was unable to make any kind of advance, not even touching it with the hand of my mind, I found myself reverting upon the predicament that was challenging me. What was in me, or about me, that propelled me to seek the edge that borders The Dark, the dark I cannot conceive? Could there be a relation between this dark and the universe that borders it? There is, after all, an edge and I stand on it. But what was most interesting to my mind is the fact that the edge was a part of our universe, not the dark. I realized that our universe is finite, because it is limited, but not the dark. I also realized that because it is finite it is, and should be, dependent; and since it is dependent it must be dependent on The Dark. An insight surged in the midst of this realization. The light that illuminated our universe and gave its being, still sustaining it, must in some way have come from The Dark, or, as I would express the same idea differently, it was born in the womb of The Dark. It is this insight that inclined me, and also my grandfather, to favor dusk over dawn. I know that logically the ideas of dark and light imply each other and that they are proportionate to each other; but I am speaking here from an ontological point of view, from the point of view that gives rise to both day and night. And when I stood on the periphery of The Dark, gazing at it, I was not merely thinking it, but also feeling its presence. Indeed, I am closer to the truth if I say that I was not even thinking or feeling its presence; no, I was what I was thinking and feeling. I was and remain clear about that fact the way I am now clear about our being here at the ledge of this grotto."

"The language you use, Kamal, to describe the relation of our universe to its source is metaphorical; it is also cast in the first person. You describe a personal experience: What can you say about the validity of your experience, or explanation?"

Seeking God

"I aver," he rejoined, "that I was describing my personal experience, but my experience is neither whimsical nor thoughtless; it arose from a careful and sustained reflection on the foundation of the world, on its meaning, and especially on the destiny of human life. I have always thought that the quest for The Divine is a personal undertaking. One can write about the journey, describe it in general, explain its events, and perhaps justify it, so that it is convincing to the reader, but it remains, a personal, private, and solitary experience. Although I have never had the opportunity to go to college, I have read many of my father's books on the subject. After I reflected on the way he lived as a family person and as a citizen, and after I reflected on the world and the way it works, I came to the conclusion that there is a very big difference between what we read and what we do, between theory and practice. I am not a scholar; I am seeker of The Divine.

"You see," he said after he cast a quick, thoughtful look at the shining disc in front of our eyes, "before I had a serious inclination to read my father's books, I was first struck, and I can say smitten, by the phenomenon of existence, the existence of nature, of animals, of human beings, and especially of the laws that govern their existence. Why? Why do these phenomena exist the way they do? This radical consciousness took possession of my mind when I was a very young man. I have, ever since, been interested in understanding the power that underlies the whole scheme of nature insofar as we can experience it. You can say there is in me an urge, a propulsive force that directs me to seek this understanding. I did not acquire it because I read my father's books; they are lifeless, and, as such, they cannot alone produce any change in my life or in the world around us. The history of civilization contains a wealth of such ideas and they have been taught to young minds for centuries, but they seem to be marginalized by those who recommend them and by those who teach them: parents, teachers, priests, politicians, social leaders. Why? What makes an idea valuable, worth adopting and acting on is the passion behind it. I am more inclined to think that passion is the moving force of the life of peoples, communities, and nations. If you take away passion from the heart of a human being he or she will lose the impetus to grow in humanity. I cannot explain to you how I came to possess an urge to seek The Divine, but I can make some remarks which may shed some light on it. Its birth in me was made possible by the kind of life I have been leading, a life shaped both by my family and by the desert, and also inspired in part by how other people conduct their lives. The beliefs and values I lived with and the way I lived them were, I think, the source of this urge. Two gems of wisdom were engraved on the wall of my mind: Be true to yourself! Love your fellow human beings! And they were engraved not because they were invoked now and then, or because violating the values implicit in them aroused a feeling of guilt in me, but because they were a way of life. This is how my parents and everyone in my family lived. You can say that these two exhortations were the structural principles of our life. When you live according to them, you find yourself thinking, feeling, and acting from their point of view. The first thing I discovered when I became an adult was the need to care for myself, not in a superficial, selfish way, but in feeling it, understanding it, and cultivating it. The importance of this discovery became acute, and sometimes acquired a sense of urgency, when I recognized that the majority of the people I interacted with led superficial lives, because they were oblivious to the demands of their inner selves, and frequently because they acted as if they did not have selves. I am not a scholar, I know, but I feel that the life of every human being grows from a seed implanted in the depth of his being. This seed is a kind of vital impetus, a spark, a flicker of life, an urge. If the conditions of growth and development of this seed are appropriate, the human being lives from this seed, from its nature. Education, and here I mean the system of all the factors that act on us in the course of our lives—family, school, work place, religious institution, means of public information—is supposed to foster this growth, but unfortunately it is absent from the larger segment of our society.

"I did not mean to burden you with my ideas, which are very succinct, perhaps simplistic, but I felt a genuine desire to converse with you. Do you know that the desire for conversation, the kind that rises from the depth of the human heart, honestly, without any hypocritical embellishments, is a cry from the soul, a cry for being?"

My eyes, which were watching the golden disc getting closer and closer to the horizon, suddenly looked at Kamal with an expression of astonishment, interrupting his meditation: "A cry?" Gently, he looked at me and, changing the course of his thoughts, he said: "Yes, the desire for conversation is a cry; it is not only an essential human need, more important than the food we eat, but the most fundamental need of our humanity."

"What do you mean, please? I really want to understand what you are saying," I inquired.

"Well, I mean conversation is the essence of our humanity. Humanity grows in and through conversation. We can say that conversation is the soil from which our humanity develops. A human being is a conversation, a discourse. You may wonder about the frame, or structure, of this conversation, or about what happens in it, especially because what usually takes place in what is called conversation in ordinary life, even in academic circles, is most of the time idle talk, meaningless monologues, or emotional explosions. No, I do not have in mind any one of these verbal conversations. For me, a conversation is a human event, an event of sharing."

"Sharing?" I asked.

"Yes, sharing," he rejoined. "It is an event in which ideas, feelings, emotions, experiences—parts of our inner being—are transmitted to the person we converse with under the conditions of respect, freedom, truth, and the desire to grow as human beings. In a conversation, I welcome you, I receive you into my mind and heart. Its purpose is not merely to exchange ideas or points. A conversation is a medium in which I reveal myself to you. Only in this way can you understand the ideas, the emotions, or feelings we try to share in the conversation. Here, my aim is not merely to understand what you say but to understand you, and I understand you when I feel and grasp your presence, when I am touched by your passion for understanding, for life, when I feel the spark that glows in your heart as a human being. A meaningful conversation is a celebration of human life."

Kamal was in a contemplative posture of mind that afternoon. He was a human presence at its best; he was a beam of human radiance. I felt his presence and was at home in it, and I wanted to linger in it, but he suddenly changed his demeanor with an air of embarrassment. "It is getting late!" he said. "I should go back to Adnan's store and fetch the meal he has been preparing for us." Then with a sparkle in his eyes he stole a compassionate look at me and left.

But he did not leave me, for the aura of his presence remained around me and within me. Something tender, something luminous, something elusive glided in my veins and found its way to my mind and then settled in my heart. I felt it; it was sweeter than honey. It was the kind of sweetness that does not merely give you a sensation of pleasure but a feeling of being upheld that makes you see more clearly, feel more passionately, think more lucidly, and envision more broadly; the kind that inflames the desire of life within your heart; the kind that makes you feel the power of hope and courage. I felt the flame of this desire in every fiber of my being. What baffled me about this realization, which fell upon me as a ray of light, is that it was shared between two human beings spontaneously. It is not an object of any kind; it flows from the human being as radiance. I wonder whether this radiance is the source of charm. Oh, how admirable, how mysterious, how noble is human presence! Even though I did not intend or expect it, a wild idea streamed through my mind: Could it be that in seeking The Eternal we must first participate in the ritual of human presence? But I was not able to dwell on this idea, because I had to welcome a transformation in process before my eyes.

The golden disc that was descending into the western sky had already sat on the horizon. It was slowly erasing the line that separated the sky from the abyss that lay on the other side. The sun that hung as a bright lamp in our sky and was a part of the world now seemed to come from the depth of The Dark. It even lost its shape and became an infinite locus of light. It became the focal point. Its rays converted the blue sky into a golden dome and the lake into a mirror that welcomed it into its depth. The oasis around me that seemed to be a formation of lake shore, trees, and blue sky vanished from the field of my vision. The ledge on which I was sitting comfortably was transformed into a ray of light dancing the dance of the sun. The whole scene became a flood of light; I was swept in this flood. I became a shining ripple in the infinity of its ocean.

I do not know how long I remained swimming in that ocean, but I do know that the flood of light that emanated from the golden disc, and which became an infinite depth of light, was not an ordinary light. The splendor that adorned its rays transcended any kind of magnificence the human mind can either create or experience. It was magical in its luminosity and exquisite in its effect. What was exciting, and in retrospect strange to my mind, is that it was not threatening, and it was not overpowering; it was friendly, gentle, and inviting. It welcomed me with open arms. And what was equally strange is that, after regaining my ordinary consciousness, I felt as if I lost something very important: I felt a pocket of vacuum in my soul. Earlier that afternoon, when we were approaching the shore of the lake, Kamal had mentioned that for his grandfather God was not a transcendent being existing in himself as a completely separate and distinct reality, but as immanent in the world he created, as its soul, as its creative impetus, and as the foundation of its laws. Well, it occurred to me that, soon after I returned to my natural habitat, if God is present everywhere, he should be the power and guiding light of every event that takes place in the scheme of nature; therefore, he should be the power and guiding light in every human encounter and in the present spectacle of the setting sun. But, we can ask, why is his presence veiled from the eyes of the majority of people, even the majority of those who are seriously educated? Why should they live in the darkness, distant from The Light?

I was unable to probe into the intricacies of these two questions, but I was and remain absolutely certain that the transformation that was unfolding before my eyes, and my consequent transport on the wings of that dazzling flood of light, was not a reverie or a daydream, but a reality, because I was not the same person after I regained my ordinary consciousness. An overpowering impulse took possession of my will: to shout, to dance, to fly, and then soar into the highest sky from the core of joy that was exploding in all directions in my heart. I was lucidly aware of my internal and physical surroundings. My desire for knowledge, my capacity for love, my appetite to ravish beauty in any of its forms, yes, these and every fiber of my being were expanding to their farthest possible limits. How could a fantasy or a reverie produce this kind of transformation, this moment of growth? The eye cannot see itself when it is seeing, and the mind cannot think, much less see, itself when it is thinking. How could I see, think, or feel myself when I was dancing the dance of The Eternal? Again, when for the first time you penetrate the tissue of the animal cell all the way to its subatomic structure and then emerge from this penetration with an adequate understanding of its elements and the causal relations that connect them with each other and with their environment, every power of your mind expands in its breadth and depth. You become a new mind. Now, imagine the being of someone who has just emerged from a dance with The Eternal, whose being was suffused with its light, with its splendor, with its life!

Yes, I was illumined by this life and I was bathed with this light, and I felt they were flowing in my blood. I became a fountain of being!

Al Basiri Oasis

Oh, it is nobler to be a fountain than to be a plant. It is nobler to give than receive, and nobler still for this fountain to derive its being from The Eternal.

I was submerged in these ideas and in the intellectual beauty of the revelation that made them possible when Kamal's figure loomed on the shore with packages in both hands. I left the ledge as soon as I could and ran toward him in an effort to lend him a helping hand. Reluctantly he allowed me to carry one bundle. He was all smiles.

"I hope you will like this meal!" Kamal said. He told me that Adnan's wife prepared it especially for us. The vegetables came from their garden and the chicken was raised in their backyard. He insisted that I should try the dates. "They are so soft they melt in your mouth. You cannot resist eating them. Besides, they are very nutritious!" Dust was falling on the oasis as we approached the rock. The first thing Kamal did when we entered the grotto was to light a candle. Then he asked whether I would enjoy a glass of wine. "Yes, I would like this very much!" I replied. And without losing any time he opened a bottle and filled two glasses, one for him and the other for me.

"To your good health!" I said with a cheerful mood.

"And to yours! Would you like to sit for a few minutes on the ledge and watch the last rite of the sun?"

"Rite?" I thought to myself as we were leaving our grotto. "He is not an ordinary human being—impossible! Everything about him betrays a deep religious nature. The way he speaks, the way he acts, and the way he conducts himself with me and others intimates a pious soul. He even looks at natural events as parts of a larger celebration. He must view human life in its entirety as a celebration. I have read in some books that we should live our life on this earth as a celebration, as though we are distinguished guests at a banquet. In our society, we tend to be religious on Sunday morning, at funerals, baptisms, weddings, in hard times, and especially when we grow older and see the eyes of death staring at us ruthlessly, menacingly. We also tend to view religiosity as a social function. A person is said to be religious inasmuch as she participates in the practices, ceremonies, rites, and symbols of her religion. Appearing religious or using religious language in the course of daily living is one more social function! The point is to keep the banner of religiosity hanging at the door of our social existence. However, the idea that calls for special attention here is that in our society religiosity, or being religious, is not an internal possession; it is a social commodity, a means to an end. Many people, including priests, use the most pious and loving language and print on their faces the most compassionate and humble expressions, mainly because they are paid to do this, just as a salesperson is paid to be nice and friendly to his or her customer. But there is a big, and I should say dramatic, difference between acting religious and being religious. A religious person lives from a religious heart, quietly, reverently, and silently: She lives from the standpoint of The Eternal.

I have always enjoyed the simile that individual lives here on earth are like the celebration of a joyful event, a banquet honoring each of us as a distinguished guest. My life is bounded by two major events, which stand before my eyes as immovable walls: my birth and my death. I came from non-being and will pass into non-being. What is miraculous and remains a mystery to my mind is that at the event of birth I come into being, I enter a world of life, of existence. Regardless of who was responsible for my birth, it is clear to my reason that coming into the world is a gift of life. Yes, life is granted as a gift. I do not choose my birth, and I do not choose my death. But if I reflect on what it means to live, I discover that this gift is an opportunity to participate in the activity of living, and that my destiny consist in realizing the potentialities constituting my human essence, particularly in growing in knowledge, love, the appreciation of beauty, and in opening my mind and soul to the ultimate that created this whole cosmic process. Yes, the activity in which I seek and enjoy a life devoted to these values, which define my humanity, is the supreme purpose for which I exist on this earth. We truly exist insofar as we expand the horizons of this activity. Realizing this purpose is our highest good. An ancient sage once said that God created the world because it is good, because it is better to be than not to be. Being as such is good; accordingly, the being of the world is good, and my being and yours is therefore good. I exist, and I exist as a human being insofar as I participate in the activity of living efficiently. However, I am not the author of my being. Thus, it is appropriate to say that I am selected, I am invited to attend the banquet of life: I am invited to participate in the rite of being. But how can I be said to participate in this banquet, and how can I conduct myself with the dignity of a good guest, if I do not partake of what it offers, namely, the opportunity to grow in knowledge, love, the appreciation of beauty, and the desire to grow in The Divine?

But when you attend a banquet it is only appropriate, indeed necessary, that you meet the hostess who invited you and worked hard to make it as enjoyable as possible, acknowledge your presence, and express your appreciation for the grand feast your hostess has prepared for you, right? Well, what if it turns out that this hostess does not seek or even expect your appreciation or the acknowledgment of your presence, most likely because you are freely and graciously invited and without any conditions? Should you not meet her? Would you not desire to know the source of the grand occasion you delighted in? But, alas! What if in meeting her you discover that the feast you have been enjoying was only an introduction, the first part of a greater, more exquisite delight? And what if you discover that your hostess is the most beautiful, the most enchanting, the most loving and lovable being you have ever met, would you not desire to delight in her presence, sit next to her, have a conversation with her, and enjoy the rest of the delicacies she has prepared for you?

The more I interacted with Kamal as a companion in this journey, the more I felt the warmth of his presence and the delight this presence produced in my heart, the more I saw that he was a participating guest in the celebration of life, that he, like me, delights in this celebration, but, unlike me, he had already met the hostess, and that he chose to sit next to her. Could it be that this is why he is indifferent to the vain glory most people pursue, thereby discovering that this glory is deceptive, and consequently developing an attitude of indifference to the vanity and glory most people seek in this short life? Could it be that he acts and reacts to the world around him from the standpoint of his friendship with the Hostess who arranged this cosmic banquet? The question that matters, then, is whether one can have such a friendship and live from its standpoint.

"Yes, in fact, I was about to make a similar suggestion!" I said, as if rising from a trance. But Kamal's body was as still as the sphinx, and his eyes were lost to what he called "the last rite of the sun." And yes, although the sun had departed, it entrusted the loyal moon with the most exuberant, gorgeous beam of silver light I had ever seen. Surrounded by an ocean of sparkling stars, and sitting on her throne in the middle of that ocean, the moon allowed her silver light to illuminate the surface of the calm lake with the most peaceful, most amiable, most otherworldly vista of light one can imagine. My eyes were provoked by its simplicity. As I gazed at it, trying to grasp it, I felt my gaze swallowed by it in some mysterious manner. Yes, I was swallowed up by its depth, by its infinity, by its sublime infinity. A shiver was jumping wildly in my heart, because I was delighting in what was happening within my gaze, and I wholeheartedly allowed it. "Is it possible that this vista—its beauty, mystery, intimacy, and grand simplicity—is one more face, one more smiling expression, of The Eternal?" This train of reflection was interrupted by loud breathing coming directly from Kamal's throbbing chest. I was alarmed, for I thought he was suffering from some kind of heart discomfort. But when I examined his face I discovered that he was calm and that his eyes were absorbed in the last faint shimmering of the dusk. Drops of sweat were shining on the furrows of his forehead under the silver rays of the moon. "Are you alright, Kamal?" I asked with a deep feeling of concern. As though waking from a dream, he turned his face, which was an icon of peace, the sort that radiates compassion, with a gentle smile and said: "I am fine, Dimitri, very fine, indeed." A halo of soft light was hovering around his head. It must have been created by the sweet hand of the moon. "Shall we offer a toast to the moon, Queen of the Night?" he added. "Yes, of course, it is most appropriate that we make an offering to The Queen!" was my answer.

We drank our wine in silence. We did not have to say anything, because we both were the beneficiaries of the sweetest kiss of joy any human being could long for; we were enveloped by the warmth of this kiss. This sweetness and this warmth were the subject of our silent conversation. They created a bond of understanding, of human solidarity between us.

"You must be famished," he said, "it might be wise to eat supper a little early tonight, because we should resume our journey before dawn tomorrow. The road as well as the weather south of this area is not friendly; we may have to improvise as we forge our way into the heart of the desert."

"Yes, I understand." With this understanding we returned to the grotto. The candle Kamal lit earlier was glowing with bright light. Without wasting any time, he opened the bags he brought from Adnan's store. As he was spreading the food on a tray made of reed, I could smell the most appetizing aroma I had relished in a long time. Having given me an explanation of every dish he placed before me, he said, "please, eat heartily and enjoy it." Then he brought the bottle of wine, which was half-full, and poured it in our glasses. "To a long life!" he said as he lifted his glass and moved it in my direction. Doing the same, I raised my glass and clacked it against his. "And to you, Kamal!"

The food we ate was delectable. To share a meal, a glass of wine, and a profound religious feeling with a human being is, in my view, a divine gift. It was impossible for me to control the flood of emotions that was seeking expression: "I am grateful!" I said, looking at Kamal. He did not look at me; he remained silent, but a moment later a tear fell from his eye onto the plate. I felt, I understood! Before we were finished, Kamal reminded me that I should eat some dates. He assured me that they were delicious. I did. I wondered whether it was possible to keep the rest for the next day. "Oh, yes! They are for us to eat and enjoy." We could feel the cool breeze of the desert streaming through the grotto as we were finishing our supper. It was time to leave the evening behind and place our souls in the hands of our guardian angels. Kamal suggested that he sleep in the adjoining grotto out of respect for my privacy and the fact that he snored. He lit a candle and took it with him along with his sleeping bag, blanket, and a rucksack.

I do not remember having a more peaceful sleep than the one I had that night. I woke up invigorated with a passionate desire to explore the heart of the desert. Both of us were ready to leave the rock at the crack of dawn. Our first stop was Adnan's store, where we were able to clean ourselves and have a good breakfast. Luckily there was no one around. We loaded the van with our luggage and the needed supplies for our trip quietly and without any delay. It was surprising to see Kamal carrying two large cans of gasoline. He must have noted my surprise, for he remarked: "In the desert, we do not know what kind of weather we might encounter. It is always prudent to be ready for the worst." This man knows the ways of the desert and he feels at home with it, I reflected in a mood of somber humility. As we were about to depart, Adnan walked hurriedly toward us and wished us a safe and successful trip. I, in turn, shook hands with him and thanked him for his kindness and hospitality.

chapter 3

Supper at Saleem's House

I NOW THINK THAT Kamal had a date with the dawn that morning, because shortly after we left Al Basiri Oasis, a very soft glow emerged into our sky from behind the eastern horizon. Its emergence gave rise to the horizon. "I wonder whether you might be interested in watching the sunrise," Kamal asked. "In a few minutes we should be approaching Jabal Al Nasiri. This mountain was popular during the Byzantine period, and it is still popular among the Bedouins who cross the desert from Iraq to Syria. Some people say that it was covered with trees until the days of the Sumerians. There is a good spot where we can have an overview of this part of the desert. We can also watch the sunrise. I have a good feeling that you would enjoy the sight of the sun as it is rising into the sky of the desert."

The phenomenon of dawn is, I think, fascinating, because it symbolizes the act of creation, the supreme act God has performed, and the greatest act a human being can perform. The coming into being of something that did not exist before is really miraculous, and perhaps the miracle of all miracles. We marvel at the creative act of the artist, the scientist, the legislator, the philosopher, the social leader, but I am interested in the first creative act, in the act that started the whole process of cosmic unfolding, because I know that an understanding of this act will enable me to move closer to its source and perhaps touch it. I feel a longing to dwell on the gate of this source, to see the lightning and witness the thundering and rumbling of the act that gave rise to this world and still reverberates in every corner of its being. But the dawn that announces the creation of our world is not only symbolic, it is also revelatory, because it is itself a revelation of the ultimate source: The Sun. It is clear and distinct to me that every created object, regardless of whether it is natural or human, reveals the nature of its creator. But the natural order, which still baffles the human mind in the different modes of its existence and in the way it functions, does not only reveal the nature of its source, but also objectifies it. Yes, it objectifies it! But unlike the creative act which results in an object or an idea by a human being, the act of cosmic creation is an ongoing process, an ongoing emanation from The Source, which overflows into its creation. It does not exist outside its creation but is immanent in its fabric, exactly the way the sun is immanent in its rays and the way life is immanent in the living organism. Its creation comes from it and derives its being from it. This is why it is immanent in it. Yes, I yearn to dwell near the gate from which the light of The Source flows into this marvelous scheme of nature: I miss my source.

"Yes, Kamal, I would greatly appreciate a visit to this mountain." In a few minutes the peak of the mountain first loomed as a dark point in the distance and then as a cone. When we reached its foot Kamal left the road and drove around a small mound. "The best path that leads to the peak begins here," he explained. It was obvious to me that he knew its geography perfectly well, because in ascending it he led me through a number of passages and winding tracks. We stood at the foot of the starting point of our ascent. "Be watchful of poisonous snakes!" Kamal warned me, as we were trying to walk through a maze of rocks and potholes. "Some but not all of them are poisonous. They sometimes slink leisurely without paying attention to any kind of disturbance around them. They think they own the mountain, because not many people come here frequently. They are ordinarily friendly, as long as you do not trespass on their space or try to harm them."

The soft glow that welcomed us as we reached the peak of the mountain was a golden radiance emanating from the center of the horizon. I was electrified by the scene that was awaiting me. It was magical! Without knowing how, I became captive to this magic. Frankly I did not resist it, because it was friendly. I was transfixed in the presence of that magical radiance. The magical does not speak the language of thought or argument or explanation; it is a blaze of charm that welcomes you into its arms willingly, hopefully, and lovingly. The magical is truth with a beautiful face; it is goodness with a loving heart! This alone is the source of its allure; and this is why we cannot resist its call. It seemed to me at that moment that both the radiance and the sand that spread around me as an ocean of being flowed from that sun, that the two were one and the same, that heaven and earth were one, and that I was neither in one nor in the other but in both at the same time. I was not thinking, for I was a drop of thought; I was not feeling, for I was a drop of feeling; I was not conscious of any particular thing, for I was a drop of consciousness; and I was not ecstatic, for I was a drop of ecstasy. How can you be distracted by the particular when you are in the bosom of the infinite, when the infinite shines in your soul, mind, and heart? When you are filled with it, you become one with it. Then you do not think it but directly see it and feel it; then every act of thought and intuition becomes powerless; then you become a drop of being, the being that you should be; yes, then you experience the infinite as silence, as eternal silence.

Sunrise is a moment of creation; but, then again, every moment we live is a dawn, a moment of creation, because every moment is an emanation from The Sun: The Source. What would it be like for a human being to conduct her life from an understanding of this truth, from the certain knowledge that our life is an unfolding dawn, and that this dawn is a ray of the eternal sun? What would it be like if every thought, every feeling, and every act originates from this truth?

Kamal was sitting in a groove several feet away from me when I regained my consciousness; he was speechless, motionless. He was completely oblivious to my existence, and I was completely engrossed by his meditative posture and by the nobility of his complexion when he suddenly made a very slight stir, as if waking from a sweet dream.

"Ah, there you are! I am sorry for abandoning you so rudely! I must have forgotten myself in that groove while waiting for the sunrise. Alas! I missed it. The sun has already left the horizon," he said with an expression of embarrassment on his face.

"Do not feel sorry," I rejoined, "because I too was relishing the beauty of the sun as it was making its way into the heart of the blue sky. Standing in this spot reminds me of the summit of Mt. Parnassus, where ancient Greek artists and philosophers flirted with the muses. But now I am more inclined to think that lovers of wisdom and beauty do not frequent this mountain in order to win the favor of the muses but in order to be close to the gods. Their passion for creation is really a passion for The Eternal."

"Yes," Kamal interjected, "maybe this lends some credibility to a tale I have heard more than once that many of the holy men who founded the monastic order of the early Christian church, not to mention John Chrysostom, used to spend several months every year on this summit trying to commune with God. But I think they chose to live in the desert for other reasons. It would be a good idea to resume our travel," he interrupted himself abruptly, "because it seems we shall have a hot day ahead of us. It would take us about four hours to reach our new destination. The remainder of the road is really tortuous. It will be much worse than the first stretch."

"It is strongly recommended, and from my point of view an imperative, that you drink as much water as you can. The weather here is, as you must have already noted, hot and dry; it tends to dehydrate the body," he said soon after we resumed our trip. He was correct in his recommendation, because I had already felt thirsty, not only because I was physically dehydrated but also because the experience I had on the summit of Al Nasiri Mountain had consumed me both physically and mentally. In such an experience the body as well as the emotions is placed under the direction of the spirit. Total concentration is a necessary condition for reaching out to The Eternal. I have frequently thought that the body is a prison of the human spirit, and sometimes an obstacle in our quest for The Eternal.

Instead of opening one bottle of water, I opened two and offered one to Kamal. He accepted it without saying a word and without making a gesture of any kind. I have been learning to speak the language of silent dialogue with him more proficiently ever since our departure from Tadmur. But what was astonishing to me was the comfort I felt in his presence. I did not feel intimidated or threatened; I did not feel I was with a stranger; I did not feel I needed to prove or justify anything I said or did; and I did not feel I was competing with him about anything. On the contrary, I do not exaggerate if I say that we mutually accepted each other in the fullness of our humanity in spite of our physical, intellectual, and cultural differences. Oh, my goodness! When the spark of our humanity is kindled in the heart, when it illumines the inner sanctum, all the concerns of this world dwarf into pettiness. We see ourselves and others in the light of our true being; we see that there is a bond that unites and grounds us in the same soil: The Divine. I kept this revelation a secret in my heart, but in a way it was not a secret, because how could I feel the way I did if Kamal did not feel the same? No, the human as such does not harbor secrets: It is made of light, and there are no dark spots or hiding spaces in the texture of light.

"I shall be happy to drive some of the way," I said. "The road has so far been very rough and nerve-wracking."

"No, at least not now. I am used to this road. I only hope that you are not ruffled."

"I am fine!" I said. "I sometimes think that the body should be chastised every once in a while." He smiled and then responded to my retort:

"Please, let me know when or if you are hungry. We can have a snack anytime you feel an urge for it. We should arrive at Saab Al Abar in about two to three hours."

"I think I can wait till then."

But we did not arrive at Saab Al Abar in mid-afternoon, as Kamal estimated, only because it was extremely difficult to navigate through a continuous trail of mutilated road. And what made the drive harder still was the heat. The temperature was in fact close to 105 F, but it felt like 110 F. There was not a cloud in the sky. We were surrounded on all sides by a vast expanse of barren land. It looked rugged, desolate. "In this kind of weather," Kamal remarked, "it is wise to drive slowly. It is also wise to cool the engine once in a while." And we did. The calm that spread around us was once interrupted by a small caravan of camels leading a large flock of sheep. Several men and women were riding the camels. Kamal stopped the van and waved to them. They answered his friendly gesture with a cheerful greeting. Then a man, who seemed to be in charge of the caravan, gave a sign to the other riders, apparently asking them to take a moment's break. He stepped down from his saddle and approached Kamal, who was expecting him. They shook hands and stood next to the camel for a few minutes speaking and once in a while pointing south and east. Although I neither heard nor understood what was transpiring between them, I surmised that Kamal was seeking some information about the weather condition in that part of the desert. Soon after the conversation ended Kamal returned to the van and resumed the drive. A little later he said: "It seems we have been lucky so far. The caravan master told me that we have just missed a very bad sandstorm that raged through this area early this morning." Then he added: "We might encounter some storms south of Saab Al Abar tomorrow." He reminded me that we were in the middle of the storm season.

"You see, I am ignorant of the ways of the desert. I shall readily comply with any decision you make. I do trust your judgment wholeheartedly. If you think it will be dangerous to continue our trip, please, feel absolutely free to return to Tadmur."

"I do not think that there is any serious reason for alarm. I am familiar with this land. We simply need to know what to expect. It is almost impossible to predict the weather conditions once we pass Saab Al Abar. Bedouins are experts in the ways of the desert. They speak its language. They know how to maneuver their way through the fiercest storms. Besides, it is, I think, critically important for you to witness a storm in action, to see it roar like a wounded bull, rumble like a vengeful lion, crush everything in its way like a tsunami, and spout clouds of sand like a tornado."

Kamal made his last remark with an air of confidence and understanding. Instead of feeling the challenge of intimidation, and perhaps fear, I was self-composed and peaceful. More than once I noticed a mirage floating in the distance. Even though it was unreal, and I did not doubt its unreality for one second, it delivered to my vision, as it must have done to others, the illusion of an oasis. I was engrossed in this phenomenon and was comparing it to the grandiose and sometimes outrageous fantasies which hover in the imagination of many people as a kind of ultimate concern without being able to recognize the difference between fiction and reality. I wonder how many a human being fails to see the difference between a fantasy and a rational, realizable purpose. Kamal interrupted my rumination by announcing that we should reach our destination within one hour. But it took us almost two hours to arrive at Saab Al Abar, mainly because driving through the fractured parts of the road was a struggle. The sun was approaching the western horizon when we reached this modest center of human civilization. We saw several herds of camels, and of sheep, grazing in fenced pastures on both sides of the road. In addition to a few simple buildings scattered on both sides of the road, clustered in the middle, I was able to see a rather extensive spread of tents on the periphery. It was difficult for me to classify it as a village or as an oasis. It is more accurate to say that it was a trading post sustained by an impermanent stream that flowed into a nearby pond and a grid of fences enclosing plots of arable land.

Seeking God

"Here we are!" Kamal said as he put the van to rest near a somewhat large tent, sending a pleasant smile of satisfaction in my direction, as if to say: "Welcome to the heart of the desert!" In fact, I began to feel, and for the first time, that I was in the desert. This feeling grew in magnitude and clarity the closer we got to Saab Al Abar. The framework of thinking, feeling, and willing, as well as the concerns that preoccupied my mind, that dominated my consciousness, and made up the world in which I had been living until I began my journey in Homs, was being gradually displaced by a new framework of thinking, feeling, and willing, and by new concerns. I began to feel that I was a part of the desert and its life. I had already started to see and respond to this world with a new interest, sensibility, and understanding. I was able to see the desert as a desert, not as a barren land, not as something irrelevant to my life and the life of other human beings. I started to see that, as a unique world, the desert is a kind of book we can read and that every element and every dimension of it is a veil that stands between our minds and the foundation of the world. The displacement of the urban world in my mind by the world of the desert was not a process of rejecting or denying its validity; no, it was a process of bracketing it for a while, of placing it on the fringe of my consciousness, of adopting another standpoint of thinking, feeling, and willing. When we adopt a cultural, religious, philosophical, scientific, or some ideological standpoint we become prisoners to it, in the sense that we think, feel, will, and react to things and events around us, even plan our lives and plan certain objectives, from its standpoint. And yet, although difficult, it is possible to make a standpoint shift, to change the standpoint we act or live by, and assume another. It is possible for me to assume an aesthetic standpoint when I perceive a work of art, or to assume a religious standpoint when I worship in a church, or a social standpoint when I am in the company of decent people. Being in the desert gave me the opportunity to assume the standpoint of the desert citizen. I sought to lift the veils that stood between my mind and the scene of nature that confronted me as an enigma. But the revelation which began to unfold before my eyes during the past few days, and which was a pleasant surprise, was that in sailing from the shoreline of my urban standpoint to the shoreline of the desert life, I had to open myself up, to free my mind from erroneous assumptions about the desert, to be willing to listen to its voice, and to learn the language it speaks. This process of opening up was, in my case,

Supper at Saleem's House

merely an intellectual act; it was an existential process of realization, of immersing my body, mind, and soul in the ways of the desert, of accepting it on its own terms, of putting in abeyance, at least temporarily, the prejudices of my urban standpoint. The mind can see things and events when it is free, and it is free when it is in command of its physical, emotional, and intellectual sensibilities, when it recognizes that the established habit of thinking and feeling the world are not absolute and that they are only instruments, in fact, languages, of conversing with nature. But Alas! Is this not the kind of attitude we urgently need in thinking, feeling, and interacting with human beings? How often do we see other persons, regardless of the kind of relation we have with them, from our individual, idiosyncratic standpoint?

Yes, for the first time, I began to feel that I was in the heart of the desert, not because I was physically in that godforsaken place, in the middle of nowhere, but because I began to see it as a desert, to feel it as a desert, and to know what it means to be in a desert. A quiet feeling of joy blessed my eyes as I watched Kamal talk to a man in front of a rather plain, two-storey building, which looked to me like two small boxes placed on top of each other. It is hard to say how long I waited for him in the van, only because I was rambling through the labyrinth of my own thoughts and feelings. But when he came back, he informed me that we would be spending the night in that settlement. He said that a special tent was being set up for our private use until the time of our departure. Then he added, "Saleem, the owner of the store, has invited us to have a cup of coffee with him. It might be a good idea to visit the bathroom while the coffee is being brewed."

A cup of coffee after a long drive seemed to me a most welcome idea. Kamal led me to the store where he introduced me to Saleem, who received me with a cordial and cheerful spirit. His eyes sparkled with curiosity and interest when he heard that I was from the U.S.A. He asked Kamal to say to me in English that not many Americans come to this part of the desert. French and especially German people frequent this area. Well, soon after I was cleaned up and refreshed I joined Saleem and Kamal for coffee. Saleem was anxious to see my reaction when I took my first sip, for he wanted to know whether it pleased my palate. A childish, pure and innocent, smile danced on his lips when he noted my obvious satisfaction with the coffee. And, indeed, it was so delicious I asked for a second cup. Kamal intimated that Saleem wanted us to spend the night at his house, but Kamal himself insisted that we spend it in a tent in order to fulfill my desire for the richest possible experience of the desert. "I have not seen this gentleman for almost five years," Kamal remarked to me after Saleem left. "He used to come to Tadmur to buy goods for his store, but now the companies he deals with ship whatever he needs on a regular basis. He seems to be flourishing. His father's family and the family of my wife are distant relatives. Let us go to the tent and get settled. It should be ready for us. You can take a short nap. You might need it after such a long, rocky drive!"

Contrary to my expectation, the tent was a spacious room, made of four solid walls, weaved out of camel hair with a small window in the middle of each one of them. The floor was covered with a beautiful, hand woven rug surrounded by two rows of cushions. Two mattresses, pillows, blankets, and other bedding objects were placed in one corner. "Sit down, stretch your legs," Kamal's friendly voice announced. "Relax while I secure the things we shall need for our journey tomorrow." I did exactly what he recommended soon after he left. I sat on the rug and leaned my back against a cushion. I was alone with myself, enfolded by a soft breeze of tranquility. Suddenly, and without noticing how, my eyes were fixed on the wall facing me. It was a delicately woven arabesque made mainly of red, black, and very few, hardly perceptible, yellow colors. It stood in front of me as a tapestry. My eyes were lost in its abstract yet vibrant form. It had the capacity to attract and sustain the totality of my vision. It was a plain but fluid, playful geometrical design. My aesthetic eyes were dancing their way through the design of this tapestry without being either bored or tired. On the contrary, they were charmed by their polyphonic harmony. I cannot remember the duration of my absorption in this arabesque, but I do remember that I was completely lost in the world of its exuberant lines and colors. What made this dance exciting and truly absorbing was the fact that it took place within the boundary of the design I perceived. There was nothing about it that lured my attention away from it. It was a pure form without any representational allusions or distractions. It stood on its own feet, so to say, without any need to rely on any external reference of any kind.

Once you begin your aesthetic dance you feel a desire to stay dancing, and you could stay dancing endlessly—an endless dance, a dance that does not aim at anything except the pleasure of dancing it forever! Oh, no! This kind of dance aims at something: to live in its beauty forever. Could it be that the desire for this dance is a cry for being? But it seems to me reasonable to say that being is not being if it does not endure: Change is a process of perishing; being is a state of permanence. Yes, this kinship with being, with that which endures, captures, in my opinion, the Bedouin's experience as well as his passion for what endures, for The Eternal. For him, the desert is the home of The Eternal! The scene I perceived, yes, the scene that was weaved by the hands of men and women of the desert, originated from the soul of the desert. I was in a tent in the desert, but the desert was in the tent. There I sat in the desert, and next to it!

A mild tingle, the kind one feels in a moment of exciting revelation, found its way to my mind. I was inclined to revisit the same tapestry in an attempt to explore its aesthetic depth once more, to feel the soul of the Bedouins who were drinking from the cup of The Eternal when they were weaving this design. But this attempt, once materialized, prompted me to explore the other walls, which were apparently made by the same hands. I turned my attention to the rug on which I was sitting. "Everything about this desert and in it seems to sing the song of The Eternal," I thought. "Was this tent made for me? Of course not! It has been made every month and every year ever since the Bedouin began to roam the desert, and it has been waiting for the lover of The Eternal ever since."

As I turned my attention sideways to examine the other walls, a young boy carrying our luggage opened the door. He placed the bags next to the mattress, and then he greeted me with a polite bow. He must have known that I was a foreigner, for he did not utter a word; but he was rather curious about me, because the inquiring look that was fixed on his face made me feel like I was a Martian! A moment later, Kamal entered the tent: "You are awake!" he said, with a mild astonishment gleaming from his eyes. "I thought you would be sound asleep by now." Gazing at those eyes with a surprise intermingled with compassion, I said: "I shall take my nap momentarily." Within seconds I leaned against the cushion the way I did a little while ago. The image of the arabesque hovered in the ceiling of my consciousness as I surrendered myself to a peaceful sleep.

It was almost dark when I emerged from my nap. I had a strong desire to walk for a few minutes before eating supper, but my desire was not fulfilled, because when I left the tent I saw Kamal and Saleem talking just a few feet away. Saleem recognized my appearance with a pleasant smile, then both he and Kamal moved in my direction, and I did the same. "I hope you feel rested!" Kamal asked.

"Yes, I feel rested and invigorated!" I said, expressing a feeling of appreciation for my concern.

"We should have our supper in about half an hour. Saleem wondered whether you might enjoy a traditional drink of the desert, made from dates. It was popular during the Byzantine and Roman periods. Some people around here still make it. It is a bit strong, stronger than wine, I should say, but I think it would be interesting to try it."

"Of course, I shall be very happy to try it. I am not a stranger to strong alcoholic beverages, especially on significant social occasions."

"Splendid!" Kamal said. Saleem was all smiles when he heard that we would have a drink before supper.

The boy who brought the luggage to our tent greeted us as he entered Saleem's house. Two teenagers, a young man and a young woman, were waiting for us in the sitting room. Their mother was standing between them. All of them moved forward when our eyes met theirs. Saleem introduced them to me. The walls were covered with hand woven rugs. One of them depicted the tree of life; another was an abstract geometrical formation. The floor was covered with a large rug. The striking feature that impressed my aesthetic sense was simplicity, no elaborate decoration of any kind. "These people live close to nature! They are in touch with her soul, and this soul shines through the way they live and express themselves." This is what I was thinking when Saleem opened a bottle of arak and poured some in each glass. He followed the arak with a dash of water, transforming the clear beverage into a milky liquid. Then giving one to me and another to Kamal, he said: "To your health, Dimitri and Kamal!" And turning his face toward his wife and children, he said in a loving voice, "To you, my dear family! My wife Hasnaa and my children are honored to have you in our house." When she heard her name mentioned, Hasnaa allowed a shy smile on the corner of her mouth, but her eyes were aglow with pleasure. Although the children were silent, I could tell from looking at their eyes that they were bubbling with curiosity and interest. I felt, as I was having my first sip of arak, which reminded me of the ouzo my father used to drink, that the members of this family lived in a medium of mutual affection and understanding, a medium absent from the life of many an urban family nowadays, where fierce, untamed individualism bordering on selfishness prevails.

I felt a streak of fire piercing through my throat as I had my first sip of arak, and I tried to pacify it by swallowing my saliva; a tear was trying to tremble in the corner of my eye, but I suppressed it. Saleem was watching me, so was his wife. He promptly asked Kamal to tell me that I should follow my sip with nuts or a cube of the cheese his wife made or with a slice of cucumber. "This should make it more enjoyable." In fact, he was right. The children asked Kamal a number of questions about me. The oldest son, Umar, wanted to know about my profession and why I was interested in the Syrian Desert. When Kamal told him that I taught philosophy, he simply stared at me with wild, excited eyes. The young man must have been acquainted with philosophy. He remained silent, but he kept looking at me with rapt attention, for he desired to have a private conversation with me, but he could not, because he did not speak English and I did not speak Arabic. But he directed a question to Kamal concerning my interest in the desert and especially why I was undertaking this rather adventurous journey. When Kamal translated Umar's question I as well as his parents smiled. It was extremely difficult for me to give an adequate answer to his question in general and to this young man in particular, for the nature of my adventure was private and resisted serious rational discourse, even though it was truly rational.

But I gave him an answer, not only because the young man was serious in raising the question but also because it was disrespectful to ignore or belittle him. For some reason, my eyes converged on his face. It was a serious face hungry for knowledge! His clear, honey-dipped eyes glittered with aspiration. You could feel in them a profound passion for life. They had an unusual magnetic appeal. No one could underestimate his presence. His forehead, which was crowned with dark black hair, with a tussle hanging on the right side, rested on two thick black eyebrows. One could tell that they covered a world of depth. His aquiline nose, somewhat large, sat between two bearded cheeks, disclosing the budding spirit of youth. I simply gaped at this image of youth and said: "I am in search of The Eternal." I was hoping that stating the general purpose of my quest might be the sort of answer he was looking for. But I was mistaken. He almost jumped to his feet when he heard the statement of my purpose, for he unconsciously knitted a knot on his youthful forehead and exclaimed in Arabic: "Do you mean The Eternal in the desert?" I simply looked at him with a blank face, for I did not understand what he said. At this point, Kamal became our interpreter. After he translated what Umar said, I let a nod of acquiescence be my answer. The young man sat still, dumbfounded. Apparently he could not grasp what it is like to seek or live in the presence of The Eternal. Or could it be that he was too young to grasp or feel an itch for The Eternal? I wonder.

"How?" His response evoked in my mind a feeling of pleasant awkwardness, pleasant because the provocation posed by this young man commanded my respect and admiration. I knew I could not deliver a detailed answer, for I was not certain that I was in possession of one, so I decided to start a train of thought that might be useful to both of us. I said: "Would you agree that the idea of The Eternal stands in contrast to the idea of the temporal."

"Yes, I do."

"Would you also agree that whatever is temporal is not real, because it is in constant change, or flux? You see, the moment a thing changes it is different from what it was; it is a new thing. The thing it was before it had changed ceased to exist. And since it is always changing, then it stands to reason that it cannot be real. Thus, what passes out of existence does not exist anymore. Again, in order for anything to exist it must linger, or endure? Is this reasonable to say?"

"Yes, I understand what you say."

"Would you also agree that everything that exists around us is always changing and that nothing seems to endure?"

"I have been thinking about this fact, and I agree to what you say."

"But the world is changing and it seems to endure. Well, is this constantly changing spectacle of nature at all possible if there is not something that endures? I mean is change possible if there is no permanence? Consider this: A changing thing comes into being and passes out of being. Can anything come into being and pass out of being by itself?

"No."

"Now, look at the whole scheme of nature. We both agreed that it is constantly changing. Can it change by itself? Let me explain this point further. When a thing changes, it becomes different from what it was in the preceding moment, and it becomes different in virtue of a new feature or aspect. Correct?"

"Yes."

"In this case, something has come into being, thereby becoming part of the thing in question. And it came into being from nothing, at least, so far as we are concerned. Would you agree?"

"It seems I must say yes."

"Well, we have no choice. Now does it come into being from nothing or by itself or by something other than itself, something superior to it in power and intelligence?"

"Why do you say intelligence? Is this a justifiable assumption?" he asked with a tremor of hesitation in his voice. But I was impressed and provoked by his question.

"By 'intelligence' I simply mean a power that acts purposefully and with a sense of design. Moreover, in making this statement I do not assume the existence of intelligence, at least, not one that is like ours. I simply make it on the basis of the kind of change that takes place. I infer the cause from the effect: Knowledge of the effect discloses knowledge of the cause. Put differently, my knowledge of the cause is derived from my knowledge of the effect. If the effect exhibits order and intelligence, I can say that the cause must also have acted intelligently and purposefully, by design."

"Perhaps. I grant that what you say seems to apply fairly commonly in science and practical life, but. . ." Suddenly, his eyes wandered away from me; a few seconds later, he shyly acquiesced: "Let us assume the validity of what you said."

Yet, I was certain that the mind of this young man, this man who has drunk the milk of the Syrian Desert, was not thinking in terms of abstract concepts or formal logical relations but ontologically, in terms of being, in terms of another logic, the logic of change insofar as it is given to human experience, for the thrust of his reaction was directed not simply at the way particular things in nature were changing or coming into being and passing out of being but at the way of the world as a whole; and he was thinking not from the standpoint of the human mind but from the standpoint of something different and greater. And yet, in spite of this realization, I thought it was wise to continue my line of reasoning.

"Let us widen the perspective of our thinking. Focus your attention on the scheme of nature as a whole and as an ongoing process of change. How did this whole phenomenon of change come about?"

"I follow you."

"Now, suppose we inquire into the cause of this change: Should we posit such a cause? And suppose we do, should it not be permanent?"

"Yes for both questions. I see the direction of your thinking. Do you mean that since everything in the universe changes, then there must be something that makes this change possible and that this something must necessarily be permanent? But, what. . ."

Our conversation was interrupted by Hasnaa's announcement that dinner was ready and that we could continue our discussion after we finished eating. All of us sat around a small table covered with an assortment of dishes I had never eaten before. "I hope he likes our food," Hasnaa remarked to Kamal, who translated to me what she said. Upon hearing this, I raised my glass and offered a toast to Saleem and Kamal and wished all the family happiness and prosperity. Everyone was eating heartily except Umar. He was in a deep, thoughtful mood; I think he was eating without being aware of how the food was transported from the dish to his mouth. His eyes did not leave the boundary of his plate. On one occasion I noticed that he stole a glimpse from his plate to mine, as if he was conducting, or perhaps continuing, a conversation with me. It was clear to me that the young man was born for a serious intellectual vocation. A strong feeling of sympathy leaped from my heart toward him. I knew there and then that the seams that held the parts of his soul together were bursting and that the wild beast of creativity was raging in his mind. I wished I spoke his language, but I did not. When everyone finished eating their meal with a spirit of thankfulness, I asked Kamal to relay to Umar that I was grateful for our short conversation and apologetic for the fact that it was short and did not shed adequate light on the nature of my visit to the Syrian Desert. The young man looked at me with a pleasant and appreciative surprise, and a whiff of thankfulness flew from his lips to my eyes. "On the contrary," he said, "our conversation was very illuminating; it helped me to understand the nature of your journey in a very interesting way."

That evening, Saleem was a jovial man. Soon after we retired to our chairs in the living room, he poured one more sip of arak into my glass and proposed a toast to a wonderful guest. His wife, who had vanished from our midst a few minutes earlier, reappeared with a small tray of sweets she had prepared for us. She hoped, she said, that I would enjoy them. She remained standing as she expressed her wish. Hasnaa was a slim, tall woman. Her hair was black, covered with a red scarf. Her eyes were large and expressed the wildest beauty I had seen so radiant on the face of a woman. They expressed a kind of earthy, transparent beauty, the kind that sweeps you away into the elegance of womanhood. There was an air of dignity in the way she stood and spoke. Kamal remarked that in his family serving sweets after the evening meal symbolized a wish for a sweet and happy life. It also symbolized the sweetness of human friendship. I looked at Hasnaa's cheerful face, met it with a smiling nod, and thanked the hands that prepared a most delicious meal and brought us all together in a rare moment of human warmth, which I would cherish for as long as I lived. When she heard the translation of what I said, the woman suppressed a smile, lowered her eyes, revealing an elegant feeling of feminine modesty, and then proceeded to remove the empty dishes from the table. Almost instantaneously her daughter jumped to her feet and rushed to the dishes with her mother. "How splendid! How noble, how inspiring family love is," I thought. "Love, more than faith, moves the human heart, and more than faith, love moves mountains!"

"It is getting late for us," Kamal whispered in my ear. But strange enough, I was not aware of the passage of time, for I was enthralled by the spirit of this family, by its realistic, open, and pious orientation. I felt the touch of this spirit in every fiber of my being. I know that my encounter with them was brief, yes, but it was an open window to their soul. I was able to see and feel the love that bonded them together and the deep feeling of contentment expressed in their faces, in the way they spoke and interacted with me and in the awesome simplicity in which they moved about me. In everything they did, they expressed innocent spontaneity, cultivated social sense, and a genuine love of life. Is the life of this family a living image of the spirit of the desert? Does it emerge into this world the way beauty emerges from the hands of the artist in the process of the creative act? Does it emerge the way the world emerges from the divine smile? Is the life of this family one of the many languages the Syrian Desert speaks? I was lost to this meditative excursion when Kamal reminded me of the need to sleep. "Yes, we should be on our way," I said, as if waking from a dream. I rose to my feet, following the lead of my companion and friend. When Saleem noticed our initiative, he, as well as the rest of the family, did the same. It was an awkward moment, especially for Umar, because he was anxious to spend more time with me. I am certain he had a strong desire to continue our conversation on the relation between the eternal and the temporal. He approached me with a warm handshake and, joining it with the other hand, he pressed it hard and said something in Arabic, apparently wishing me a safe and successful journey. He was followed by his sister and brother, then his mother, and finally his father. I wished I could spend more time with this lovely family to know them better and to discover the secrets hidden in their hearts. It was a heart-rending moment of leave-taking, of leaving something precious behind.

"But, goodness! Can such pearls of human presence, of shining sparks of the human heart, be left behind—here, there, or anywhere?" I reflected as my eyes were still enjoying the exuberance of their smiling faces. "No, the place of such pearls is the human mind, that mansion where our thoughts, feelings, and desires come into being. They come and stay there not the way clothes stay in a closet but as incentives with eyes and ears, as nutrients that nourish our next act. Once received, these pearls become incorporated in the structure of our being. They thrive there as moments of human growth. These pearls are drops of life falling from the soul of The Universal; they lift the place where they stay to a higher level of being. They are bright, sparkling stars. They illumine the place where they stay and disclose its universal nature. Believe me, I have seen with my heart, yes, with my heart, the light of these pearls when I was enveloped by the warmth of this desert family, by the mysterious power of the love that united them as a community, by the grace with which they welcomed me to their presence. I have always thought that love is infective, that it has the capacity to shatter those walls that separate human beings from each other, thus creating the conditions of human growth and development. But now I see what it means for love to be a bond that unites people and why it is the only basis of human solidarity. The glory of this bond is that it does not look at causes or consequences. It has no mathematical skills whatsoever, because it does not know how to calculate: how to add, subtract, multiply, or divide! It simply flows from the heart freely, abundantly, the way a river flows from its spring and the way light flows from the sun. Flowing, which

Supper at Saleem's House

defines the logic of giving, is its essence and reason for being. Its destiny consists in this flow.

A canopy of glittering stars were hanging as a chandelier over us when we left Saleem's house and walked toward our tent. It was a magnificent sight. Kamal hesitated a little and then looked upward, gazing at that canopy, as if he was lost in the world of its magnificence. Curiosity took the better of me, so I looked at the chandelier and invited the eyes of my imagination to savor its radiance. "Are these pearls that glitter in the dark sky of the desert, the same pearls that illumine our way in this glorious evening, also drops of The Universal, the same pearls in a different light? What would the world be like without these drops? Could it be that the light that emanates from them is the spirit that gives unity and meaning to the scheme of nature and human life? How did it come about that I, this infinitely finite speck, this infinitely rich world of being, stand in solidarity with this stranger, who is in fact no stranger, under the same chandelier delighting in the splendor of these dancing pearls? How did it come about that I feel at home with this stranger? And what is this home but the human heart, the same heart that cries for recognition, for growth, for freedom, for compassion, for immortality, for the ultimate?" Kamal was gaping at me when I was leaving this stream of reflection. My vision moved away from the scene of the chandelier to the scene of peace in his eyes. Our eyes met. They spoke, and they spoke the language of silence, the language of our humanity, the language of the true universal. We understood each other: We communicated. It was a glorious moment, an unforgettable moment.

The tent was waiting for us. This was the first time we spent the night under the same roof. As soon as we entered the tent, Kamal, who was proficient in the ways of the desert, immediately lit a gas lamp and then spread the mattresses, one on each side of the tent. He covered each mattress with a sheet and a blanket. He placed a pillow at the end of each mattress. "Please, cover yourself well, because it gets rather chilly at night. If you need anything, do not hesitate to wake me up." A few seconds later he added: "It is better to have a good sleep than to wake up early, because our drive will not be smooth tomorrow."

"Thank you, Kamal. I wish you a good night," I said. I was about to thank him for a most meaningful day, but immediately checked myself. I know in today's society it is almost socially imperative to thank a person for the smallest thing he or she does for you, which betrays a materialistic or hedonistic disposition toward life in general, but how can I really thank someone for being a loving human being? Is love a commodity? And would a loving person understand me when I thank her for a loving act she performed for my sake, especially when her act has flowed from her heart the way water flows from its spring, and more especially when this water has flowed from the spring of The Eternal? Would a nurse, having assisted so many patients lovingly and felt pangs of pain during her work, expect a thank you from anyone, or would she only worry about the well-being of her patients? The only way we can express, or recognize, thankfulness for acts of love is to try to become more loving. More loving is the silent language of thankfulness. Moreover, why should I receive thankfulness for an act I performed if in loving I become a richer, better human being? Is it not logical to say that I am the one who should be thankful for being given the opportunity to love and to grow in love, and therefore, in my humanity? With this consciousness in my heart, I undressed and put on my pajamas in the privacy of darkness and surrendered my waking consciousness to Hypnos.

I am frequently visited by dreams, sometimes strange, sometimes weird, and sometimes pleasant, but I do not remember having any dreams that night. It was a peaceful night. When I woke up the following morning, Kamal was already up and around. He had already moved most of our luggage to the van and was in the process of preparing our breakfast.

"Good morning!" he said, when he noticed that my eyes had welcomed the light of day. "I hope you had a good night's sleep!" he added. His face was glowing with life. He directed me to a section in the back of Saleem's house where I could clean myself and change my clothes.

"Yes, I had a very peaceful and deep sleep, thankfully. I do hope that you slept well and that you feel good this morning." He did not speak, but he answered me with a gentle nod and a kind smile in his eyes. I was convinced at this point of our friendship that, although he spoke in detail when a special need arose, Kamal was not inclined to ordinary talk, but to silent speech, except when verbal communication was necessary. Could it be that he preferred to express himself by bodily gestures poetically? Later on that day I wondered about this aspect of his character: Why? Could it be that he thinks that ordinary language is an inadequate medium of communicating individual and sometimes private and unique feelings and ideas? Could it be because ordinary language stands between his heart and the heart of the person with whom he tries to communicate? But then, how could words, that are abstract verbal entities, grasp the wealth of private ideas, feelings, and emotions of the human mind? Could it be that he came to the conclusion that public language has become a barrier behind which people hide their real selves and that he himself had nothing to hide? But then, is it not possible for bodily gesture to be deceptive, fake? Yes, this is possible, but not when you see with your own eyes the light of the gesture and feel the warmth of the heart that speaks to you. Even when I hear Hamlet's speech on being and not being presented on stage, and even when I know that what I hear is acting, I believe what I see and hear so far as the actor expresses himself from the heart, not necessarily his individual heart but the human heart as such.

Breakfast was waiting for me when I returned to the tent clean and refreshed. It was composed of eggs, cheese, milk, bread, dates, and fruits. As before, the dishes were placed on a hand-woven "tabaq," a tray made of reed that grows on the edge of the oasis. Kamal, who was sitting next to the tray, was gazing at the wall of the tent under a golden beam of light that was streaming through the side window. The design on the wall was literally dancing in the medium of this beam. "Was he praying? No, because he was not a praying man. He never used religious language in my presence, and he never made any reference to any religious matter. He must have been worshipping. And why not? I always believed that beauty is the royal road to love, and that universal beauty is the royal road to The Divine. Beauty is magical: It has the capacity to inflame the desire of love in the human heart, the desire for union with the beloved. By its very nature beauty is attractive; it is enchanting. Whether in nature or human beings or human works, beauty is the living image of The Divine. But how, or why, can the beautiful arouse the desire of love? Here I do not have in mind the sort of beauty that is generally appreciated by the majority of people, whose aim and function is to produce temporary pleasure, but true beauty, whose aim and function is to make the heart swoon in the arms of profound joy. Let me suggest a modest proposal: Can this sort of beauty awaken the daemon of love in the chest if it does not derive its being from The Divine? When you contemplate its splendor, you feel the power of magic. When you feel the beats of your heart racing with time, when you feel that your heart desires to leap out of your bosom and unite with it, you are already standing at the door of The Divine. Yes, your yearning for the beautiful is a yearning for its source. The language of beauty is the master language of The Divine. The beautiful does not speak the language of the scientist, the philosopher, or the theologian. The language of these thinkers is abstract, lifeless, but the language of The Divine is spiritual discourse; it is communication in action. It transforms the life of thought into action, and the life of action into worship! It is the kind of communication that energizes the impetus of growth, the power of understanding, and the desire for joyful life!

I felt awkward when I saw Kamal's attention lost to the dance of the sunbeam on the wall of the tent. He sat still like a meditating Sufi, and, in truth, he was a Sufi. I stood next to him watching his posture and his gaze in awe. The radiance of the golden beam on the wall was reflected in his gaze. His eyes were glowing with this radiance. I have never thought in my wildest dreams that I could encounter such radiance! Yes, holiness is a radiant ray of light, and this ray resides in the heart. Artists have tried to represent it in poetic, pictorial, sculptural, and musical form. But how can one feel the radiance of holiness, say in a painting, or know what it is really like, if he has not been touched, stung, by it?

Kamal was oblivious to my presence. He was absorbed in the dance, enchanted by its beauty. I could not help but think that for him life is a ritual, a celebration of The Eternal. It is one thing to worship The Divine on a certain day or at a certain hour, it is another to lead a life of worship, in which you live The Divine in whatever you think, feel, and do. What is the use of being religious if you do not live from the standpoint of The Eternal, if it is not the light and moving force of what you think, feel, and do?

"I have been waiting for you!" he said, with a pair of cheerful eyes. Waiting for me to eat breakfast, or to join him in the sacred dance of the sunbeam? Frankly, I was embarrassed to ask, not because I was a timid or dishonest person, but because I was touched, illumined by the light of his worship. Although he was waiting for me to share breakfast with him, still, sharing breakfast with him would be sharing another religious ritual, another act of worship.

"I feel hungry; I have a strong appetite for food this morning," I replied, and then sat opposite him. "What a meal!" I exclaimed. Though different from the last breakfast we had, for it was simple, it looked inviting and generous!

"May this food enhance the sense of life in your heart!" he said. Having made this warm wish, he started eating. For the first time, I noted that Kamal did not speak when he ate. He ate in silence; but I could readily notice that he enjoyed the activity of eating, for he was eating heartily, more than any person I had ever seen before in my life. You get the impression that this activity was both a means and an end in itself: a means, because it promotes physical well-being, and an end, because it is intrinsically enjoyable. How could it be otherwise if the food he was eating and the activity of eating it are essential ingredients of the process of living, of being human? Human life, in all its dimensions and in every act of realization, is valuable: Life is sacred; if it is sacred, no part of it can be profane!

I did not feel awkward because he was eating wholeheartedly or ceremonially, but because I discovered one more imperfection in myself. I have frequently noted that such a feeling harbors guilt in my mind and a desire to meet the need it creates. I have never ignored or hesitated in meeting such a need. But that morning I felt that meeting this need was more of a challenge than a shortcoming, mainly because it was not the result of negligence but of a discovery, of something I simply did not know. So I joined Kamal quietly, and I can say reverently, not out of fear of Kamal, but because I began to view the ordinary activities of my life as integral parts of my existence, organically related to my life as a whole. The more I watched him eat, and he ate silently, the more I saw the value implicit in this general practice, the more I felt its meaning, and the more I tended to believe in it as a way of eating my meals. I recalled there and then how my grandmother, who was known for her piety, used to demand, when we were children, that we eat silently. But, as you know it is hard for children to remain silent. When we ate we had to obey my grandmother, for she loved us tenderly. She protected us when we violated the strict rules of our parents and was there for us whenever we needed anything. Well, one day, giving in to a feeling of curiosity, I asked my grandmother: "Why should we remain silent when we eat?" Her answer was simple: "Because the angels descend from heaven to bless the food. If we speak, they will not descend." Regardless of whether this answer was metaphorical, or just a way to silence us, or to invoke a higher authority to justify the need for silence, it evoked a sense of reverence for life. Kamal was a shining example of this sense.

To tell the truth, the breakfast I shared with Kamal that morning was one of the brightest moments in my life; it was a moment of revelation, of gleaning deeper and deeper into the meaning of my life. The silence which suffused our encounter was a living spirit; it invigorated my mind and sent a ray of joyful peace to my heart. Could it be that this kind of peace is the fountain of the creative impulse in our minds, the desire to live and grow in our humanity? This may strike my reader as a rhetorical question, but it is not, for I felt animated by this impulse as I was assisting Kamal in preparing ourselves for the next stretch of our journey. The radiance of this spirit was not restricted to the way I felt during the breakfast meal, but permeated the whole of my being. I felt its pulse as I moved around in the tent and as I moved my bags to the van, I felt it when I stood outside in the open air examining the cacti plants on the side of Saleem's building, and I felt it when I cast a look of admiration at the morning sky. It was almost time for us to leave when Saleem and his oldest son accompanied Kamal to the van. They wanted to wish us a safe and comfortable journey. I was deeply touched by their warmth. They smiled with their eyes and lips as they approached me and shook hands with me. I felt their sincerity and was upheld by it. Saleem exchanged with him a few sentences in Arabic, which I could not understand; but Kamal translated them to me: "If you need anything, just call us." Tears gathered in the corners of my eyes. I could not control my emotions. Impulsively, I moved towards Saleem and embraced him tightly, not only with my arms but also with my heart. Then I moved to Umar and did the same. Kamal extended a similar embrace to both of them. As I left them and proceeded to my seat in the van, next to my friend, I noticed Hasnaa and the other children standing on a small balcony of their house. They were watching us with anxious eyes. I stopped for a moment near my door and waved my two hands to them wishing them joy and prosperity. They waved back. There was lightning in the sky of my soul.

chapter 4

Al Naseri Mountain

THE SUN WAS RECLAIMING its throne in the azure dome of the desert when we left the oasis. It was a hot day, but what made the impact of its heat pierce through my skin into my bone was a strong wind blowing from the south. "It gets excruciatingly hot when this wind reaches our region. Please, let me know when it becomes annoying or unbearable. I shall be happy to turn the air conditioner on whenever you feel an urgent need for it. Gas is scarce in this part of the desert; the less we use it, the better it will be for us, especially since it is hard to foresee what the weather will be like in the next hour or day. But in general our drive should be fine today, because we shall be driving on a clearly marked road, even though it will be rough."

"So far, so good," I said. Land extended unobstructed by any kind of elevation on both sides of the road, except for sparse patches of dead desert plants. We were driving in the middle of nowhere. Not a falcon, an eagle, or a sparrow, intelligent and persevering birds, birds that are proficient in the ways of the desert, was in sight. The only kind of motion I felt was the sound of the engine, which became loud and screechy when Kamal had to drive over badly mutilated asphalt. I reflected on these plants, on how they grow and struggle every spring, on how they seek to assert their existence in the world, only to be stifled shortly afterward by the heat; I reflected on how they, in spite of the deadly strike of the heat, try to resurrect themselves, again and again, every spring. We frequently allow ourselves to be lost in the web of our mechanized world, to become integral parts of this big web without wondering why, or how, we are parts of this machine or even whether we are destined to be such parts. It sometimes seems that young people are taught, or conditioned, to believe that their destiny is to perform a certain function in this machine without questioning whether this is their true destiny without even seeing, much less recognizing with the eyes of their minds, whether they are mortal or perhaps have a different or better purpose in life. A more puzzling breeze of thought wafted through my mind: "I wonder whether it even occurs to them to take a short break from their routine, rigid schedule to sit on the side of a mountain or the shore of a lake or a bench in a garden and think about this machine, about who directs it, whether the purpose for which it exists is justifiable. I wonder whether they can also think about the existence of the whole scheme of nature, whether it is the result of a freaky accident caused by some blind force lurking in the belly of nothing, or whether it is some kind of wisdom. I wonder whether they can, just for a moment, ask why the plant or the lion exists and why it struggles for life, why the earth moves around the sun, why the sun shines every morning, why the wind blows the way it does, why the stars glitter at night, why the rain falls, and especially why this whole scheme of nature exists in the first place." My mind was floating with this breeze of thought when Kamal suddenly said:

"We should reach Al Naseri Mountain in about half an hour. It would, I think, be important to visit it, because it is a very interesting geological formation and a cultural landmark."

"A cultural landmark?" I caught myself exclaiming silently. I was really astounded when I heard this description coming from Kamal's mouth. "A geological formation," I would understand, because I have learned that the Syrian Desert has been a geologically active area, but a "cultural landmark"? His proposal aroused my curiosity. "A cultural landmark?" This time, I directed my question to Kamal.

"Yes," Kamal replied, "legend has it that one of the pioneers of early Eastern Christian theologians in the fifth century, a Syrian monk called Dionysius spent some of the early years of his life in a monastery on this mountain. A number of monastic orders were established here in the third century and they remained active until the end of the fifteenth century. Most of them have been demolished in the course of time. Some fathers of the Eastern Orthodox Church say that the basic structure of St. Timothy monastery, where Dionysius stayed, is preserved."

This revelation acted on me as a wake-up call, as a reminder of the significance of the desert in the rise and development of the Christian worldview, of what the desert meant to the early fathers of the Church and what the Christian fathers meant to the desert. Is the Syrian Desert a minaret where The Eternal calls human beings to worship? Did the early Christian Fathers hear and understand its call? Did they build their monasteries as places of worship—yes, worship? Oh, dear reader, let me be clear at the outset that by "worship" I do not mean standing in church for an hour or two like a gentle lamb singing and saying prayers and going through a prescribed ritual of some kind, all with the air of humility, reverence, and devotion; I rather mean a serious, genuine desire to transcend oneself into The Ultimate; I mean an activity of self-examination and the endeavor to commune with The Ultimate. The purpose of self-examination is self-understanding—understanding who I am and what my source is; for how can I make the tremendous leap into The Ultimate if I do not know my nature and that my destiny consists in union with it? And how can I know that The Ultimate is my source and destiny except by searching for it in my heart? Paradox, you say? I understand. When you delve deep into the depth of your heart, when your eyes are stung by its flame, when the fountain of knowledge opens up to your mind, you see that the spark that kindles in your heart points to The Ultimate, and you also discover that the paradox your philosophical logic prides itself with will pass into harmonious consistency with this reality.

By itself, thinking, whether it is in the form of argument or meditation, does not lead to communion with The Ultimate, for it is an intellectual event; as such, it remains in your mind, although it might point to The Ultimate. Communion with The Ultimate is an existential encounter in which the totality of my being, with which I identify myself in the world, leaps out of my bosom and delivers itself to The Ultimate in an act of passionate embrace. This is why having faith or assenting intellectually is not enough—enough, that is, to make one a lover of The Ultimate. To be a lover, to live from the standpoint of The One, in accordance with the light of the divine spark, one has to rise from her worldly slumber, cleanse herself with the light of The One, and then, pure and passionate, knock at the door of The One. If she does this, she will not be received by a priest, an angel, or an attendant of some kind, but by The One. She will not be received with a smile or a gesture or sweet words but with open, warm arms.

I was stung by the fire of the spark in my heart. I tasted it, and it was sweet. But the sweetness was not the sweetness of honey, nor of nectar. It was the kind that charms you, that makes you drunk, that makes you an addict. As an addict, you know you cannot go on without having a cup of it every moment of your life; so, you give up everything you have, and wander in search of The Source, without which you cannot exist. I confess I am an addict. I am a seeker of the source: The Eternal.

Kamal knew I was in the middle of intense reflection. He is a very empathetic person. Although he had the capacity to feel, and perhaps think, what I was feeling and thinking, he did not violate my privacy. How can a person who has been touched by the hand of The One commit such a crime? Impossible! Kamal remained silent until the storm of reflection in my mind abated. "Would you like some water?" he kindly asked. "We should not forget to drink some kind of fluid in this part of the desert; and please, do not forget to ask when you need water or anything!" On the contrary, such a person is a healer, a doctor of the soul. His vocation in life is to build, to help people find their way when they are lost, to give them courage when they are overpowered by problems, and to make them hopeful when they are crushed by disaster. "Yes, Kamal, I would like some water," I said. "As a matter of fact, I shall share some with you."

"Behind your seat there is a box of bottled water. It comes from a spring northeast of this area. They say it is medicinal. It is not bottled commercially. Natives buy the bottles and fill them one by one." I followed his instruction and instead of fetching one I fetched two bottles, one for each of us. I opened his bottle and gave it to him. He smiled without looking at me. I felt his smile. It lingered on his face for some time. "Did he see or feel its radiance?" Of course not! He simply drove on with a steady eye on the road, which was becoming increasingly rough. But he was a very skilled driver, for he was weaving his way around the potholes with amazing facility.

Shortly after I quenched my thirst, I noted a dark object in the sky. It was at first indistinct, but my eyes pursued it in an attempt to discover its identity. Kamal noted the object and my interest in it. "We must be approaching Al Naseri Mountain," he said. "What you see in the sky is a falcon. He and his family nest in one of the ruins there. They remain in this part of the desert until late summer, then they travel to the north mainly to avoid the blazing heat of the sun. This specific falcon is a scout. He will soon vanish, but he will return with other members of his family. They seem to enjoy human company. People around here are friendly to them. There is perfect harmony between human beings, the desert, and the animals that inhabit it." Kamal was right, because within fifteen minutes a flock of falcons flew around us in the most interesting formation, as if to welcome us to their territory. They remained flying in front of us until we reached the foothills of Al Naseri Mountain. "This is the most significant mountain range we shall encounter on our visit," Kamal added after a few minutes. The most interesting part lies on the eastern side. We shall have to drive on a very rough track for about fifteen minutes. So, please be patient. The track was hardly visible, but Kamal drove on it as if it were visible to his eyes. The more I travelled with him the more it became certain that he was not only a true son of the desert but an embodiment of its spirit. There I sat, next to him, breathing his spirit and feeling its warmth. "It would be appropriate," he remarked, "since it was already noontime, to have our lunch here at the foot of this hill before we make our ascent to the summit. We can have it in an interesting grotto just at the point of our ascent. But before we reach this point, I would like you to pay close attention to the form and texture of the rocks as we drive around the northern side of the mountain. It is made of a rare species of granite. An old man, who was learned in the history and geography of the desert, once told me that Queen Zenobia excavated the stone of her palace from this mountain." He stopped the van, turned off the engine, and then added: "Let us go out for a few minutes and look at the rock formation." I did as he recommended.

    The moment I left the van, I found myself standing before a huge mosaic. Apparently, the tremors which spread from the center of a nearby volcano sometime ago fractured this side of the hill but did not raze it, mainly because granite is not that easy to raze. A mosaic, another arabesque formation! An idea rose to the forefront of my consciousness: "Is it possible that the language of the desert, and maybe of The Eternal, is geometry? Is this not the most existential language in describing or explaining the cosmic process?" My vision was glued to this rock for some time, to its intertwined lines, soft yet warm colors, and sheen. It was embraced by its pure elegance. But I was not merely taken by the aesthetic pleasure this elegance produced in my soul; I was also taken, even more profoundly, by the living spirit that made it shine and dance with elegance, by its infinite depth, by the warmth of this depth. A wild idea flashed through my mind: "Could it be that not only this arabesque but also every natural form is a veil behind which

Seeking God

The Eternal shines in its infinite splendor? If this question bears any truth, we can certainly ask: "By what art, or skill, can we learn how to remove this veil?" But this idea did not linger in my mind; it vanished before I could apprehend it. Was it because I was not yet ready to deal with its assumptions and implications? I cannot say, but my absorption in the arabesque was interrupted by the searing heat of the sun. When I regained my normal consciousness Kamal was watching me with a glowing smile on his face. "You must be hungry!" he said with a deep sense of inner satisfaction. My answer was a modest yes. We returned to the van slowly and silently.

But we were at the grotto within two minutes. It was a spacious cavern. It is reasonable to characterize it as a haven in that part of the desert. It must have been visited by many travelers during the past years, perhaps centuries, because its walls, even the ceiling, were covered with writing in different languages: English, French, German, Greek, Arabic, Japanese, Spanish, and Slavic. Some of them seemed recent, but the majority seemed rather old. "This is not a grotto," I mumbled. "This is a museum that houses the memories of travelers, lovers, scientists, and adventurers." I inspected the different forms of writing with a childlike spirit. I wished I could understand what they signified or meant. But the mere fact that I was there, that I was a witness to this tapestry of memories, of human expression, incited in me a feeling of sympathy, of connectedness with a kind of human presence. People visited this desert and lingered in this cavern! A mysterious feeling of humility and elation passed through my soul. I was humbled by the sublime presence of The Universal, by its transcendent presence, not only in the spirit of the desert but also in the human spirit; and I was elated by the fact that I was both a witness and a participant in this presence. I was overwhelmed by it. Without knowing how or why, I looked at Kamal with baffled eyes. He never reacted to the spiritual turmoil, sometimes volcanoes, in my heart the way he did that moment. He must have seen or felt the flashes of The Eternal that were coursing through my mind without even recognizing their magic, and he must have felt the intensity of my emotional excitement: "Yes!" he exclaimed. His "yes" was carried to my ears with a breeze of compassion and understanding.

Kamal had already prepared our lunch when I received this gift of recognition from him, this gift of communication, of sharing, of solidarity! It was a simple but a wholesome meal. After we finished eating,

Al Naseri Mountain

he asked if I was ready for the ascent. My answer was a grateful nod. He looked into my eyes and smiled. "We should take some water with us," he remarked, "because the track that leads to the summit is rather long, rugged, and winding. This mountain is more than thirteen hundred meters high. The ruins are situated at a lower elevation; we may or may not reach the highest point. We shall see. One more reminder, please! Do not forget to bring your hat with you."

Luckily, both of us were wearing thick, sturdy boots, because the track was, as Kamal emphasized, very rugged and sometimes hard to follow. It was frequently covered with rocks and sand; but Kamal, who led the way, knew its outline by heart. He pointed out that the dead plants that covered the lower part of the mountain are ordinarily green during springtime. "There is not much rainfall in this region. The land is arable, but heat and lack of rain stand in the way of vegetation. Some desert animals thrive on dead plants." After a short pause he added: "Within two or three minutes, we shall have covered the distance. Both of us should be due for a short rest. What do you think?"

"Frankly, Kamal, I was going to ask for it. I waited a little only to test the endurance of my body. This is the first time I undertake such an ascent. It is a sweet challenge for me; and it is sweet only because I am undertaking it with you." As it was his habit, Kamal remained silent. It began to dawn upon me that he had, so far, been silent concerning spiritual matters. "Could it be because he believed that the spiritual as such is sacred, unspeakable?" I asked silently. Kamal stopped near an overarching cliff which cast a sizeable sheath of shade. Let us rest our muscles for a few minutes here. He pointed to a somewhat large rock on which we sat. I drank some water and then gave myself the liberty to contemplate the desert that stretched before my eyes as a creamy carpet. A swarm of mirages floated on it gently and leisurely. A number of falcons flew over us and around the mountain. "They must be its guardian angels, yes," I said. At first, they seemed to be the only sign of life here, but that was not really the case, because very soon a hissing sound attracted my attention. Two lizards, one chasing the other, zoomed quickly before our eyes. They did not pay any attention to us; they simply went their merry way. Kamal watched them with playful curiosity. "They must be enjoying themselves." He smiled and then added: "They are playing a game of hide and seek, or perhaps flirting with each other!" I was once more absorbed in the swarm of mirages, of the infinite nothingness from which they were born and into which they were dying when Kamal reminded me that it was time to continue our ascent.

"Why did the Christian monks choose to worship their God on mountaintops? Why did they choose a solitary way of life, away from the clamor of society, when the first and last command they received from The Master was to love their fellow human beings?" These questions were fluttering in my mind and were begging for answers as I resumed my climbing behind Kamal. During our ascent the track became more and more winding, and I became more and aware of the pull of gravity. I was aware of this pull with every step I made. Climbing was beginning to become a struggle for me. But I kept on going, and I kept pace with my friend, who certainly felt my struggle. "It will not be long before we reach the ruins," he remarked. I knew he was trying to inspire courage into my will, but I felt something else: He was trying to feel with me and to be with me in my attempt to overcome the downward pull of gravity. With a heaving chest, I responded: "I never thought I would have a contest with gravity. But let me tell you that I welcome the challenge of his contest."

"You will win." He said

"It is easier to descend than to ascend."

"It is disappointing to give up in the middle."

"I would agree; but why do you think this is the case?" I asked with a sincere desire to know his opinion about this aspect of human endeavor.

"If you remain at the bottom, any bottom, you would not know the difference between top and bottom, and so you would remain in a dark cloud of ignorance of what it is like to be at the top. You would languish in your ignorance and you would not feel the pain, and thrill, of doubt, or even of knowledge. But if you know that there is a top, and if for some reason you fail to experience or know what it is like, or what it is like to stand on the top, you would necessarily suffer a feeling of deprivation, particularly of knowledge forgone, a nagging sensation of having lost something important. This deprivation acquires a tragic character especially if knowledge of the top is crucial to the understanding and realization of your life's purpose." Kamal suddenly stopped, adjusted his hat so that it cast adequate shade over his face and then looked at me with his serious, penetrating eyes. "Let us sit next to this big rock for a few minutes. You need to rest a little. This is your first climbing experience. Look at your chest heaving!"

With this warm expression of concern, he led the way to the rock, which, in virtue of its large size, cast ample shade on the northeastern side. I was touched by his proposal and followed his footsteps thankfully. We sat on the ground and leaned our backs against the rock. In this position, we faced the horizon that welcomed the sun to our earth a few hours ago. "Think of the matter this way," he began. "An ascent is a climb to some kind of peak, a point beyond which one cannot go, of course, bodily. We may distinguish four types of ascent: natural, as the summit of a mountain or the tip of a steeple; ontological, as the summit of being, or the fountain that gives rise to all that exists; social, as the summit of religious, political, or legal authority; and ideal, as the standard of human perfection. Each one of these types is an end-point, a point at which the ascent stops. For example, the highest point on the face of the earth is Mt. Everest; the highest point of the universe is The Ultimate; the highest point in social organization is the ruler; and the highest point in human life is the ideal of human perfection. Now let us focus our attention on the last kind of summit. By its very essence, a summit is a point that is beyond our present reach; we need to move toward it in order to reach it. It acquires the character of summit because it is an end or a last point or because it is more in value or truth, power or being. We speak of an ideal of human perfection only because human beings are not given to the world as complete or perfect but as a possibility for perfection or completion. The process that leads to this point is called growth and development. Our bodies are, like trees, rocks, or animals, given as ready-made objects at the moment of their creation, but not the fabric or outline of human nature. We are not born as human beings but with the potentiality to become human beings. For example, we are not born as thinkers, lovers, appreciators of beauty, or as social or religious beings, but with the potentiality to think, love, appreciate beauty, and be social or worshippers of God. There is no need for us now to examine how or even why this is the case, but only to recognize that it is the case. Accordingly, since we are born as potentiality for becoming human, and since we become human in the process of actualizing this potentiality, the more we succeed in this actualization, the more we *are*, in the sense that we exist as the human beings we are supposed to be. Humanity, then, is a goal. It may seem ironical, if not paradoxical, that the ultimate goal of human beings is to become and thrive as human beings, not as lumps of flesh. As a process that unfolds in time in the activity of daily living, this goal is a summit, an end-point whose realization signifies human perfection. Well, the question that glares us directly in the face is this: What is the ideal, or standard, of human perfection, not from this or that standpoint, not according to this or that established authority, but according to a synoptic vision, to a comprehension of its ultimate essence, the kind that transcends any kind of particularity, idiosyncrasy, or human limitation? We raise this question because the actualization of any potentiality whatever cannot take place, or even begin, without an end-point, a plan, or a standard according to which the actualization process proceeds, on the one hand, and without an adequate grasp of the very structure of the potentiality itself, on the other. Otherwise, it will take place arbitrarily, capriciously, or whimsically. The vision of the end-point should meet the demands implicit in the potentiality. But, then, how do we arrive at an adequate conception of the ideal of perfection? An ideal is a standard that is superior to any other standard. We cannot quest for such an ideal merely in the human mind, regardless of its sagacity, depth, width of comprehension, or loyalty to truth, mainly because it is not its own source, nor in the world as we experience it, because the world is, like the mind, a creation, or a creation-in-progress. Since the mind is finite, it cannot be the author of the standard of its perfection, even though it can point to its source and possesses the means of seeking it."

"Yes," Kamal continued with a glitter in his eyes, "our quest for the ideal of human perfection should aim at the fountain from which all things flow: nature, wisdom, power, goodness, beauty, and holiness, not to mention the infinity of the aspects that make up the realm of being. And let me stress that this is the greatest quest a human being can possibly think or even dream of. Imagine a speck in relation to the infinite, but also imagine a speck that is a possible infinite. How can this two-fold possibility become real? The actualization of this possibility is the essence of the quest for the ideal of human perfection. Marching forward in it is marching upward to the summit of human existence. What does it take to march on the road that leads to it?"

Soon after raising this last question Kamal fell into deep silence; his face was a clear embodiment of thoughtfulness itself. He did not look at me but at the distant horizon, as if he was having a silent dialogue with someone. He suddenly emerged from this silence with a gentle smile. "Dimitri," he said, "it is getting late. We should be on our way to the summit. The ruins are waiting for us. We have a rendezvous with them."

Why did he stop his conversation with me so suddenly? The general remarks he made in an effort to answer my question were condensed, incomplete, almost cryptic. Did he purposely refrain from offering an answer because my question does not have a final answer, or because he wanted me to discover the answer myself, or perhaps because arriving at such an answer cannot be the result merely of philosophical thinking but also of ontological seeking? And, most of all, did he want to impress upon my mind the fact that an ascent to any meaningful summit, especially the summit of all being, is a solitary undertaking? Did he, by planning my journey into the Syrian Desert, intend for me to have an experience of climbing to a summit? Let me, at this point of my narrative, confess that climbing a mountain in the midst of a desert, any kind of desert—social, intellectual, religious, physical—is not an easy venture. I knew there and then that Kamal was not only my guide and friend; he was also my inspiration: a model to emulate in what it means to be a human being.

The sun had already left its zenith and was on its way to its western shores when we approached the ruins. Turning back and looking at me with a cheerful face, "How do you feel?" he asked. "Very soon we shall have a respite, and a reward, because we shall be able to rest a little and get acquainted with the spirit of a people."

"I feel good, very good indeed, Kamal. I am anxious to see the ruins." We stopped near a huge cliff for a moment, and then he pointed the way eastward around this cliff. In less than a minute we found ourselves standing at a ledge overlooking a rather large expanse of ground covered with several mutilated architectural forms, mainly walls, broken columns, and roofless rooms. Before moving onward, I surveyed this architectural relic as a built environment against the wider environment that enfolded it; then I focused my attention on the eastern horizon, that line where the sun starts an act of creation every morning—of being, of life, of human progress. "It is here at this line that the eternal intersects the temporal," I reflected. "I wonder whether the early fathers of the church chose this mountain and this spot for this simple reason! Was their passion a passion for The Eternal? Did they live here to be close to The Eternal? They certainly knew that The Eternal does not exist here, there, or anywhere, and that it does not at all exist, since it is the foundation, substance, and mind of all existence, in short, The Source. The source of all existence surpasses existence, simply because it is the source of all existence! If we say it exists, we imply that there is something superior to it in virtue of which it exists, which is impossible. Did they choose to dwell here to make a statement, to remind the people of the meaning and destiny of their lives? Is the horizon a divine metaphor?" Kamal was waiting when I woke up from this short reverie. He looked at me with compassionate eyes and asked: "Would you like to pay a visit to our first find?"

"Definitely!" I said, as he led the way. Kamal must have inspected, and felt, every stone, every corner, every column, every enclosure in these ruins, for he showed unusual familiarity with them. We began with the main entrance, then, having passed through a foyer, we found ourselves in a somewhat larger courtyard punctuated on all four sides with rows of broken columns or bases of non-existing columns. A wide passage separated the remnants of these rows from parts of what used to be a solid wall overlooking what must have been living quarters. At the northern side I was able to notice a passage that led to a large structure, which, according to Kamal, was the library. I tried to reconstruct the courtyard in my mind; I even imagined myself walking in it a few times and knocking at the door of a side study room where monks must have met on certain hours of the day to review the results of their thinking and reflections on the nature of certain religious ideas and practices, to share their feelings and revelations on the their attempt to move closer to The Divine Light, and to consider new proposals for the betterment of the spiritual and material well-being of society. Oh, how I wished to be standing incognito in one corner, smelling the air that carried the scent of their souls, listening to the clamor of their ideas, feeling the intensity of their passion, and examining the message of their ideas!

I was struck speechless and motionless in the grip of the hand of time when I suddenly felt the warm presence of Kamal around me, and within me, embracing me with two gentle eyes radiating human love, the kind that makes you feel the pulse of The Eternal in your heart. Did it occur to you, dear reader, that the radiance of love speaks more eloquently, more truly, more profoundly than any language created by human beings? Did it ever occur to you that love is the horizon at which The Eternal intersects the human, where the human becomes divine and the divine human? Did it occur to you that the only language The Eternal speaks is love, that human beings babble when their speech does not originate from a loving heart? I felt Kamal's presence, and I understood it. I was not ashamed that he was a witness to my secret thoughts, feelings, and yearnings. He was, and remains, my friend.

I accompanied him to what must have been a gate that led to a large area covered with large blocks of marble and parts of broken columns. One could also see some remains of other architectural structures. The most obvious structure was a chapel. Our legs moved toward it spontaneously, as if it was a center of gravity. Most of the walls had tumbled down. The floor, made of blocks of stone, was fractured in many places. Four bases of huge columns were still intact in the middle; they must have carried a dome. Part of the main cupola in the altar area sat on the western side of the chapel. I walked toward that area and stood at the step that separated the nave from the altar, the divine from the secular space. My eyes looked eastward at the point where the sun dawns at our world every morning; then they looked upward, not at the dome that ceased to exist but at the real Dome that protects our world; and then I looked at the nave where the community participated in the celebration of the divine liturgy.

Some strange ideas flashed through my mind as I stood there gazing at the infinite horizon: Why did the early fathers build a chapel here at the top of this high mountain in order to celebrate the divine presence in the human community and the world? I understand that a chapel is a sacred place, but how about the whole scene of nature? Is it not a sacred place? Does it not exist as a divine ray? It would be a grave mistake to think that The Divine can be closeted in any kind of enclosure. I wonder whether the ecclesiastical establishment in its entirety—priests, doctrines, buildings, theological works—is itself a barrier that separates human beings from The Divine! What is the end of all religious study and instruction, religious rites and doctrines, and religious places of worship but to enable human beings to feel, directly, passionately, and wholeheartedly, the presence of the divine, not only here or there but everywhere? "The religious as such has lost its meaning," I mumbled involuntarily; it has lost sight of The Divine. Even the word "religion" derives its meaning from reverence for the gods, from that encounter in which human beings confront God or feel related to God. People do not live anymore from the standpoint of The Divine; on the contrary, the divine is being used in the service of personal, limited, and misguided interest.

These reflections left the domain of my mind and reverberated throughout my being. They quivered on my lips. Kamal was there waiting for me, and next to me, when I recovered from my short flight into reflection. We walked eastward to the limit of this architectural site and then several feet further to the edge where we stood for a few minutes. The first thing that attracted my attention was the steepness of that side of the mountain. It seemed as if space collapsed in one chunk into the abyss of being. Looking down into the infinite depth of that abyss was an awe-inspiring experience! Yes, I thought to myself, those monks must have communed with The Divine, not in that chapel, but on the edge, in the very bosom of The Eternal. This bosom is the only chapel where human beings can celebrate the divine presence!

A whiff of exhilaration danced in my soul as we walked back to the main ground of the monastery. Kamal was explaining the function or significance of every part we visited. I felt a special attraction to the stones that were scattered everywhere. I took the liberty to sit on the base of a column. I felt it; it was coarse and solid. It was eroded by the chisel of nature. It was real! Then I took an overview of the monastery that once existed. I found myself returning on the road of my memory to the times of the early fathers. What force, or hope, drove them to leave everything behind and establish a place of worship here on the edge, close to The Eternal? Where are they now? Why is this desolation? "Ruins!" a voice shouted from the depth of my mind, "These stones and vacant, abandoned spaces are nothing but ruins. They are traces of life that does not exist, of a light that faded into nothingness! These stones signify one certain truth: perishing."

These dark, sad ideas were buzzing madly in my mind. An expression of confusion froze in my throat, and a curl of sarcasm quivered on my lips! I felt the squeeze of nothingness around my neck the way a criminal feels the noose around his neck just before he abandons his last breath of life. Can it be that this spectacle before which I now stand is no more than a patch of nothingness? Am I sitting in a graveyard where even evil spirits would refuse to live, much less visit? These cruel ideas, which visited my mind before and wrecked my peace for a long time, seem to have returned to me on my visit to the Naseri Mountain with a vengeance. Did they fall from the ceiling of my consciousness because I am having a close encounter with The Eternal? But they did not return alone, merely as abstract ideas in the mind of a philosopher who is seeking to discover their meaning or truth with a disinterested attitude; they returned as drops of consciousness, with eyes, ears, and a tongue from the depth of my being. They were not merely logical drops aiming at a logical debate or conversation with me; they were ontological drops of consciousness. They were living moments of consciousness. They did not want me just to think but also to see and to comprehend what I see, to believe what I comprehend, and to take a stand on the basis of what I happened to believe. Yes, I am in the desert standing on a barren mountain and sitting in an empty spot, practically alone in the middle of nowhere. But, alas! Am I really now sitting in a graveyard, or ruins, of meaningless scraps of human artifacts? Can it be that these two eyes that fell from the ceiling of my consciousness and now stare at me provocatively and defiantly, maybe sarcastically, and, I am inclined to think, menacingly, are the eyes of doom, of meaninglessness? Is the quest I have been undertaking nothing but a scornful strike of vanity?

Standing with this ultimate challenge, of this thorny quandary, and in spite of the fact that I was enveloped by what seemed to the ordinary eye an infinity of barrenness, I was able to look into those two eyes and quietly and confidently say: "Yes, these ruins are alive, not dead, and they remain sacred." This response was not the result of a sudden conversion or enlightenment; it had been growing and evolving from the soil of my heart, from its inner depth. It was not planted there by an external authority, because it was not merely an idea or an emotion or a feeling, and it was not the result of an episode of logical thinking, even though it was essentially logical. It was the result of an intuitive disclosure under an inner light, a light that comes from within, from the sun of the heart. The light of this sun penetrates the appearance of things and reveals their essence. It enables you to see this essence not only in its own light, as it is in itself, but also as it is in its causal relations. It enables you to see it not only as a part of a whole, not as this or that immediate or intermediate whole, but also as a part of the universal whole that encompasses the totality of being. The more I see the brilliance of this light, the way it reveals the truth of what I see and feel and the authority with which it enables me to grasp the truth of what I see and feel, especially the transcendence of its character, the more my conviction in what I see and feel becomes faith.

As I sat in the lap of those ruins I had an illumination that the monks built a home for themselves there in that spot because they were poetically inclined: They chose to lead a poetic way of life. They must have proceeded from the belief that the whole order of nature is itself an emanation from The Divine Sun, that every place in this order is a sacred place, that every element of it, whether it is a rock, or a tree, or a bird, is a candidate for having a communion with The Divine. How can anything that comes from the hands of God not be sacred? How can any ray that emanates from the sun not be an emanation from its essence? It was clear to me that any spot in this whole wide universe can be an appropriate place of worship. But why this spot? Why designate any particular spot? And why live on a mountain in the middle of the desert? They chose this spot because it is an edge, and it is an edge because it sits over a downward abyss and under an upward abyss, under The Divine Dome over a bottomless nadir. Yes, they chose this spot because they wanted to live on the edge of being as such. For them, this spot was a religious metaphor. They wanted to live in this metaphor. Living in it was an expression of deep yearning for The Divine, for being one with it.

And it was a metaphor for another reason. They wanted to provide a model for living for the Christian community, and the whole world, about what it means to lead a good life, a life worthy of our humanity, worthy of the divine spark that graces our hearts by its very presence. I have frequently heard that the monastic life is an expression of a deep-seated selfishness, because the monk is primarily interested in his own happiness, or salvation, without regard to the happiness or salvation of others, while the essence of the message of Christ is to love our fellow human beings, and this, by leading a life of giving. Did Jesus not devote all his life for the well-being of others—caring for the poor, the wronged, the sick, the outcast, the greedy, the thieves, and the weak? Did he not prize the communal way of living as a condition of the good life?

Let me at once point out that the monastic way of life is in principle inconsistent with the secular way. We should always look at the monastery as a religious metaphor, not as a prison of selfishness. And as a metaphor, it is intended to reveal the wealth of possibilities in the monastic way of life. When I say of a woman that she is a rose, I only want to emphasize the delicious fragrance and brilliance of her beauty, which ordinary language cannot communicate. As a human being, a monk cannot afford to neglect the needs which are essential to his growth and development as a human being. Could it be that leading a poetic way of life, that is, living metaphorically in exemplifying the meaning of human growth, a passion for The Ultimate, a genuine understanding of the transience of all created things, and the true meaning of religiosity, which lies in self-formation in the presence of The Divine and not formally in applying particular instructions and practices imposed by a certain ecclesiastic elite, yes, could it be that living this metaphor is, in a way, an act of love? Could it be a way of holding the torch that illumines our way in seeking the good life?

I am in no way suggesting, or implying, that the ordinary or secular way of life is less valuable than the monastic way of life, because, to my mind, there is many a monk who walks unrecognized on the streets of human life, quietly, silently, invisible to people around him, who is, in all likelihood, a monk par excellence, and, on the other hand, there is many a monk in a monastery who should not be there. A true monk does not necessarily abandon the world or frown upon it or denigrate it; on the contrary, he is a person who loves the world and cares for it. How can he be a monk if he is not a son of the world? He does not spend his life in abstract meditation in order to become numb to the world or to be oblivious to its problems and hardships. No, he is the kind of person whose life is itself a meditation, a meditation in action; and his life is such a meditation insofar as it is productive, and it is productive insofar as it promotes the well-being of others. Promoting the well-being of others is the ultimate test of true monastic life. I do not know of a holy man or woman, or a sage, now or in the past, and in all the cultures of the world, who is not a servant of the people in some capacity and in some way, or who does not touch the lives of others. Who said that leading a poetic way of life, in which one lives close to the abyss of being, cannot be a fountain of productive love? In writing these meditative thoughts, I do not mean to advance an apology for monastic life but only to stress that it is a life in quest of The Divine, that this life once flourished on this mountain, that this mountain was once a kind of lighthouse that pointed the way to The Eternal, that the monastery is a metaphor, and that these ruins embody the essence of this metaphor.

This metaphor came to life when my eyes lingered on the capital of a Corinthian column, on the function it performed in making the chapel that once existed a symbolic house of the human spirit; then I moved to the steps that separated the altar from the nave, then to the cupola, and finally to the outline of the sacred table, where the priest performed the liturgy service. These remains, taken singly and gradually collectively as an architectural whole, are meaningful artifacts; they are not merely natural or random objects. They are purposeful, and the purpose they embody is a human purpose. This feature was obvious to me, because the form which expressed this kind of purpose is a human language. I understand this language; I understand the meaning implicit in it. Allow your aesthetic imagination to reconstruct the chapel out of the remains that are strewn around you and you readily find yourself standing before an actual chapel, or within it, where human beings worshiped God centuries ago. Again, allow yourself to understand this aesthetic construction further: Pay a visit to the sanctuary with a religious attitude during an early morning or evening service, and you will find yourself standing in a place of worship on the top of a mountain in the middle of a desert, and, yes, you will find yourself standing over an abyss of being. A rather wild, aggressive question slipped into mind as I was in the arms of this short meditation: "Is it possible that the realm of the past is a realm of nothingness? Am I really now standing on the top of a barren mountain? It cannot be! Alas! How can it be if I feel the sacredness of this place, and how can I feel this sacredness if I do not grasp in my mind what it means for such a place to be sacred: the whole system of beliefs, values, practices, symbols, and customs which constitute the mosaic of a way of life? I feel the warmth of this life rising to my temples, I feel the spirit that emanates from this warmth, I feel the yearning for The Eternal that pulsates in this warmth, and I feel the radiance of the divine glowing around this mountain."

No, the past is not a realm of nothingness; it lives in the present, and the present reveals its glory. We may view these remains as dead relics, as rags of nothingness, as inconsequential parasites on the realm of being, only if we choose to ignore them. But I am convinced that such a choice would be a gross betrayal to the testimony of our minds and hearts, to the eyes within that see, know, and judge what they see and know by the sweet touch of truth; it would be a betrayal to the inner urge for self-fulfillment and especially to the yearning that shouts for The Eternal. Such a choice would be a cowardly surrender to bad faith, to a false way of being in the world. These remains stand as a testimony to the life that filled the air of this monastery, the air of this metaphor, for a long time centuries ago: It exists silently in their form; it is a cry for The Eternal. I hear this cry; it reverberates in my heart.

I was not aware of his presence during these ruminations, but Kamal was sitting next to me quietly and meditatively on the base of a broken column. His eyes, like mine, were having a silent dialogue with the chapel. "What is he thinking?" I wondered. I gaped at him silently and thoughtfully. He was an image of serenity. He was a microcosm of the spirit that throbs in the heart of the Syrian Desert. He must have felt my gape, because it originated from my soul, not from my mind. The language of the human heart is, by its very essence, communication, the kind that makes a meaningful difference in those who communicate. A smile was fluttering in his eyes when he turned his attention in my direction. "Are you ready for the next stretch of our ascent to the summit?" This question did not come from him as a reminder or as a token of courtesy but as a friend with whom I was on a quest for The Eternal. "Yes, I am ready, Kamal."

We retreated slowly and silently to the track that led to the summit, leaving behind the remains of a life that celebrated the divine presence of The Eternal long time ago, or so it seemed, but in fact it did not, because flickers of that life lingered in my mind. They were darts shining in every corner of my consciousness. I felt renewed. I felt a surge of passion rising in my heart; it was neither abstract nor aimless: it was a passion for The Sun. I wanted to embrace it and live in its fire forever. I felt like I wanted to get out of myself and fly into the height of being, into that source that gives birth to everything that exists, that makes the world flourish, and that makes beauty dance in the garden of human life. This feeling was swelling in me and it was intensifying the higher we ascended. Normally, it would have been difficult for me to climb a high mountain, but not that day. The tide of passion, of life, that was flooding inside me generated an amazing burst of strength both physically and mentally. As a matter of fact, I felt light, almost transparent; I felt as if I was flying on the wings of one of those falcons that welcomed us to the mountain earlier that day. I was free, free from physical gravity, the kind that pulls human beings down and tethers them to the surface of the earth. Those monks who lived in that monastery on the edge of the mountain, on that border that overlooked the abyss of being and non-being; those monks who stared at the horizon as they waited for the sunrise every morning and for the sunset every evening, so they could watch the stars that glittered under the gentle rays of the sun; those monks who sought to lose themselves in the bosom of The Eternal—no, those monks were not dead. Their spiritual passion and yearning dwell in the monastery, and every stone there embodies a part of that life. Every stone is a spiritual whisper, a flicker of light! I heard this whisper; it conveyed wisdom to my ear. I saw the light; it illumined my way as I moved closer to the summit. Why not? Do we not read the book of a culture in its remains? And do we not feel the pulse of its spirit in the meaning it embodies? Of course, we derive not only insight and understanding but also inspiration from this spirit. I realized there and then that the monastery we just visited was a biographical book: the story of the desert monk, of the man who drank from the divine nectar in one of his mysterious moments and became intoxicated with The Eternal ever since, of the man who was stigmatized by the divine light and felt afterward an everlasting repugnance to the darkness that fills the mind of many a human being.

A smile was warming its way joyfully to my lips when Kamal pointed out that we were approaching the summit and that the track we were following would soon come to an end in a few minutes. From that point onward we should choose the most convenient way to the top, mainly because the foot of the summit was rocky and jagged. He asked me to watch my step, because the rocks, over which we would be walking and sometimes climbing, were smooth and treacherous. And he was right, for we suddenly found ourselves in a pyramid of steeply rising rocks, which to my naïve eyes appeared as a thicket of rocks. It was an imposing sight! I could not resist an inward desire to stop and contemplate that fascinating geological formation. Each one of those jagged rocks looked like a steeple, and the whole thicket looked like a chorus of steeples rising upward into the infinity of the sky. "They must be singing the Gloria to The Eternal!" I thought to myself. Yes, I could hear it, and I heard the beauty of their voices. I heard their aspiration, their longing. My heart leaped out of my chest and joined them in their glorious chant. Kamal must have felt the state of exhilaration I was in, for he was standing next to me gaping into the sky: His eyes were singing the Gloria with the chorus. I felt his presence and welcomed his solidarity. It was indeed a glorious moment. We walked between these steeples silently and slowly found our way upward. I could not help but look backward for a moment simply to form a perspective against the final stretch of our ascent. What a perspective it was! It seemed to me that the thicket of steeples within which we were twining our way was rising with us. It, too, was striving to be free from the pull of gravity. It too was striving to be free in the bosom of The Eternal. My heart was beating to the melody of the Gloria as we continued our ascent to the summit. "We shall now go through very narrow pathways and we shall have to squeeze our way through jagged rocks on either side." Kamal remarked as we plowed our way into the thicket of steeples. "Please follow me from now on," he added. I followed his instruction and very soon found myself pressing my body through a narrow trail. "How are you doing, Dimitri?" Kamal asked. "I am fine," I said. "I am in good hands!" He did not respond to my retort. He simply marched on. Within a few minutes, we found ourselves on the top of the mountain. It was mid-afternoon when we were surrounded by open space on all sides. Contrary to my expectation, it was not a cone-like structure; it was a flat, albeit raggedy rocky surface. We walked around it. It seemed as if it was sitting on the tip of the steeples we just passed through. As my eyes surveyed its topography, it occurred to me that this peak was a station, a last station, I should say, in one's ascent to the summit, to that point which overlooks the territory of being in its entirety. "A friend of mine once told me," Kamal said, "that the monks who used to live in the monastery tried to build a kind of sanctuary on the eastern side of this elevation." Then, pausing to lead me to the spot where the remains, mainly rectangular rows of stones, were still visible, he added: "But their project did not succeed, because every structure they erected was destroyed by the wind. The weather can be woefully harsh around here."

We stood at this site for a few minutes, and then he led me to a nearby rock next to which there was a niche similar to the ones we usually find in a church altar in a cathedral chapel. It was clear to me that this embrasure was carved by human hands and it was intended for meditation. I approached it and cast a careful look at it, at the way it was chiseled, and especially at the way it faced the East. "Yes, it is a religious site!" I mumbled. "This is where lovers sat and communed with The Eternal." Without knowing how or why, I eased myself into that recess and sat on a rock that was lying in one of its corners. The first and only thing I noticed when I looked around me was infinite space. I almost felt that I was in the presence of infinity itself were it not for the vague horizon in the distance that embraced the space and presented it to my eyes as a sea of pure being. I gazed into the distance for a few minutes without any kind of distraction whatever. But then how can one's attention be distracted in such a sea, where his vision becomes one with infinity, where infinity fills every corner of the mind within? I thought that the seeker of The Eternal did not sit in this niche in order to empty his mind of its content but to fill it with the spirit of infinity, to become one with it.

The sun had already moved to the other side of the mountain when I sat there within the sweet arms of infinity. I was concerned about Kamal, for I did not want him to wait long for me, so I left the niche and looked around. He was nowhere to be seen. I knew that he was having his private meeting with The Eternal. Well, I returned to my spot and sat on the rock again. But instead of communing with the infinite I found myself wondering about my relation with Kamal as a human being, not with the intention of intruding into his soul, for this is morally impermissible, but with a desire to know, to deepen my understanding of his ways with the desert and ultimately with The Eternal. He had been my guide and my friend, and I knew without any shed of doubt that he would do all he could to open his soul to me and do whatever he could to help in completing my quest. Besides, he did not hesitate to help me to take advantage of every opportunity that might expand the dimension of my experience of the desert, and he did not withhold any knowledge that might illumine my vision of The Eternal. "Alas!" I reflected, "is this man really a son of the desert? Is he a god-intoxicated man? Is he addicted to the light of The Eternal? I know I have a desire to drink from its cup, I know that nothing in the world would be more pleasing to my palate than its nectar, and I know that this desire has been intensifying the deeper I plowed my way into the desert. But what is it like to be in love with The Eternal, to long for it every moment of your life, to bathe in its light every morning, and to cherish its warmth every day?"

I thought about the source of this yearning, about the daemon that underlies this kind of addiction, perhaps an acute awareness of being as such. Could it be that the experience of change is the most disturbing, the most devastating experience in human life? And what does this signify? Sitting in front and with the ocean of infinity that shone before my eyes as a divine presence, as the presence of Light itself, I now saw, and with a clearer vision, that change signifies perishing; it signifies not only the non-being of everything that exists in this world, including my work, but also my own non-being: nothingness! This thought, which appeared as a clear and distinct idea in the light of divine presence, sent a shudder through every fiber of my soul. Dark clouds moved into my heart. They brought with them electrifying thunder and lightning. I felt the sharp pangs of this shudder. I felt uprooted, unsettled. It was desolating, mortifying, for it undermined the foundation of my consciousness of the world and of myself, of the way of life I have so far lived—the tapestry of its beliefs, desires, values, habits, sensibilities, the aspirations that made up the structure of my inner and outer self, and especially the purpose for which I struggled to live every day of my past life. I am not too much amiss if I say that this is what it means to be uprooted. It means to be here, there, but nowhere. It means to be you and not you: paralyzed, helpless! I was afraid. I was afraid, not of falling into the abyss that lay a few inches away from me, nor of the physical emptiness of the desert, but of despair, the disease of all diseases.

Has it occurred to you that despair is worse than death? Death signifies your non-existence, and so the non-existence of pain and suffering. But despair is a different matter; it is death in torment, and torment in death. It is damnation itself. A strong whiff of nausea streamed through my nostrils. I felt the urge to vomit, but I could not. I tried again and again but to no avail. There was nothing to vomit. How can we vomit anything when we drink from the cup of nothingness? This nausea was a very tight and formidable net; I was caught in it the way a fly is caught in the net of a spider without any possibility of escape. I struggled for some kind of exit, but there was no exit. I became frantic and moved about aimlessly and fitfully. I was in this state for a while, but not for very long, because I could not endure the oppressive feeling of nausea, so I collapsed, not from lack of will, or from cowardice, but from fatigue. This collapse was a kind of respite, because it afforded me a moment of self-reflection: My own non-being loomed clear in my consciousness. It did not take me long to realize that the net I was in was of my own making, that the cup of nothingness I drank was concocted by me. I recognized that the only exit available was a retreat into myself. Was this the message conveyed by the feeling of nausea? Was the draft of nothingness a call to self-examination, to examine more carefully what it means to embrace The Eternal? How was I to understand the God-intoxicated man who has been my guide and friend?

Into myself I plunged in search of its inmost desire whose satisfaction is a condition for the satisfaction of every other desire or pursuit. But this desire stood in front of my consciousness staring at me with bewildered eyes. "The question you have to answer," those eyes were again whispering in my ear, "is the question of being: to be or not to be, to live or to die. Choose life! Being is good." Being is life; life is good; therefore, being is good. The logic of this voice was clear and forceful. Yes, I want to be, but what does it mean to be? How can I be in a world of change, in which everything seems to die the moment it comes into being? To be is to endure, but everything is an ongoing process of change, of annihilation. Is the world around me a passing show? So it seems, and yet, the consciousness that is now agonizing over this question, and in fact over the meaning of its destiny, endures, for if it does not, how can it continue its train of thought and its quest for The Eternal? How can it recognize the actuality of change and annihilation? Its body and every idea, emotion, or striving in its mind changes and will pass away, but there must be something else that endures, and without this something every human endeavor, no matter how great or valuable it is considered by the wisest of the wise, would be a strike of vanity, of fantasy. It might be viewed by others, in some way, as important, but in relation to the person in question—to her accomplishments, interests, or survival—it would be nothing, a passing breeze of air. Am I a passing breeze of air? Is Kamal a passing breeze of air? I am certain that he knows perfectly well that the scheme of nature, our bodies included, is a constantly changing show; that he does not consider himself, or his life, a passing breeze of air; and that he does not consider the scheme of nature a passing show, even though it is constantly changing.

I know that philosophers have advanced arguments to prove the existence of God, and they usually equate him with The Eternal or The Ultimate, but so far as I know no one of these arguments is convincing, for how can that which transcends human reason, that which is not an object of direct human experience, be the subject of logical reasoning? And in the first place, why should we try to prove the existence of something we do not directly experience, or have direct knowledge of? Do we try to prove the existence of genies? What prompts us to try to prove the existence of such an extraordinary being? Does nature not exist?

Al Naseri Mountain

Do I not exist? Does the sun not shine every day? Does the flower not blossom every spring? Do I need to prove the existence of something I directly see or live? Yes, these and the whole scheme of nature exist: Of this fact, I am absolutely certain. I am inclined to think that the quest for The Eternal does not begin with the arguments, or proofs, of the philosophers; for these are lame attempts to justify an already existing, necessary belief. Besides, they are abstract and indifferent to the realm of existence. Even if they are sound arguments for the existence of God, such arguments do not entail any certain knowledge of him. And how can we assert the existence of something we do not know? A cogent argument does not bring something into being; at best, it sheds some light on a belief or a hypothesis. An abstract argument begins with a thoughtful, sympathetic, and inquisitive contemplation on what exists. It results from reflection on the order of nature, on the mystery that shines in every one of its acts, on the voices it whispers when we feel the life that pulsates in it, the intelligence that works in and through it, and the beauty that adorns it. Only when we hear these voices, only when we confront the passing show of nature as worthy of understanding, and only when we listen to the music nature sings do we feel curious to know the mind that steers it, or how it functions the way it does. It is reflection on the scheme of nature—in its mystery, intelligence, beauty, order, or the sweeping dominance of change—that prompts us to ask the question of all questions: Why does the world exist rather than not? Put differently, why is there something rather than nothing? This question does not originate from the mind of the philosopher out of idle curiosity; on the contrary, the mind of the philosopher as a philosopher originates from its existential encounter with the mystery of the world, from the fact that it is intelligible, and from the fact that it is the ground of our own quest for meaning in this short life of ours.

Reflection on the scheme of nature is not merely an act of intellectual comprehension of what we experience, in which we simply conceptualize what we perceive as an external object, as an object we appropriate in some manner; it is a dialogical contemplative event in which we first understand what we experience and then seek to communicate it. Communication is never a passive activity. It is an active, productive one in which we grow in the capacity of knowing, feeling, and acting, mainly because we grow in the capacity of understanding and wisdom. Otherwise, communication would be a form of babbling.

The aim of this dialogue with nature is not only the discovery of its true identity but also the source of its being. In a dialogical encounter of this kind we delve deep into the source. We go beyond what appears into what underlies it and makes it possible. I have always thought that the scheme of nature is a musical composition, a beautiful symphony. Who does not feel, indeed live, the soul of the composer in listening attentively to this symphony? And who does not want to have a private audience with its composer? Do you not desire to witness the source from which this beauty emanates?

I am a lover of beauty, and I am a seeker of my source and the source of the world. I am now confident that the eyes that asked me to choose between being and non-being, life and death, were no more than an echo of a deeper voice originating from the bosom of my own being, from that kernel which gives rise to everything that I am. I can now see that this voice is not a whisper, nor is it a reminder; no, it is a cry for being. It is a cry against non-being. How can it be such a cry if it is not a witness to being, if it is not baptized by its light and stung by its fire? But what does it mean for this cry to be a cry? Please, imagine a drowning person, who cannot swim, crying for help, or a lover crying for his beloved. Reflect on the structure of this cry, on its source and aim. If you do, you will certainly glean, under the light of your reason, that it is not only a primary desire for being, for life, but also a yearning for it; and that its satisfaction is an indispensable condition for the swimmer or the lover or anyone who utters such a cry. But you will also see that to be a human being is to be a cry for being, to walk through the ocean of change and land safely on the shores of being: your homeland. Could it be that Kamal has already made this journey? Is this why he is at peace with himself and in tune with the rhythm of nature? Is this why his eyes are always radiant with a special light? Is this why he loves the world and is at the same time indifferent to it? Does he know the secret of change? But how can he be indifferent to the world if he does not know its secret?

I was distracted from this flight into the land of wonder by a mild gust of hot breeze. Suddenly, I jumped to my two feet and left my niche behind in search of Kamal, but he was not visible anywhere in the vicinity. Then I inspected every possible space within my field of vision on the summit, but he eluded my eyes and ears. I was absolutely certain he was a most efficient and responsible human being. "His meeting with

The Eternal must be longer than he expected," I thought. "But, then, where is he having this meeting?" I was afraid to answer or even dwell on the implications of this question for fear I would be violating his privacy, which I prized with a deep sense of respect. The only thing I could do was to wait for him. I knew he would join me as soon as he could. So I took advantage of this lull and simply walked around the rocky terrain of the summit. I climbed one of the big rocks and scanned the extensive vista of space that spread around me as a disc limited only by the horizon. At that point, I did not allow my imagination to speculate on what lay beyond the horizon but only on the fact that I was standing on the summit in the midst of this amazing disc, on the fact that this whole disc spread before my eyes as a perspective and that my mind could grasp it as a whole. It occurred to me as I was surveying the depth of its being that the monks frequented this summit because, for them, it was a simile. The summit was the farthest point from the world of change and the closest to the world of The Divine. They wanted to be as close to God as possible. All they had to do was to step over the horizon. If they did, they would be in the lap of another horizon, which would, in turn, reveal the next horizon, and so on infinitely. Yes, they knew this process quite well, but they also knew that this process was the way to The Eternal and that this way would not be possible without a comprehensive vision of the world as a whole. To see a thing in perspective is an essential condition for understanding it. But the monks frequented the summit for another reason. They wanted to see the world as a whole from the standpoint of their vision of The Eternal, not from the standpoint of this or that finite being. They were convinced that no knowledge that pertains to the world is adequate if it is not attained from the standpoint of such vision. Only the light of The Eternal can reveal the true nature of the world: its genesis, structure, and destiny. Could it be that this rock, this steeple of the desert, was a stepping stone the monks used to leap from the finite into the bosom of The Infinite?

Kamal's shadow was emerging from behind my back. "This rock is one of the most interesting spots on this summit," he said as I began to acknowledge his presence with a cheerful spirit. Where he was or how he suddenly appeared remained a mystery to me, but it did not matter, for I was confident of his prudence and trustworthiness as I was of my own existence. And yet, it was clear to me that he was being sanctified by the light of The Eternal, for his complexion was an icon of peace, of holiness. I felt a strong impulse to touch him, because I wanted to feel what it is like to be purified by the splendor that lingered in his depth, but I refrained from doing either. I felt the warmth of his presence, and this feeling gave me great satisfaction. "Yes," I said, "it enables one to have a comprehensive vision of the desert." He smiled and then remarked: "Yes, a synoptic vision." He was silent for a few seconds. It seemed to me that he wanted to elaborate this remark, but he did not, for he reminded me that it was getting late and that we had at least one more hour of driving before we could reach our next destination. Frankly, I was reluctant to leave that summit, at least not before three or four days; I had a strong desire to spend more time in the niche. I wanted to fly to the horizon and sit on it for a while and watch how it vanishes into a new horizon. Yes, I had a strong desire to know how space, the space of ordinary life, evaporates into nothingness as it approaches the All-Encompassing horizon. And yes, I had a strong desire to stand on that rock again and lift my eyes into the blue dome that protects our world and, if possible, to fly into its center and take a peek into The Depth. But this desire was not fulfilled. I have always respected Kamal's wisdom: He knew the ways of the desert.

The sun had already left its zenith and was moving toward the western frontier when we started our descent. At first we had to forge our way through a maze of scattered rocks intercepted with many dead plants. "These plants," Kamal said, "give birth to the most beautiful flowers in springtime. The falcons are enamored by their beauty. I think this is why they never leave this spot. I wonder what it is like to view this summit from their vantage point. An old man who used to spend much of his time roaming the Naseri Mountain said on more than one occasion that the monks who used to live around this summit used to feed the falcons. They used to talk with them, play with them, and nurse them." I was puzzled when I heard this anecdote. "Most interesting!" I broke in.

"More than this," Kamal retorted, "I really believe that the monks understood the ways of the falcon. They even befriended them, not only because they are God's creatures and so reveal The Divine, but especially because they tried to learn from them the art of flying. Any serious human being would, if she observes the ways of the falcon, wonder why it flies the way it does and why, like the lark, seeks to soar into the depth of the heavenly dome. The falcon is free from the cares of the earth as well as from gravity—in a way. It flies almost effortlessly on the wings of the wind. I sometimes thought that the monks wished they could sit on its wings and soar with it into the depth of the infinite sky, for their greatest wish was, and remains, to approach, as far as they could, the farthest possible limit of being available to the human mind." Kamal's narrative was interrupted by a shriek I made and tried to suppress but could not. Absorbed in Kamal's narrative, my right foot hit a small boulder that sent a jolt through my body. I would have had a bad fall had it not been for Kamal's strong arms that caught me before I hit the ground. "There you are!" he said with a glowing smile on his face.

"I am not sure, but it must have been a hard blow," I said. Casting a quick glance at my face, he slipped his right arm under my left shoulder and led me to a nearby rock elevation, where he made me sit for a few minutes. "How is your foot? Any pain?" He inquired.

"No!"

"Let me look at it," he recommended. I complied with his request, so I removed my shoe. He squatted and felt my foot. He pressed it on all sides. "Do you feel any pain?" He asked every time he applied pressure on the various places he felt.

"No!" Then he massaged it gently for a few minutes.

"You will feel fine!" he said with a sense of satisfaction. A few seconds later, he added: "It might be wise for you to sit on this rock a few more minutes. Some rest will be good for the soul and the body!" I felt a desire to insist that we continue our descent, but I could not, only because I was trustful of his good will and prudent judgment. "The heart of this man was fashioned with the hands of Care," I thought, as he left me for a few moments, perhaps to respond to the call of nature. "A loving heart is a nurse: a nourishing and a mending heart. It is a source of giving and a power of healing." When I was a teenager I heard that love is an emotion and that it is blind, perhaps because it is felt as an unstoppable force or striving, but I am now convinced that it is not an emotion, although it moves on the wings of emotion, but a power, and that it has eyes, ears, feelings, a heart, and a logic of its own, and that it always aims at the good. It is made of goodness and sanctified with the hands of freedom. The more I reflected on this insight, the more it became clear to me that Kamal was a pearl of love! Love is neither boastful nor arrogant, neither stingy nor profligate, neither vain nor self-forgetful, neither fault-finding nor punitive, neither indolent nor ambitious. It is always itself: an ever flowing fountain of life. It gives life, because it is a life-giver. What it gives flows from it naturally, without conditions or expectations. Giving is its reason for being, and giving is its destiny. The only satisfaction it enjoys is the satisfaction of being itself: a fountain of giving.

I was awakened from this short reverie by Kamal's voice: "How do you feel now? Is it hot for you?"

"I am rested and ready to resume my descent."

"Splendid!" With this gesture of approval, we continued our descent, and within a few minutes we found the track that led to the bottom of the mountain. I should here remark that Kamal was constantly inquiring about my foot, always making sure that I was fine! The afternoon sun was sweltering; but I welcomed the heat, not because it was harsh and frankly hostile to my body, and I was indifferent to bodily pain, but because I wanted to walk in the light, the light of The Sun. Life flourishes in the light; I am a life and I wanted to live. The impulse to life is the strongest impulse in my being. What could be the source of this impulse? Is it a freaky eruption in the course of cosmic evolution, a kind of anomaly? This may be the case, but what is the source, or cause, of this evolution, not only of its process but especially of the existence of the process itself? My soul shall not know the meaning of peace until it knocks at the door of this source, unless it witnesses that light that is the source of all light.

The landscape that we left behind as we began our ascent of the mountain was now emerging slowly in the field of my vision when we began our descent. The golden sand of the desert was glittering under the dancing rays of the sun; it was a symphony of golden colors, of light—of divine light. I listened to this symphony with anxious ears, and anxious heart. Its divine beauty filled my heart. I was enamored by this beauty. I must have forgotten myself for a few moments, because I suddenly noticed that I was smiling. Who could possibly stand indifferent before the majesty of this kind of beauty? A scientist? Perhaps. But I am not a scientist; I am a lover of the beautiful. "Be careful!" Kamal said, interrupting my aesthetic experience. "The ground here is shifty, slippery. One can easily twist an ankle or break a hip." Kamal was right, for soon after he made his warning I felt that the ground on which I was standing was shifting. I slowly learned how to measure the speed and movement of my steps. However, let me confess that the descent from the summit downward was an adventure. I had to concentrate the totality of my attention on the track. Detecting my anxiety, Kamal recommended a recess: "How about a break? We can rest for a few minutes at that bend." I welcomed this recommendation without any hesitation. My heart was palpitating when I sat on a rock Kamal had pointed out. "Who said that descending a mountain is easier than ascending it?" he said with an angelic smile in his eyes.

This remark fell upon me as a thunderbolt; it unraveled some vague ideas and feelings in my mind. It enabled me to view the totality of my adventure of the mountain in perspective, as a series of interconnected experiences. The mountain as a metaphor loomed in the foreground of my imagination as a journey into the meaning of human life in general and my life in particular. The point was to explore the meaning of ascending and descending and of standing on the summit. My life, as well as the life of every human being, is an activity of ascending, standing on the summit, and descending the mountain of life. Yes, my life is a mountain! It is a process of growth and development from the moment of birth, of rising to a pinnacle of achievement, regardless of how great or small it might be, and then of descending into a valley of silence! Both processes are difficult and painful, and both are good and exhilarating. The process of growth and development, of ascent, is the hardest task human beings face in their lives. It is an activity of choosing and creating themselves as the individuals they are. They derive their deepest satisfaction from the realization of this activity. But, then, when they reach the pinnacle of this activity, when they stand on the summit of their achievements, they discover that the next stretch of their lives is a stretch of descent, and they discover that the struggle of descent, of the attempt to free themselves from the downward pull of gravity, is no less painful than the struggle of ascent. We would like to remain on the summit, but we cannot, because our nature is weaved of the thread of time. We belong to the earth, after all! As we descend the mountain of our life, we grow new eyes, which are forbidden to youth, by means of which we can see our humanity's most intriguing secret: the fact that there is a valley of silence waiting for us at the end. When we see this valley with our new eyes, and these eyes see existentially, we know what it means to be finite. We see the actuality of finitude directly and we comprehend it with a feeling of realism. I know many people do not wonder about the meaning of their lives, much less the meaning of their finitude, but this does not obviate the fact that this aspect is an essential ingredient of human nature and life.

I have read most of the philosophers' works on the nature and meaning of life, and I have lectured on the subject many a semester. I even reminded my students, those young people whose eyes cannot grasp even the paradoxes of time and perishing, that they are mortal, that their lives would not be genuine, and that their happiness would be shallow if they did not proceed in designing and implementing the projects of their lives from the realization that they are mortal and that the valley of silence will be waiting for them as the last station of their lives. But to confess, I have never had an existential encounter with the valley of silence the way I did that afternoon with my own eyes when I began the descent of the Naseri Mountain. The lucidity of that encounter startled me: I felt a shiver in my weary feet and then in my gut. We frequently find ourselves caught in the tyrannical machine of social life without paying adequate attention to the actuality and significance of our mortality. Oh, how the burdens of social demands and vanities of life veil the truth of our finitude! It seemed to me while I was sitting on that rock resting next to Kamal that, metaphorically, the descent of the mountain was a struggle the way ascending it was a struggle, but with a difference: While the descent was a struggle to build ourselves, to complete ourselves, the ascent was a struggle against death. We are meant to live, to continue to live, to live well, and always to live better. Sitting over the valley of silence, staring at the abyss that lay beneath it, and contemplating my mortality brought into sharp focus the contrast between finitude and infinity: Can I think finitude and comprehend it, which is an indubitable fact of existence, without implying the existence of the infinite? I exist and I think both; I am able to think the here and the now, this and that object, but I can also proceed in my thinking to the farthest possible limit of both physical and intellectual existence. Why? How? And why do I want to continue to live, not merely as a physical reality but as a human being? There must be something in me that resists the descent into the valley of silence, and there must be some wisdom in the bosom of this something. I want to see it with my heart, feel it, and take a peek into that Fountain from which everything that exists flows.

It was a slow, nerve-wracking descent. It would have been impossible for me to reach the bottom of the mountain safely without Kamal's assistance. I slipped more than once and would have fallen flat on my back had it not been for Kamal's strong arms. I would have easily broken my hip or a vertebra! He was always there for me as my guide, teacher, and protector. On several occasions, as I have already remarked, I reflected on the meaning of his presence: Why was he there for me at that point in time and in that place? I could not answer this question, but it was obvious to me that my ascent would have been impossible without the wisdom and generosity of his heart. One cannot, I think, walk on the road of self-actualization alone. And yet, the quest for the infinite is a solitary venture. Its point of origin is a particular mind, its energizing power is a particular will, and its destiny is the divine. I can receive guidance and psychological and material support, but no one can think my thoughts, feel my feelings, and will my actions: No one can will my destiny and no one can assume responsibility for the actions I perform or the kind of life I live. But the fact that it is a solitary venture does not at all imply that it is a selfish or lonely endeavor, because love is its beginning and its end, and, perhaps more important, the binding force that holds together everything in between, giving it meaning, making it a journey worth taking, and thus building a life worth living.

chapter 5

In Saada

IT WAS LATE AFTERNOON when we reached the bottom of the mountain. "You must be very thirsty," Kamal said the moment we set foot on the ground of the desert.

"Yes, I am thirsty!" I retorted.

"We should be on our way in a few minutes," he said as we walked toward the van. Kamal handed me two bottles of water. Then, he inspected our luggage and supplies. "Everything is fine!" he remarked in a rather faint voice, as if he was talking to himself. Within seconds, he was seated behind the steering wheel with a deep smile of satisfaction on his lips. "How do you feel?" he inquired as he started the engine. Although my answer to Kamal's question, which came from a good heart, was correct, it was inadequate, because the feeling that filled my heart was indescribable. It would be more appropriate to characterize it as a moment of delightful comprehension, of enlightenment; for I felt as if the boundaries of my inner being were stretching and expanding in all directions. I felt as if scales fell off my eyes, as if the fountain of life in my being was flowing more abundantly. A serene calm floated in my heart. There was something magical, enchanting, about Naseri Mountain. Every element of it spoke the language of the desert, and every word it spoke sang the song of The Eternal. It seemed as if the mountain was the desert's permanent prayer to The Eternal!

I was captivated by this delicious, indescribable feeling, which was pounding vibrantly on the walls of my soul when Kamal remarked: "We shall leave the main road in a few minutes and take a track usually frequented by caravans; it will be rough for a while, but it will be a shortcut to Saada, our next stop. Then we shall take a poorly paved road to our final destination for today. This part of the desert is known for its rugged terrain and unpredictable weather. It is practically barren. One can hardly see any kind of vegetation around here. But thankfully it will be a short distance."

As it was his habit, Kamal did not say much, but the few pieces of information he relayed to me now and then were adequate; they were more than enough to keep me oriented in the ways of the desert and what we should expect in the imminent present. This idea provoked a train of thought in my mind. "He must have a highly developed sense of communication, of what it means to be with other human beings," I mused, as he tried to steer his way into the bumpy road. He knew the difference between idle talk and serious, meaningful conversation, the kind that connects two human beings at the level of humanity, the kind that makes a positive, constructive difference in the way we think, feel, and act, that creates human presence, that keeps the flame of life kindled in the heart. The more time I spent with him, the more I became proficient in the art of silent conversation, in which we do not only feel the humanity of others, recognize their presence, and orient our mode of being with theirs, but also open up to them, share ourselves with them during that encounter. How can we understand what they say or feel or desire, if we do not understand them as human beings, if we do not accept them for what they are? Yes, Kamal was verbally silent most of the time, but I knew, and I felt, that he was constantly listening to the voice of my mind and the beats of my heart, for he was there, as alert as possible, to meet my intellectual and material needs when I expressed them. The truth of this synergy became very clear to me as we approached Saada. Why not? After all, he understood the ways of the desert, and he understood me.

Saada was a rather small settlement. It appeared on the scene of our vision as an agglomeration of a few buildings, tents, and barns. Some palm trees began to come into view when we approached the periphery. Several flocks of camel were resting in their shade. A number of Bedouins emerged from the trees and watched us as we reached the settlement. I cast a steady look at them with a deep feeling of curiosity. They seemed an icon of simplicity, of innocence. "Are these people sons of the desert?" My mind wondered as my look lingered on their faces. "What would it be like to spend a few days with one of these caravans?" When innocent, the human face is an image of The Divine; it represents God's presence on earth. It represents the sublimity of The Divine in the fullness of its being. Having an encounter with the sublime in nature or art can be thrilling, humbling, and illuminating, and it can be instructive; but having an encounter with the divine sublime is not merely awe-ful but also enchanting, and I can say blissful, because it is elevating, exhilarating, ennobling, upholding. It uplifts us to the source of our being. I cannot remain indifferent to this kind of image. My heart leaps to it with admiration and respect. I do not see its color, shape, or size, and I do not pay attention to whether it is frowning or smiling. The Divine appears one and the same in any one of its expressions. Besides, I have always valued the human face, regardless of whether it is sad or happy, puzzled or placid, anxious or peaceful, friendly or hostile. Appreciating the human face only because it is pleasant or useful is an insult to human dignity. Should we not respect the human in us for its own sake, because it is an emanation of The Divine on earth?

Kamal parked the van in front of a small store. His mind was on practical matters: "We need to replenish our water, bread, and cheese. They make good cheese here. Have you ever had camel cheese? You should try it."

"Gladly!" I rejoined. The store looked like a typical country shop. As soon as he saw us, the manager rushed toward us and warmly embraced Kamal. They must have exchanged warm greetings in the past, because their faces were buoyant with gladness. A moment later, Kamal pointed to me, mentioned my name, and said something in Arabic. He must have introduced me to him, for the manager came closer and shook hands with me with a pleasant smile on his face. "Sorry, no English!" he said with an air of embarrassment. I smiled and shook hands with him again, trying to assure him that I understood and appreciated his desire to meet me. Then, having talked for a few minutes, Rafiq, the manager, went to the back of the store and returned shortly afterward with a box containing the goods we needed. The two men chatted for a few more minutes and then parted the way they met, cheerfully.

Although it had left its zenith a few hours ago, the sun was still pouring scorching beams of heat over the desert. Kamal was right. The road on which we traveled in the afternoon was truly rugged. Most of the pavement was eroded, and I could hardly recognize its outline, but Kamal drove on it as if it were just another road! His innate knowledge of the whole region was amazing. It seemed to me that he foresaw every pothole, every turn, and every leveled stretch of the road. Suddenly and inexplicably I turned my attention away from the road to Kamal's face:

In Saada

It was an image of self-composure and peace. Even though his eyes were focused on the road, they were in a serious reflective mood. A gush of curiosity filled my mind; I wanted to know the object of his reflection. I wanted to take a peek into this private affair with the desert, the way he feels it and understands it, especially how his eyes see the rays of the divine in it and commune with it. I wanted to know the source of the peace that filled his heart, the confidence that enlivens his mind, and the secret that makes his soul dance with tranquil hope. But most of all, I wanted to stand on the well of his passion for The Eternal. Did I have the right to indulge in this kind of desiring? Would this constitute a clandestine invasion of his privacy? Honestly, I cannot, now in retrospect, answer these questions, but how can anyone be in the presence of such a noble human being without feeling the itch to know the source of the divine aura that emanated from everything he said and did? How can anyone smell the fragrance of such an aura without trying to know its source? Would I be violating any kind of privacy if I were to probe into the secret of the divine presence in the tree, the mountain, the lion, or the moon? What if Kamal is, and I believe he is, a divine spark on earth? Does the question of privacy arise? I wonder!

The beams of my gaze must have crashed on his profile, for a mild smile glided on his face. "I hope you are not tired, or perhaps hot," he said without facing me. "This son of the desert, this friend of The Eternal, yes, this human being, with whom I am having the distinct honor to explore the ways of the Syrian Desert does not speak from the top or back of his mind but from the bosom of human presence, from the radiance of this presence. Such presence does not have verbal, psychological, social, or physical walls or barriers of any kind. In this sphere of being, we exist with one another in the simplicity and innocence of our humanity the way Adam and Eve existed in the Garden of Eden. We commune with each other and we communicate from the bosom of this communion. When I love you, and human love is the highest form of human communion, I feel your feeling, be it of pain, joy, dejection, anxiety, sadness, weariness, or loneliness, without being told. In this kind of existence, I see what I feel, think what I see, and will what I feel. I share your feeling, I cherish it, I cultivate it, and I celebrate it in everything I do. Does it take much to have this kind of communion when I look into your eyes, hear your voice, touch your hand, or see the way you walk? Love rises to its highest glory in the medium of human communion.

"No," I replied after a long silence, "frankly, I am neither tired nor hot, and to tell the truth, I am indifferent to my physical surroundings. I just feel an inner itch, a nagging desire, to delve deeper into myself, into the source from which my life flows. I know such a source exists, because when I examine the theatre of my mental life in an attempt to understand the secrets of its inner workings: how I think, how my passion crackles like thunder in the sky of my mind, how I dream, how I make decisions before I act, how I hope, how I imagine. I feel that there is something that sees and oversees the drama that unfolds on the stage of this theatre in the course of my daily life. The way this something weaves and steers the story of my life is simply puzzling to me and at times I think miraculous. I know it is the seer and the overseer of my life story at the same time, but I cannot comprehend it in its dual role, I cannot have a comprehensive vision of the fullness of its essence, and I cannot comprehend why it exists the way it does or why it exists at all; and yet, I know it is an essence of some kind. And what is more puzzling to me is that I see and appreciate the miraculous aspect of nature around me, of how this universe is structured and how it works. I know people do not dwell on this question, because they are absorbed in the enterprise of daily living, which is overwhelming most of the time, or because they have become familiar with it, and so they take it for granted, or because they think it is a trivial question, having committed themselves to a philosophy, a religion, an ideology, or a worldview, but this does not in any way obviate the fact that the spectacle of nature is an ongoing miracle. Yes, Kamal, I have an itch to have a vision or some understanding of the power that underlies my inner being and the being of the world."

"Do you think there is a relation between your own source and the source of the universe?" Kamal asked in a quiet but thoughtful voice. His eyes remained focused on the road, but his attention was focused on me, on what was going on in my mind.

My response, though personal and sincere, was inevitably colored by years of academic exposure: "I confess that I have frequently meditated on this question. Sometimes my meditation began with an examination of the origin of my own self, seeking an understanding of its essence and the ground in which this essence is founded, and sometimes I began with an attempt to understand the origin and meaning of the universe. Invariably, I discovered that a quest for the one leads to a quest for the other. I realized that any knowledge of the origin of the world, regardless of its extent or kind, necessarily has implications upon how we should live, no matter how long or short our life might be; and similarly, any knowledge of the origin of myself necessarily leads to an inquiry into the origin of the universe, for I and every element of nature, and I can say nature itself, are creatures; they are contingent and, as such, cannot be fully understood apart from the ultimate ground of the whole scheme of things. What is noteworthy is that our bodies, in which our humanity is anchored, are integral parts of nature; they are governed by its laws, the same laws that govern the living and non-living things. Add to this the fact that there is harmony between the working of our bodies and the working of our humanity. It sometimes seems to me that our bodies exist as means to an end and that the end is growth in spiritual life. I would not be too much amiss if I say that the human body is an instrument in the pursuit of our destiny as human beings: human growth. It is, after all, the locus of human individuality. So far as I know, I cannot exist as this particular individual without this particular body in and through which I am now speaking these words. Thus, any inquiry into the origin of our humanity is intimately connected with an inquiry into the origin of the universe. Accordingly, the same mind that is curious about the origin of the one should be curious about the origin of the other."

"Though logical," Kamal rejoined, "and to my mind plausible, what you say is somewhat abstract. I wonder if there is another mode of reasoning that may clarify the relation between the source of the universe and of the human self, the kind that shows the practical relevance of our knowledge of this origin to the meaning of human life and destiny. I have discovered early in my life that, though pivotal and an essential condition of human progress in any sphere of human life, and we may say intrinsically valuable, knowledge cannot be an absolute, final end, but a means to the attainment of human ends to their aspirations. We do not live in order to know; we seek to know in order to live, and the life we live should foster human perfection. What is the use of knowing the true nature of justice, freedom, beauty, or goodness, if we do not apply this knowledge in our lives; what is the use of saying that God is absolute in power, wisdom, and goodness, if we do not acknowledge him in our personal lives; and what is the use of knowing that physical exercise is useful for the human body, if we do not exercise? Quest of knowledge is a mode of having, while living is a mode of being. I am convinced that, regardless of how or by whom we were created, we are destined to be, to live, not simply to have, no matter the sort of things we need or desire to have. Being is the primary demand of human nature, because our humanity is given to us as a potentiality: It is a possibility of being, and since it is a possibility, our being is none other than the process of becoming who and what we are in the activity of daily living. But if our being is a process of becoming, if our essence is given as a potentiality for becoming real, then it is imperative that we know how to become, or how to live, or what beliefs and values should be the foundation of our lives."

"What you say," I broke in, interrupting his train of thought, "raises a question that has been gnawing at my mind ever since I was a young man: the question of time, or change." But the question, much less its articulation, froze on my lips, mainly because I was overwhelmed by its enormity, so I succumbed to a mood of meditative silence in which I tried to sort out its dimensions and ramifications. As he did in similar situations before, Kamal did not make a stir of any kind. He sat next to me as a sphinx. His eyes were lost to the distance that hovered in front of him over the desert as an abyss.

"Time exists," I continued after I became clearer about my question, "only because we experience change in nature and in our minds. Time is a function of change; it is also its measure. We experience time as long or short inasmuch as we experience change as long or short. The experience of time originates from the experience of change. The way we experience the duration of change determines the way we experience the determinations of time: seconds, minutes, hours, days, and so forth. We are temporal beings insofar as we ourselves change, and we exist in time insofar as nature itself is an ongoing process of change. What has always baffled me is that the whole scheme of nature is a spectacle of change. Nothing seems to endure; consequently, nothing remains the same as itself. This is why we can say that the phenomenon of change entails perishing, and the concept of change implies the concept of perishing. And this is why we can say that, from the temporal point of view, everything that exists in nature is finite, in the sense that it has a beginning and an end. Everything that exists, be it a tree, a river, a sun, a moon, or a galaxy, comes into being and passes out of being.

"Metaphorically, we can liken the spectacle of nature to a river of change. Every particle of water in it is in constant change, but the river as river endures. What makes it endure? Moreover, even though a thing is a trajectory of change, it relatively retains its identity. Although the house I am living in is changing, and one day will cease to exist, it nevertheless remains the same house as long as it exists. It seems to be a synthesis of opposites. This seems to apply to everything that exists, including nature as one cosmic process. Now, what makes a thing endure in spite of the fact that it is constantly changing?

"The things that make up the spectacle of nature endure for a period of time and then cease to exist; they simply perish; but they come into being and pass out of being within this spectacle, and they could not have made an appearance in the realm of being by themselves, mainly because they did not exist before they came into being and because they could not choose to endure, since it is obvious that nothing persists. What causes them to come into being, linger for a while, and then pass out of being? If the spectacle of nature is a river of change, and we have to grant that it is, if this river is an ongoing trajectory of change, something permanent must underlie it, for this trajectory itself cannot proceed and cannot exist in the first place, if there is not something that keeps it going and if this something does not endure. Change itself cannot be experienced as change if we do not also experience something that is permanent in or behind it; and the concept of change is inconceivable if we do not assume the existence of the concept of permanence."

"Would you apply this line of reasoning to your own existence as a human being," Kamal suddenly intervened, "or at least how does it apply, if it does?" Kamal's perceptiveness and his ability to be in sync with me in exploring this line of reasoning were simply astonishing. He asked his question neither to quiz me nor to help me in the development of my train of thought, but only to underscore the critical importance of this point, especially its relevance to human life. He was in full command of the line of thought I was developing, and he was aware of the significance of the question of the source that gave rise to the universe. I realized later on that he was trying to have a dialogue with me, in which the object of the conversation was not only understanding the ideas I was trying to communicate but also sharing something important with me. For him, genuine dialogue is an occasion of human communion, of sharing ourselves: love. How could Kamal have raised his question at that very juncture of my exposition had he not felt my inmost desire to justify my quest for The Eternal?

"My existence as a human being is different from that of natural objects such as cats, rocks, or trees. A natural object remains relatively the same from the moment of its creation to the moment of its annihilation. The change it undergoes is a process of gradual degeneration into non-being. The rock remains the rock it has been throughout its existence. What keeps its relative identity as that rock is a different question and need not concern me in this context. But the point that calls for special attention is that its lifespan is the stretch of time that falls between the beginning and end of its existence. What I say is based on the assumption that natural objects are, so far as we know, given to the world as ready-made objects. Their structural make-up changes, but not the essential features which constitute their identities.

"But the case is different with human beings. A particular human being is not given to the world as a ready-made object but as a potentiality for becoming one. Here, humanity is given as a schema, as an abstract possibility, that can acquire a particular structure or identity under certain conditions. All human beings share this schema. Its possession is what entitles a biped to a membership in the class of human beings. But the particular identity of a human being, or the essence that distinguishes him from every other human being, is a personal achievement. The 'I' that thinks, feels, and wills in me, the 'I' that distinguishes me from Socrates and my neighbor John, is a project, a plan I design and realize in the course of my daily living; it emerges and develops in this course of existence. It acquires its distinct individuality from the kind of beliefs and values according to which it lives. Unlike any natural thing, which is a physical object and functions according to certain laws, the 'I' as a world of thought, feelings, and actions, is not a physical object we experience with the five senses. Like the physical object, it is a trajectory of change, but with a major difference. The change it undergoes is not a process of degeneration but of development, of continual coming into being. The more I develop, the richer I become as a human being. It seems that my vocation in this world is to develop, and I develop inasmuch as I actualize the human potential in me: in knowledge, prudence, love, justice, and the appreciation of beauty and holiness. I exist in order to become the human being I should be. You see, I am a project; therefore, I am a task! The path I follow in pursuing this task is founded in the ideals of reason: goodness, beauty, truth, and holiness. Let me confess that walking on this path is the greatest challenge of human life; it is perhaps the most intimidating endeavor we can undertake. I know many people shy away from this path by devoting themselves to the pursuit of pleasure, wealth, power, fame, health, knowledge, or some personal interest, but it seems to me that perfecting our individual selves is our destiny. It is also the most satisfying, the most joyful activity the human mind can conceive. What if I gain the whole world and lose my soul?

"And, yes, I can hear a sarcastic, mocking whisper in my ear: 'Fool! You speak loftily, naively, and hastily. You will lose your body and your soul! Like the cat, the storm, or the tree, you shall not endure; your life is short and even if it were longer, you shall never be able to perfect yourself. And suppose some power, benign or malignant, has given you the time you need to perfect yourself—so what? What is the significance of this self-perfection? All your accomplishments, and every trace of you, shall vanish into nothingness: Perishing is the supreme law of the universe. You may felicitate yourself by the fact that you are different from the stone or the tree by being human, that is, by the fact that you create yourself as a human being. You know, as you used to admit throughout your academic career in your conversations with yourself, as well as in your meditations on the relation between the finite and the infinite, that nothing is real and therefore nothing exists unless it endures, that the real abides, for otherwise we cannot know of its existence. What is the use of your self-creation and of your delight in what you create when the hands of death will silence your voice forever? Why struggle, walk on the road of self-denial, suffer all its indignity, insults, deprivation, alienation, and mental anguish when you know you will be buried in the graveyard of nothingness? Have you seen or heard of anyone who has returned from the house of the dead? What makes you think that being human is a blessing and not a curse? You are not only conscious of your surroundings but also of yourself: You are a self-conscious being. Is this self-consciousness the source of the curse and of the false feeling, which has in time become an urge, that you are entitled to immortality? Is this false feeling an expression of grandiose self-love, of hubris? Do you really aspire to become a Greek or Roman god, or perhaps a Christian angel? Some of those who contemplated this silly predicament decided that the only kind of immortality, which is really a form of self-appeasement, is to procreate and perpetuate the family and the species, or to create great works of art, science, philosophy, and social monuments whose value can linger in the minds of a few people in the near or distant future. But suppose those few great minds succeed in leaving behind such a legacy, where will they be after they die? What baffles any logic is the prevalent preoccupation with the desire for immortality as if it is an absolute privilege or a fact of the world. The stone comes into being and passes out of being without complaining or making any fuss about its mortality; so does every other living and non-living thing in nature. What makes you think that if you live after the death of your body you will be a happier or a better human being or even a human being? Is your desire for immortality a desire to escape from the pains, uncertainties, fears, failures, frustrations, and insurmountable challenges of your present life? Vain glory!'"

Kamal's face, which was always an image of self-composure, suddenly became tense, and I daresay apprehensive, soon after I reported to him the message of the whisper. Although his eyes remained fixed on the road, having left the rough stretch some time ago, I could clearly see that he fell into a pit of deep thought. Thoughtfulness was radiating from his face. Then he leaned forward with a shade of perplexity in his solemn complexion, as if he was intentionally hugging the driving wheel of the van. He remained in that position for a few minutes and without looking at me said: "Are you in any way interested in the immortality of the soul?"

"No!"

"Do you mean to say that the man Dimitri, the man I am speaking with now, the man who is a flame of life, having tasted the meaning and the joy of life, does not wish or hope to linger somewhere forever?"

"Yes, I do not have such a hope, wish, or desire."

"What is the purpose for whose fulfillment you would gladly give everything you own?"

"I have reconciled myself to the fact that I shall perish. To tell the truth, I am indifferent to death. I have seen people suffer from pain, fear, anxiety, depression, loneliness, poverty, alienation, injustice, oppression, but not from death. Death is a cessation of life, and no more.

So far as I know, this event is neither painful nor pleasant; it is simply a natural occurrence, and, as such, indifferent to human feeling. There is a difference between the pain of death, the pain that is caused by it, and the agony over death, the pain that precedes it. Fear of it is what causes the agony.

"Those who fear death, or hate it, or treat it as their worst enemy, do so not out of fear of dying but out of a deep-seated attachment to life. The desire for life is the primary impulse in human nature. But my concern is not with the mortality of the body but with the human dimension—with that part in me that thinks, feels, and wills, the part that can transcend the physical dimension; that can fly into the realm of truth, goodness, and beauty; that can sit on the throne of reason and try to understand the laws of nature; and that can sing the song of heaven on earth."

"And what about the human dimension that concerns you?"

"I know I was born some years ago and shall leave this world a few years from now. Where did I come from? Where am I going? What is the meaning of my stay on earth? I did not choose to be born, and I will not choose my end—why am I brought here? I discovered, during the peak of my adolescence, that I was given to these parents, this society, this town, this neighborhood, this culture, this religion, and this age! Am I a marionette? I am not seeking an explanation for doing what I am now doing or the kind of life I am leading, which, if made, is a reasonable and justifiable demand. I am seeking an explanation for the meaning of my existence. Is this existence a phantom, and my life a phantasm? If so, in whose mind? Is it an accident? If so, why and how did this accident take place? Has the story of my life, as well as the life of the world, been weaved by a fool?

"No!"

"Then, what is the point of toiling, of leading a life of growth and development, of trying to surmount the insurmountable in going through the effort of self-creation, in short, of actualizing the human potential, which is the foundation of my being, if the human mansion I build will soon pass into nothing?"

"I have a feeling that the answer to your question is immanent in the source and meaning, in the experience, that gave rise to them, for frequently our questions, especially when they are serious, disclose the seeds of their answers. Would this spectacle of nature exist, and would you experience it as such, if there were not a sufficient reason for its existence? Would you, as you yourself acknowledged in your present adventure, experience the fact that everything that exists is a trajectory of change, if there were not something permanent that underlies it and gives it direction? Would you think and articulate your own questions if there were not an intellect, a thinking being of some kind that steers this spectacle for a good purpose? And would you feel an urge to quest for the meaning of your existence, even though it is short, if you did not already experience meaning, not only in your own existence, but also in the existence of the world?"

This torrent of questions landed on the ground of my mind with a loud bang. Kamal knew very well that I was a serious seeker of The Eternal, and he knew that I was passionately committed to this quest. But he also noted that I was seeking a justification of this quest. He was a perceptive thinker; for he was convinced that an answer is not genuine, nor is it useful, if it does not originate from the labor of one's mind, from inner concern and critical desire to answer the questions that prompted the mind to raise them. It did not take me long to see that the way he organized his questions, with whose meaning and thrust I was familiar, a fact he knew very well, was intended to spotlight the validity of my quest for The Eternal.

As Kamal was forging his way into the depth of the desert the way Captain Ahab was forging his way into the waves of the ocean in search of the white whale I was trying to find my way into the thicket of the questions he presented to me, all of which either revolved around or in some way pointed to the question of the meaning of existence. I knew, as he did, that the world exists and that we cannot ignore the question of its existence, for it would be logically impossible, indeed arbitrary, unless we begin our inquiry into its nature from the fact that it exists. This line of reasoning does not make any assumptions either about the nature of its cause or about whether the cause transcends it or is immanent in it. The question of existence is implicit in the existence of what exists. Whenever we say something exists we are logically entitled to ask why and how it exists. But the significance of this question lies in the fact that it necessarily leads to the source that gives rise to its being.

I was able to see clearly and distinctly, as I was warmly enveloped by the silence of the desert, that the question of my mortality is superficial, if not senseless, that there is an enduring power, creative and wise, which underlies this whole spectacle of nature, that although everything in this spectacle will sooner or later perish, this power will endure, and that because it endures it is truly real, therefore, the true object of my attention and knowledge. The revelation of this insight became stronger and clearer the more I experienced the divine in the desert, in its sand, mountains, hills, oases, sky, stars, wind, residents, animals, and culture. I am now convinced, more than ever, that the justification of the quest for The Eternal is not, or cannot be, adequate, if one does not have a direct encounter, or union, with it, if one does not feel its presence, see it with the eyes of his mind as it is in itself, and take a glance, if possible, at the dynamics of the fountain of its creativity. Reflection on the inner working of the scheme of nature and human life can instigate the question of the meaning of life, but it cannot, in and by itself alone, provide a convincing argument, or a justification, to seek it as the ultimate principle that underlies the world and the meaning human beings need to fulfill their destiny. An adequate, perhaps final, justification, to seek a union with it is not possible unless the seeker stands in its presence or at least on the horizon that overlooks its infinite domain and sees with all his cognitive faculties the kind of being it is. The judgment of reason can be convincing, and it can be logically valid, but it cannot deliver a final explanation, unless it is also confirmed by direct testimony, or experience: witness. The question for me is not to know but to be; I do not want merely to know The Eternal; I want to be with it, I want to love it. I have frequently read the arguments of those who claim that we should believe in The Eternal in order to understand what we believe in and of those who claim that we should first understand The Eternal in order to believe in it. Those two approaches are one-sided. How can we separate the existential encounter with The Eternal from the endeavor to understand it? Any claim to knowledge that is not grounded in an experience of the object is abstract and as such lacks certitude and, therefore, efficacy. To be knowledge, the claim must be founded in a direct, concrete experience of the object—of its ground, implications, and constitutive elements. This kind of knowledge is definitive; it can be used as a basis of effective, authoritative action. The source of the scheme of nature is immanent in its structure the way the artist is immanent in her work, the way the sun is immanent in the space it illuminates, the way life is immanent in an organism. How can anyone contemplate, that is, think and feel, the infinitely intricate structure of nature without at the same time thinking and feeling the radiance of the divine presence in it? This very feeling is the impetus that propels the interested heart to quest for The Eternal and to cling to it the way a lover clings to his beloved. How can we seek something that does not exist, and how can we ignore something, especially that shines with goodness, beauty, and truth, if we do not experience it? But the quest for The Eternal is not an attempt to appease an itch of curiosity; it is a desire to satiate the longing of the heart to be at home—to be in touch with its source, to see the miracle of the creative process, to see how the basic truths and values that matter in our life flow on the wings of this process, for living according to them is the source of the ultimate peace we essentially crave as human beings and the understanding that illuminates our way in our endeavor to achieve our destiny.

But, alas! A gentle voice cautions me not to give free reign to my rational speculation, even though it is based on a genuine, yet modest, encounter with the divine radiance in nature and human works. The voice I hear, however, is none other the voice of reason itself, not abstract reason, but the reason of the heart.

chapter 6

On the Way to Amana Mountain

THE SOFT RAYS OF the golden sun were slowly receding from the blue sky of the shining desert. The first impression that struck my attention when I regained my normal consciousness was the serenity of the atmosphere that filled the landscape around us. I do not recall having such an experience of calm. The terrain we were traversing was flat, smooth, and completely arid. There was no sign of plant or animal. All I could see was a limitless pond of sand reflecting the light of the golden sun. Nothing stirred around us except the rhythmic vibrations of the van. And the dusk—yes, the dusk! It was not any shade of grey or dark or even brown. It was a fine, elusive cast of the gentlest purple you can imagine; and it was not in any way a natural hue. It was not an emanation from a particular source but an all-embracing presence. Although it did not seem to be a part of nature, it illuminated the desert and revealed its very being: stillness, stillness of the infinite. Suddenly my eyes were attracted to Kamal, who was thrusting his way into the divine stillness. Alas! His face was a vibrant reflection of its tranquil silence, and he was one with it. It was an image in which this tranquility acquired a living form. His eyes sparkled with an aura of quiet joy. A quiet, indescribable feeling, the kind that transports you from the natural world into the sacred chapel of your heart, suffused my mind. I knew that we were approaching a critical phase of our adventure. Everything around us spoke the language of silence. I did not have a feeling of awe: I was engulfed by awe.

Kamal's gentle, yet supple, voice shattered the walls of this awe. "We are gradually moving into the heart of the desert. It is somewhat different from the parts we have so far seen. It has a character of its own. My grandfather used to say that you should come to this region if you want to hear the song of the desert, if you want to feel its allure, if you want to touch the hand of The Eternal. But, strangely, not many people come here. Once in a while a composer, a spiritual eccentric, a painter, or a poet visits this area. Most of them sit on the fringe but rarely go beyond it. Some of them have musical ears. I have an inkling that they desire to listen to the Hymn of the Syrian Desert. One serious visitor confided to me that all the ancient Greek Muses were born here. He also mentioned that Zeus met the beautiful Phoenician princess, Europa, on the fringe while she was listening to the desert hymn. He fell in love with her and carried her off with him to Crete. Zeus was wildly enchanted by the magical powers of the Muses. He must have had a craving for beauty, not only in women but also in nature, philosophy, and art. I do not understand why only a few visitors take the plunge into the abyss from which humanity originates! But, I am inclined to think that lovers are the only people who desire to take such a plunge. Lovers are adventurers, but, more importantly, they want to live, and the only way they know how to live is by celebrating the rite of life and drinking the nectar of life from its source. They become one with this nectar when it flows through their veins. In time, it becomes the fountain of their being—of their thinking, feeling, and willing. They are keen on understanding the world and living from the standpoint of The Source."

"But why?" I intervened impulsively.

"Longing."

"Longing for what?"

"Their source."

"What do you mean?"

He did not answer me immediately, but after a moment's hesitation, he added: "their human source and the source of the world." Kamal made this simple answer with a pensive look on his face. I felt, from the way he spoke and clinched his fingers to the driving wheel that he really was trying to express himself differently. So, I thought it might be useful for me to press him for an elaboration of what seemed to me a rather brief and vague response.

"But why do they have this longing?" I asked.

"They have it because it exists in them as an essential impulse; it underlies everything they seek or do in the world. It lurks behind and within every major goal they pursue in their lives."

"But why do most people seem oblivious to its existence? They live as if it is irrelevant to their lives."

"To exist as an essential impetus is one thing, and to acknowledge it in fact is something else. Most people think that survival, in this or another world, is dearest to them, but the way they factually live does not show that they acknowledge the primacy of this impetus. The key to an understanding of this painful phenomenon lies in the fact that our humanity is given as a potentiality and especially in the institutions society adopts for its actualization. How can they acknowledge it if the power that recognizes it, namely, reason, is not adequately cultivated?" He raised a challenge I have been battling all my professional life as an educator.

"I see the basis and logic of this problem. But, please, let me revert to my original point: Why do people long for their source?" Kamal had frequently shied away from verbal conversation. This was the first time he showed some willingness to pursue the logical implications of a belief he firmly held. Any insight he could reveal on this critical question would, I was certain, enrich my experience of the desert. So I took the liberty to be a dialectician.

"Some say that they long for their source, as I have just pointed out, because they want to understand themselves, because, in general, knowing the source of something reveals its nature. Thus, if people understood their source, they would understand what they are, and if they understood what they are, then they would know how to live. Knowing how to live is a central concern of human beings."

"Yes, I understand this point; what do you, Kamal, say? Is the longing for The Source a longing for understanding?"

"It is certainly a longing for understanding in general and self-understanding in particular; it is also a longing for being with The Source."

"Being with The Source?" I repeated emphatically.

"Yes."

"Why?" I insisted. I noted at that point of our conversation that although the words Kamal was using in answering my questions were ordinary, he was not using them in their ordinary sense. I was anxious to know what he meant by being with The Source.

"Let me first point out that we long for The Source, not merely because we are curious about it or because our knowledge of it is useful in our practical life but because it is good, because it is loveable, and what is good is lovable. The good as such is attractive, and, so, desirable. As you know from your personal experience, people pursue what they consider good for them and shun what they consider bad for them. The same applies to animals in the wild and the plants everywhere they thrive.

"I understand what you say in general, but what do you mean when you say we long for The Source because it is good? In what sense is it good? I know what it means for an apple, an idea, or a human being, to be good, but in what sense is my ultimate source, the source that transcends everything my senses can perceive and my mind can conceive, good or desirable?"

"Yes, I do not use 'good' in its ordinary or even in its philosophical sense but in a much deeper and richer sense, a sense not exclusive of human beings but including the totality of what exists. I use it in the universal, ontological, non-anthropomorphic sense. Now I want you to perform an experiment in your imagination. Please remove yourself from the world and stand on the mountain that overlooks the totality of the universe. Imagine the world coming into being from its source the way the rays come into being from the sun. Of course, prior to the existence of the world nothing existed, regardless of whether the world that later on exists is within or outside its source. We can even say that, from the standpoint of human beings, nothing existed prior to the existence of the world. Would you agree?"

"Yes, what you say seems logical to me and plausible."

"Now, let me ask you: Can we say of nothing, or of pure non-existence, that it is either good or bad?"

"I do not know what you are aiming at, but let me state that such a judgment is not possible, because we cannot evaluate or judge what does not exist."

"Precisely! But suppose, standing on that mountaintop, and just before the creation of the world, one were to ask you: Is it good, or better, for the world to be than not to be? What would you say?

"Well, it is hard to answer your question, because your supposition is wild, truly provocative, since imagining the existence of that mountaintop is inconceivable if we assume a state in which nothing prevailed or existed."

"But this supposition is logically permissible, because we are now making it. This implies that the supposition of nothing as well as of the mountaintop was only hypothetical speculation; it was intended to provide a conceptual framework, a basis, for explaining the sense in which

The Source of our being and the being of the world is good. Just a side remark: We talk about nothing, even though we know it does not exist!"

"I follow your line of reasoning."

"Then let me repeat my question: Is it good for the world to exist rather than not?"

"Of course, it is good to be, and it is better to be rather than not. But in what sense is it good? I must insist on an answer to this question?"

"When we say it is good for the world to be, we mean it is in itself good, or intrinsically good. Its goodness consists in the fact that it exists, or derives its goodness form the fact that it exists. Let me point out that in talking about the existence of the world I am not talking about mere existence but about the existence of a miraculously designed and created reality. In and by itself, mere existence is a chimera. Meaningful, or true, existence is always the existence of something concrete, to which we can refer and about which we can discourse. I know that what I am saying may seem strange to many people, because they are in the habit of making judgments of good and bad on the basis of what is useful or on the basis of some value they may prize; but I am asking you to extricate yourself from this framework of thinking and focus your attention on whether it is better for the world to exist regardless of any reference to any human interest or mode of thinking."

"I follow your train of thought."

"Now, if the existence of the world is good, should it not follow that its source must necessarily be good?"

"The inference is valid."

"Would you agree, then, that if the world exists, it derives its goodness from its source?

"I agree."

"And would you also agree that the existence of the source is greater than the existence of the world, for always a cause is greater than the effect it produces?"

"Yes, but what you say is rather abstract. Exactly in what sense is it superior?"

"In the sense that the world derives its essence and existence from the cause, its source. Let me express the same point differently. As a cause, the source does not only produce but also gives the world its essence. There is an affinity between the cause and the effect, because the effect shares its essence with the effect, but not the reverse, because the cause may produce more than one essence. For example, an artist may produce a painting. In this case, the painting drives its essence from the artist as its cause, and, in this respect, there is affinity between them. But the artist can produce other paintings and can also produce other types of artistic work. In this case, we can say the artist is superior to her works, because she creates the painting and because she creates other paintings and types of painting. But the source of the world is infinitely greater, not only because it created it, and is still creating the world, but because it is the original source, the source of everything that can possibly exist. And when we speak of the original source, we necessarily imply that it would be contradictory to say that another original source exists or may exist next to it."

"I see the logic of the idea you are trying to explain."

"Would it follow from what we are saying that the original source is absolute in being, which implies that nothing greater can exist?"

"What do you mean?"

"I mean if it is absolute, it is greater in being than anything the human mind can conceive. It should follow from what we have so far said that if being is good, the being of the world must necessarily be good. Would you agree?"

"Necessarily."

"And would you also agree that since the good is lovable, the absolutely good must be absolutely lovable?"

"Necessarily."

"Now," Kamal continued with some hesitation in his voice, "let us focus our attention on the relation between The Absolute and human beings. We have already agreed that human beings share their humanity with their source because they issue from its womb." With a playful smile on his lips, he added: "Please, do not object to my use of the word 'womb.' I use it metaphorically."

"Not at all!" I said. "In fact it is quite appropriate and I can say very expressive."

"It seems to me that the human essence was one with its source, of course, if it flourished in the womb of that source and in a way its home. Do you object to this description?"

"No."

"Can we say that the event of separation from its source at the moment of creation generated a profound desire to return to it, mainly because it received its being and life within its womb?"

"What you say is reasonable."

"And can we also say that this desire was generated not merely because the source was absolute but because it was good, and, more accurately, because it was absolutely good—in other words, that absolute goodness is the source of our longing for our source?"

"Yes!" I agreed with a puzzled voice, and then quickly added: "What is the meaning of this longing? For, to have a feeling of longing and knowledge of its basis is one thing but to raise the question of its meaning is something else. So many people, as we pointed out earlier, ignore and in some cases dismiss it as superfluous. They live as if it were an irksome or silly question, and would belittle you, if not ridicule you, if you were to mention it. On the contrary, they immerse themselves in the world on the assumption that the beginning and end of their destiny lies in the world."

"I understand the thrust of your question. Longing for the good is not longing for this or that good, but for The Good itself; it is longing for love, for life. The light and exuberance of this life dims when we become distant from it: The more distant we are, the stronger the feeling of longing is. We long for our source because we want to be united with it, filled of it. Yes, we have the urge to be filled of it. Nothing fills us, and nothing gives us the sense of completion we crave, except this kind of union. And when we are filled of The Good, we become a spring that flows of goodness; we become an ever-flowing stream of love. We become the source we should be. A source of his kind is not, and cannot be, pain, pleasure, or any kind of excitement. The only kind of satisfaction it feels is joy, and it is more accurate to say that joy suffuses every fiber of its being.

"In our union with our source, we are neither spectators nor visitors; we are participants in the dance of life. We stand within the source, at the fountain of our existence. We drink from its nectar, and we celebrate the ritual of cosmic creation. We meander leisurely through the garden of The Good from which the world flows. Has it occurred to you that the world is an eternal flow from and back to The Garden? Here we stand face to face with the universal of all universals; we see clearly, think truthfully, feel lucidly, and will articulately; and here we learn the secret of self-creation."

"Back to The Garden?" I interrupted.

"Oh, yes! The existence of the world consists in its continual return. If it derives its existence from The Garden, it should return to it continually; indeed, its existence is its continual return. Can it exist without its source? No! It would collapse without it. Passion for existence is the ultimate source for the yearning for The Good, and this is ingrained in the fabric of everything that exists."

"You speak metaphorically, of course?"

"Yes!" Kamal said without hesitation. "In truth, every word I use in my conversation about The Eternal, including the word 'eternal,' is a metaphor or an element of a metaphorical expression, because any sort of experience we have of The Eternal transcends anything that exists in the world around us. Unfortunately, our categories of thought and the whole web of human ideas, consequently, human language, are grounded in our experience of the physical world insofar as it is given either as an agglomeration or as a conglomeration of things. Ideas such as world, infinity, God, or eternity are, although derived from experience, essentially metaphorical, primarily because they do not denote any particular object in the field of perception. At best, they point to something that lies beyond the natural world. I aver that when the human mind soars beyond the natural world, or when it delves deep into its genesis and probes into what lies beyond, it discovers that its sensual and intellectual powers cannot function once they cross the final border of the physical world. They simply capitulate before this wondrous, indescribable domain. Neither concept nor percept, neither emotion nor image, can either articulate or even feel the content of its vision, not because what it experiences is not a meaningful reality but because it is different in its essence. It is not material or spiritual, yet it is their fountain; it is not beautiful or sublime, yet it is their source; it is not good or bad, yet it is their ground; it is not spatial or temporal, yet it is their starting point; it is not divine or human, yet it is their spring; it is not transcendent or present at hand, yet it transcends essence and existence; in short, it is not any particular this or that, yet it is the source of every this and that! No superlative can adequately express the nature of this vision. We can say that it is, but not what it is. This is not because it does not exist, and does not have a nature, but because it is beyond description. Although the wondrous panorama that makes up the mosaic of this vision is in every aspect different from anything the human mind has ever experienced, nevertheless, it can make the leap of transcendence into The Garden, only because it is made of the same stuff. This is the only reason why it can soar into that domain and at the same time be in it."

What Kamal said was insightful and in some way challenging. I felt a strong need to interrupt him more than once about the impact of our visit to The Garden and especially the kind of relation that holds between the knowledge one attains and practical life, not from an academic point of view, with which I was quite familiar but from the practical point of view, but I could not, because, contrary to his usual way of speaking, he presented the last part of his conversation in haste, as if a concern of some kind was encroaching on his stream of ideas.

My fears were quickly confirmed, for, having taken a long breath, which conveyed a feeling of seriousness, he announced that we were approaching Amana Mountain and that we should reach its foothills in about five minutes. Darkness had already fallen on the desert when Kamal was trying to give me an explanation of the basis of longing for The Eternal.

chapter 7

Amana Mountain

IT WAS PITCH DARK. The only thing my eyes could make out was the unfolding road ahead of us under the steady headlights of our vehicle. The air of solemnity that filled the desert gradually crept into the van. I felt its touch; it was warm, friendly. My heart beat fast. A strange feeling danced with its beats. I did not understand why or how it slithered into my heart, but it did. We cannot always explain the cause and purpose of our feelings, or even of our moods, but they have causes.

Kamal was in the habit of giving me an account of our itinerary for every landmark we visited, but nothing was forthcoming in regard to Amana Mountain. His unusual silence excited a feeling of curiosity in my mind. "Is there something special about this mountain?" I asked silently. "Is there a settlement nearby?" But my curiosity was quelled when Kamal suddenly declared that we had arrived at our destination. "We shall spend the night at a small cavern on the northern side of the mountain," he explained. "This side is safe from the wind that might blow from the south. It can be strong sometimes. But I think the desert will be quiet tonight." Within a few minutes the van came to a standstill.

The moment the engine fell silent, Kamal turned the interior lights on, looked at me with genial eyes, and said: "Here we are!" His face was glowing with gladness. "Are you hungry?" Without waiting for an answer, he added: "After such a long trip, both of us should be famished." And without any hesitation he stretched his arm to a box behind his seat and pulled out two flashlights. He gave me one and inserted the other in his back pocket. Then, he went to the back of the van and pulled out a rather big box he must have packed in Saada. It contained our supper. "Can I help you? I would like to!" I said emphatically. The only response he gave me was an approving yet gracious smile. He pointed to a parcel next to the back door. It contained blankets and pillows for both of us. Since my load was lighter than his I turned on my flashlight and led the way, but the way was a bit unfriendly, because it was covered with a thick layer of smooth sand. Our feet sank in it with every step the way they would in a thick sheet of snow, but with a difference: The sand is denser and heavier. A wild idea flashed through my mind: "Is getting drowned in the sand more oppressive than getting drowned in the snow?" I wondered, but my wonder did not last long, because Kamal stopped before an opening, which must have been the door to the cavern. "Here it is!" he said as he illuminated the cavern with his flashlight. It was a rather large enclosure punctuated by what might have been stalactites and stalagmites. Kamal chose a place for us between the rock formations. I think he made the right choice, for the ambience of the place made me feel an integral part of nature. Being in harmony with nature has always created a deep sense of satisfaction in my heart. But my satisfaction at that moment was deepened as I watched Kamal prepare our supper. Though simple, the meal we ate was appetizing and enjoyable.

His diligence, modesty, and contentment in whatever he did never ceased to impress me. He was an inspiration. His love of life shone in every action he performed and in every conversation he conducted. Both of these qualities seem to be lacking in a large number of people in contemporary society. As usual, we ate our meal in silence. When we finished, he cast a thankful glance at me. "We may have to stay more than one day on this mountain," he said. "We shall spend some time with a monk who dwells close to the top."

"A monk?" I asked, with a big stare in my eyes.

"Yes, a monk. He has been living here for more than thirty years. He is now almost eighty two years old. I think you would enjoy his company. He is still a vibrant and attractive character. If there is any human being who is knowledgeable and proficient in the ways of the Syrian Desert, it is he. He would never admit this fact, but I am certain he is a true son of the desert." The stare that glowed from my eyes did not shrink or wane and the impact of the surprise in my mind did not fade; on the contrary, my curiosity was inflamed. I wanted to know all about him and especially why he chose this mountain as his permanent dwelling.

"Does he belong to a particular religious order?" I asked.

"As far as I know, he does not. One day, when I was having a conversation with him about monasticism, he expressed the belief that the idea of religious orders is contradictory. There is only one kind of monastic life, he said vigorously, the kind that seeks The Eternal. The idea of religious orders betrays attachment to some religious institutions and certain ways of being religious, but the only attachment a monk should uphold is attachment to The Eternal. The ways that lead to it are infinite because it is infinite in its being. The only language the monk should speak is the language of The Eternal, and the language of The Eternal is the language of life: love. To live is to love, and to love is to live. This may sound somewhat cryptic, but I think his ideas are radical, provocative. A friend of mine who visits him frequently told me that he is a philosopher."

"A philosopher?" I asked, getting excited about the prospect of meeting a philosopher in a desert.

"Yes, but not one who theorizes about the nature of the world. He is a philosopher of clothes."

"Of clothes?" I asked my question with a blush of astonishment. I knew that philosophers have reflected on the nature of the varieties of human experience—scientific, religious, political, aesthetic, mathematical, educational, or economic—but I had never known a philosopher who theorized about the nature of clothes or the experience of clothes. In what ways can clothes be relevant to philosophical thinking? Although I could not find a place for clothes in the sphere of philosophical speculation, this question bubbled noisily in my mind."

"This is what my friend told me. I have never had an opportunity to discuss this question with him." My astonishment surrendered to a mood of bewilderment. Kamal noticed the mental state I was in. "How about a walk under the stars of the heavenly dome? It should be pleasant at this time of the evening. Besides, we had a long and tiring trip today. A breath of fresh air would do us a lot of good."

"Yes, I would very much enjoy a walk with you." Kamal was right. The moon sat majestically near a constellation of glittering stars; she was gracing the desert with the most elegant light I had ever seen in my life. The motif of this light stood in clear contrast to the pleasantly dark blue of the sky on which the royal choir of heaven sang next to her. There was magic in the air. We stopped and gazed at this display of magnificence. I allowed my mind to be enchanted by its loveliness:

The same desert that was sweltering under the sun during the day had turned gentle and dreamy under the moon in the evening! The same desert that was stern and harsh a few hours ago was now soothing and peaceful! I was able to see more clearly what it means to say that the scheme of nature is a spectacle of change and that the mirror of this change reveals in its continual course of transformation the infinite richness of The Eternal.

Suddenly, I felt a peculiar stir in my heart, a kind of mild but thrilling explosion, joyful explosion, I should day. I felt that the seams of my mind, will, and feeling were slowly bursting, opening up. A streak of delicious pain swept through my body and soul. I knew something unusual was happening inside me. I could not, and cannot now, describe it, but I was certain of one fact: My heart was enfolded by a warm, tender waft of peace, not the peace of quiet but of inner harmony. I was in touch with the totality of myself; every part of my being, physical and psychological, functioned harmoniously with the rest of the parts. The subject in me, which had always acted as the overseer of my life, and had never been directly accessible to me as an object of thought, disclosed itself in the fullness of its being as a bright spark from which my life emanated. I realized that self-consciousness is not an inscrutable or contradictory concept philosophers concocted in the night of their idle speculation. No, it is a moment of existential self-consciousness: a moment of self-clarification, self-understanding, and self-containment. I felt as if the self that dwelt inside me and managed the domain of my inner life was, in fact, a mirror that reflected, not only the radiance but also the harmony that embraced me and Kamal under the magnificent spectacle of the starry heaven; that I was not a drop of solitary existence, but one with the outer harmony that flowed tenderly from the infinite source I have been seeking; that the life that pulsated in my veins was a drop flowing in the river of that very source and that the harmony I felt a few moments ago was a living echo of the harmony that fills the heart of The Absolute. Yes, the self-consciousness I experienced was not a conceptual gymnastic performed in my mind by the hands of abstract logic; it was a moment of self-consciousness in which my mind confronted itself in the heart of its source. There in that source it saw itself clearly, truly, and wholly. A tremor of exhilaration ran through my heart. I cannot say how long it lasted, but I must have been in a deep reverie, for I was awakened from that mental state by Kamal's hand gently tapping my shoulder.

My heart was throbbing and singing and my eyes were swelling with tears when I recovered from my reverie. It took me several seconds to collect the thread of my ordinary self and acknowledge its existence. To tell the truth, I felt a little embarrassed, for I seem to have lost control of my ordinary senses for a while, but my embarrassment quickly vanished when I saw Kamal's friendly eyes gracing me with their kindness. I felt at home with him. Friendship is a protective, healing power. We continued our walk silently in the vicinity of our cavern. On our left, the peak of Amana Mountain stood as a steeple soaring into the depth of the infinite under the bright light of the moon. "Even the mountain prays in the desert. It, too, longs for The Eternal!" I reflected as we walked in the silence of the evening. "But, alas! The mountain itself rises from the desert itself. Its aspiration is the aspiration of the desert, its voice is the voice of the desert, and its longing is the longing of the desert." I rejoiced in this aspiration, I heard this voice, and I felt this longing!

"We should rise early tomorrow morning," Kamal said, shattering the peace that floated around me as a spring breeze. "It is, I think, prudent to part company with the evening and seek refuge within the arms of Hypnos, as the ancient Greeks would say." Kamal was in tune with time. He felt its rhythm in all its determinations and acted accordingly.

"Yes, I am ready to rest within the arms of that god," I remarked with a sense of satisfaction. We took a different path on our way back to the cavern. Kamal pointed out some interesting rock formations. "These are remnants of the volcanoes that erupted in this area about eight-hundred years ago. Some people think that precious metals can be found inside them. This is why you can see holes and cracks in almost each one of them. Human beings have always been fascinated by gold. And yet the real gold is ready at hand within the human heart."

I did not react to this pearl of wisdom, but I stopped for a moment and felt a rock that was lying in wait for us as if wishing me to touch it. It was hard, harder than any rock I had ever felt; it must have come from molten lava flowing from Amana Mountain not long ago. "Yes," I reflected, "nature, not time, is the moving image of The Eternal."

The doorway of the cavern was lit by moonlight. Before going in, Kamal went to the van that was parked in the vicinity and within a few minutes returned with a parcel of our sleeping gear. He lighted a candle and then spread our sleeping bags on two small, elevated banks carved inside the walls of the cavern, one for him and the other for me; they looked like two beds carved in the walls. "I am certain that many tourists before me slept on these beds," I said to myself silently.

"We should have a tranquil sleep night," Kamal remarked, and then he retired to his bed. I did the same.

"Good night!"

"Good night to you!" Kamal answered. I fell asleep sooner than I expected.

The morning sun rays were dancing at the entrance of the cavern when I opened my eyes to the world. Kamal was not around. I put on my clothes hurriedly and was about to look for him when I suddenly heard footsteps approaching our desert bedroom. They were Kamal's. He stood in front of the doorway with smiling eyes. His face was radiant with cheerfulness. "How about a bath?" He asked. "There is a pond around the corner. You may want to bathe in it; it is deep enough for a swim." He gave me a towel and showed me the way. Frankly, that was a most welcome proposal. I accepted his offer instantly and gladly. I took a very refreshing swim! When I returned, Kamal had already prepared our breakfast. As soon as we finished eating, he told me that the pond received its water from a spring that flowed from the mountain until late summer. It dried between the months of September and December. No organism of any kind grew in it, mainly because it was very hot. This region received ample rainfall during wintertime, which was short, but then all signs of life vanished by the end of the summer. There was, however, a continually running spring on the eastern side of the mountain.

Soon after we ate our meal, we took our sleeping gear and food box to the van and then began our ascent to the mountain. Unlike Jabal Saada, this solitary mountain in the heart of the Syrian Desert was excessively rugged; it did not show any sign of civilized activity. But Kamal, who knew the ways of the desert, also knew the ways of Amana Mountain. He led the way through the rocks as if following a visible track. He chose the western side in order to avoid the heat of the rising sun. "This is not a very high mountain," he said. "We should reach the cloister of Father Sergios in about one hour."

"One hour is a long time," I said.

"It seems," he retorted.

As usual, he was right; the higher we climbed, the steeper and more difficult it got to find our way through a dense forest of rocks that covered the higher part of the mountain. "No wonder, tourists do not visit this lonely place!" I thought as I was I was struggling to keep pace with Kamal. Sometimes we had to squeeze our bodies sideways between the rocks in order to be able to move upward, but, much of the time, we climbed over the rocks. I do not remember ascending such a mountain in my life. Almost halfway into the ascent, I asked Kamal whether we could take a short break. "Of course!" he said agreeably. A few minutes later, he pointed to a clearing and remarked: "How about a recess there?" I accepted his recommendation without hesitation. I was really tired. My legs were getting tense and my heart was beating fast, not because I suffered from a case of hypertension, but because of the daunting effort I was exerting in my attempt to climb between and over the boulders. I breathed a sigh of relief when we sat against a somewhat big rock facing the western horizon.

Kamal noticed my physical state. "One would think that the ascent would get less burdensome, the more distant one gets from the center of the earth," he said cryptically." "Or, perhaps," I broke in, "the closer we get to The Absolute!" Although he remained silent, a soft smile danced in his eyes. I understood his smile, and I felt his understanding.

It occurred to me as I was gaping into the infinite distance that the quest for The Eternal becomes increasingly difficult as we approach our destination. This realization loomed in my mind as a vague intuition. I tried to discover its source or exact nature, but I could not. However, it was clear to me that some forces inside me were resisting my inmost desire to continue my quest, as if they were trying to quell the fire of its passion, as if they were trying to whisper in my ear that my quest was a flare of vain whim. And yet, it was clear, and, I would also say, certain, that a feeling of profound joy accompanied every new advance I made in my quest for The Eternal. Joy is not a sensation; it is the sort of feeling that arises from the depth of reason, from our experience of the true, the beautiful, the holy, and the good—from our experience of growth as human beings. How can any rational person ignore or belittle the value of this kind of experience? As far as I am concerned, this feeling was a confirmation of the meaningfulness of my quest.

An exhortation by an ancient sage suddenly hovered in the forefront of my consciousness: "The unexamined life is not worth living." I have frequently reflected on the oracular meaning of this advice and came to the conclusion that its author wanted us to question the truth of the values we live by, always making sure that they are justifiable, for he was convinced that living according to rational principles is the royal road to happiness. But, today, I discovered a new, commonly neglected meaning implicit in this exhortation: the insight that any attempt to justify our basic beliefs and values necessarily leads to an understanding of their source. The principles that justify them must be universal and enduring; otherwise, they cannot have a claim to truth, nor, therefore, a capacity for justification. What is true must always be true; it cannot change with the seasons. It bends with neither fashion nor passion. The laws that govern the universe were not made by human hands, and they were not made for today or tomorrow but for all time and for everyone. They were made by the same power that gave rise to the human essence.

My meditation was interrupted when Kamal reminded me that it was time to continue our ascent, "primarily because," he said, "the sun will soon reach its pinnacle. We should try to avoid the heat of the sun as much as possible." He pulled a bottle of water out of his rucksack and added: "We should drink plenty of water in this kind of weather." He was right, for the heat was already seeping through my skin. I followed Kamal's directions, as I always did. "Ready?" he asked. "Oh, yes, I am!" I felt a surge of enthusiasm about the second part of the ascent. I did not know whether this feeling came from drinking the water or the meditation in which I dwelt on the meaning of my quest for The Eternal. But I was ready to continue our journey. Kamal was always giving me directions on how to climb and walk among the rocks. He really was versatile in the ways of the desert! But, then, how can we be on a quest for The Eternal if we are not versatile in the ways of every aspect of nature? The Eternal is not an object that sits in a certain office or lives in a certain mansion or rambles in a certain park. It is the infinite from which the different types of reality emanate. It is immanent in each one of these types of reality. It is the indwelling principle of life and being of everything that exists.

A wild idea surged into my mind as I was striving to follow Kamal's footsteps: "In all its aspects, living and non-living, nature is sacred because it is an emanation from The Eternal. Each one of them was created and consecrated by its blessed hands; thus each one offers an occasion to commune with The Eternal. Accordingly, the distinction between the sacred and the profane is a fiction created by the minds of some people. The ancient Greeks did not make such distinctions. They built their temples to house the images of their gods, not to worship in them. They worshipped next to the temple in the open space of nature. Building temples for their gods was their way of honoring them. They viewed the gods as forces of nature, as expressions of The Infinite that revealed itself in the whole scheme of nature. Yes, nature is sacred, and because sacred, we have no right to abuse it.

I was still reflecting on the implications of this idea when Kamal announced that we were approaching Father Sergios's cloister. His announcement instigated in me a feeling of expectation, and, I can say, of suspense. "Why would anyone want to live in this lonely place, in this heat? What kind of person is Father Sergios? Kamal told me that he was a philosopher of clothes, but why would a philosopher of any kind live in the heart of the desert? And why should it be important for me to meet him?"

These and related questions were thronging my mind when we were suddenly free from the forest of rocks that practically covered the whole mountain. "Here we are!" Kamal said triumphantly. The open space that welcomed us after a rather arduous ascent produced a cheerful feeling in my heart. "Father Sergios lives on the western side of the mountain, but he spends much of the time on the eastern side. He has a small chapel there. He calls it a chapel, but it is really a hut. I think he uses it as a shelter from the sun. He should be somewhere in the proximity of the hut at this time of the day."

In a few minutes, we noted a figure moving in the field of our vision. "It is he!" Kamal pointed out. He must have noticed us, for he suddenly stood still. His eyes were fixed on us when we came closer to where he was standing. Within a flash of a second, he lifted his arms upward and shouted "Kamal, my friend!" Then he rushed toward us. Kamal did the same. They embraced, and their embrace lasted for a few seconds. I stood there watching them, stunned with amazement. It was a heartwarming sight. I could not help but allow a smile of respect on my lips. Moments later they faced each other silently, but their silence was a dialogue, and the medium of the dialogue was their sparkling eyes. When they finished their conversation, Kamal turned his

Amana Mountain

attention toward me and said: "Father Sergios, I want you to meet my friend, Dimitri. Father Sergios was a slim and rather short man. His hair was white as snow. Though time has formed wrinkles on his face and neck, he seemed to be in good health. His erect body was covered with a pale grey tunic. He looked more like a living manikin than an inhabitant of our cities or villages.

"He is an American."

"Then I should speak with him in English."

"I thought you were Greek!"

"No, I am American." I said. My roots are Greek. My parents immigrated to the U.S.A. in the latter part of the 19th century.

"No wonder you look like Greek. Do you speak Greek?"

"No!" Even though I did not know anything about this hermit except the fact that he was a philosopher of clothes, I felt a strong, yet spontaneous attraction to him. Who would not feel an attraction to a warm, genial person, especially to a person who speaks with his eyes—the windows of the soul? I moved forward and shook hands with him.

"I am very pleased to meet you!"

"We have been touring the desert," Kamal said. Since we were nearby, I thought it would be a good idea to pay you a visit. Besides, I wanted you to get acquainted with my new friend, Dimitri."

"Of course," he retorted. "I would have been disappointed had you bypassed my mountain." Then, he showed us his garden, which was highly atypical. It consisted of several small patches of land mostly hidden between boulders. He must have chosen those spots to avoid constant exposure to the sun. Each one of these patches was devoted to a kind of vegetable or fruit. I was impressed by his gardening skills. "Let us go to the chapel for a few minutes. You must be tired after a long and hard climb over those rocks." The hut, as Kamal called it, was no more than 600 ft. away. It consisted of two small rooms. In one, there was a small elevation in the middle of which sat a candle in a saucer, and, in the other, there was a small cot. Next to the cot, I noticed a folded rug and a big square box. "Please, sit on the cot, Dimitri," treating me as a guest of honor. Then, he unfolded the rug and asked Kamal to sit on it. He sat next to him and both of them faced me. The chapel part of the hut was almost carved into the mountain and the other parts were built of stones from around the mountain. The only opening to this simple abode was the main door, which was made of wood. One corner of the living room was used as a kitchen. In addition to the box, which must have contained the basic tools he needed to prepare his meals, I noted some cooking pots and a small chest of drawers. It was clear to me that the life this monk led was truly ascetic. The few pieces of furniture that attracted my attention were not in fact worthy of notice. But I noted them only because they reflected an air of simplicity, of closeness to nature.

"I missed you, Kamal," he said. "It has been long since we last met."

"I missed you, too, Father."

"Tell me, how is your family? I hope they are flourishing!"

"They are doing well, thankfully."

"I know you and your friend, Dimitri, must be tired. Please, do not be upset if I leave you alone for a few minutes. Rest a little." Without waiting for a response he left us for almost half an hour. He returned with a basket of fruits containing figs, berries, and prickly pears. He pulled two tin plates from one of the drawers and filled them with fruits. "You must try them!" He made this courteous gesture and left us again only to return in a few minutes with a jug of water. He opened the drawer again and fetched two tin cups. "Dimitri, you are not eating! You have not touched the prickly pears. You must try them; they are good." Within a few minutes, he picked one, sliced off the two ends, made a longitudinal slit in the middle, and then pulled the skin sideways. A light orange fruit sat in the middle. "Now, try it; use your fingers. This is the way to do it," he insisted. With a thankful smile I followed his directions. The fruit I ate was sweet as honey. Frankly, I had never eaten, much less seen, this kind of fruit before. I looked into his timid eyes and said: "It is delicious. Thank you!"

"I am glad you liked it. I read once when I was a young man that cactus grows in the American desert. But the species that grows here is different."

"Yes, it grows in the western part of the U.S.A., but prickly pears are not available where I live," I remarked.

"The U.S.A. is one of the richest and largest countries in the world," he said. "Where do you live?"

"I live in Antioch, Mississippi."

"Mississippi!" He retorted with a wild surprise on his face. "You live close to the mighty river, then. I remember reading about your state. It has a rich cultural heritage. I was impressed by William Faulkner; he is one of the literary giants of the world. I was especially impressed by his moral vision, by his deep understanding of and respect for humanity."

"Some critics may disagree with you, but I think that Faulkner is indeed our favorite literary mind, though I myself am partial to Tennessee Williams. Our state is known for a distinguished tradition in artistic creation."

"Yes, it is." He fell silent for a few seconds and then, changing the subject of our conversation, he asked: "what is your vocation, Dimitri?" This change took me by surprise.

"My vocation?" I repeated the question, not only because I was not expecting this sudden turn in our conversation, but also because I really did not understand the intent of his question: Did he mean my professional occupation as a human being? It was not until later on, having ruminated on the main events of my visit to the desert, that I saw a relation between his question and my visit; for no ordinary human being enmeshed in the ordinary affairs of the modern world would be interested in exploring the ways of the Syrian Desert. Again, why did he ask this particular question?

"Professionally, I am a teacher of philosophy, but vocationally, I am a student of philosophy."

"Most interesting! You teach philosophy?" he said with gleaming, inquiring eyes. It became immediately clear to me, from the way he phrased his question, that he had extensive knowledge of philosophy. He inflamed my curiosity. I simply looked at him intently and answered: "I am not certain whether I do. The university at which I am employed thinks I do. I have been teaching there for almost twenty-five years.

"And what do you think?"

"I cannot answer this question adequately."

"Why?"

"Because I am not yet clear about what it means to teach in general and what it means to teach philosophy in particular."

"But you have been teaching it, and for how long?"

"Twenty-five years."

"What makes it difficult to give a clear answer, especially since you are formally employed by an educational institution? How can a person perform a function for so many years without knowing precisely what he is doing?" Father Sergios's penetrating questions created an uneasy feeling in my mind; they were a call for critical self-examination.

"The prevalent understanding among students and educational institutions in general is that teaching is a process in which ideas, or a certain type of knowledge, is transmitted, directly or indirectly, from the teacher to the student, as if ideas were mental objects to be transmitted from one place to another. This general understanding assumes that the human mind is a receptacle in which we can store ideas. It also assumes that an educated person is one who can store and recall the ideas stored in the mind by the faculty of memory. Although painfully adumbrated, let me say that the inner logic of this general understanding, which was common in the past, remains widespread in practice at the present.

"But I came to the conclusion some years ago that ideas are not objects, or entities of some kind, and that the human mind is not a kind of receptacle. An idea is an occasion for the comprehension of meaning, and the mind is a faculty that can perform many cognitive functions. Comprehension of meaning is one of these functions. It constitutes the event of understanding: To understand is to comprehend a content of meaning. The mind is a flame of consciousness; it is the source of knowledge, selfhood, will, emotion, and the feeling that we are self-conscious beings, or individuals. You can liken the mind, metaphorically, to a plant. The plant is a process of growth. The mind grows inasmuch as it grows in its comprehension of the infinite diversity of meanings implicit in our experience of the human and natural worlds: scientific, aesthetic, religious, political, educational, and cultural. The structure of the meaning comprehended can be articulated into an idea; but as an idea, it contains only the general features of the meaning, not the fullness of its richness. These features are abstractions from the content of the comprehended meaning. But what constitutes real understanding is the comprehension of the meaning in its entirety. Now, you can, by means of memory, transfer a general idea, of course, as an abstraction, to or from the mind; but you cannot transfer an act of comprehension or understanding. This act is an event, and this event takes place consciously and willingly by the person who performs it. And if this person does not choose to perform this act, comprehension of meaning does not take place. I discovered that students forget most, if not all, of the ideas they 'learn' but they never forget what they comprehend. What they comprehend becomes a part of the constitution of the student's mind.

"In my view, comprehension of meaning should be the supreme goal of education, namely, teaching and learning. Thus, the teacher does not teach by transmitting ideas through lectures or books to the mind of the student, and the student does not learn, by memory, to receive ideas and store them in his or her mind. Teaching takes place only when an occasion is created for the comprehension of meaning, and learning takes place only when the student willingly succeeds in comprehending a content of meaning. Ideas, which are intellectual abstractions, are only vehicles, and we can say instruments, that provide an occasion for the comprehension of meaning. Accordingly, as a conscious and free activity, learning takes place in the mind. No one can force students to undertake it. We can force them to memorize but not to learn. Only when certain factors—teacher, book, conversation, and guidelines—are conducive to the comprehension of meaning can learning take place. Learning is self-learning. It is initiated and conducted by the student.

"The role of the teacher, as teacher, then, is not to impart ideas but to create the appropriate conditions that enable the student to take the initiative to seek and to grow in understanding. I do not underestimate or in any way belittle the role of books, lectures, or writing. Indeed, these are essential conditions of the teaching process; they are ingredients the teacher uses to create occasions for the comprehension of meaning. But, how can I be certain that I have created such conditions? I cannot answer this question for two reasons. First, I am not sure whether the methods I have chosen in my teaching were effective in creating appropriate conditions for learning and, second, I cannot be certain of the extent to which they were effective even if they were effective, because the learning experience is a subjective fact and because students practically vanish from my life as soon as the academic year is over. But, if we mean by teaching the activity of imparting ideas, I confess I have never been a teacher. I have always tried, in my work, to transform the traditional method of imparting ideas into a method of creating the conditions of self-learning. Whether I succeeded, only God knows."

"Then," Father Sergios asked, "if teaching is not an event in which an idea is transmitted from some source to the mind of the student but one in which a content of meaning is comprehended, what is your role in the teaching-learning process?"

"Assistant. Midwife."

"Midwife?"

"Yes, the task of the midwife is to assist a pregnant woman in the birth of her child. Similarly, the task of the teacher is to assist the student in the process of learning, or comprehending new meanings. The pregnant woman gives birth to a child; the student gives birth to an act of comprehension. Here the act of comprehension is a potentiality; it is actualized, brought into reality, in the process of education. The outcome is true knowledge: noesis. In every activity of learning a new dimension of humanity is born. This is the essence of human growth. I subscribe to the view that education is not restricted to school or university education; it is a lifelong process. It is a process of human growth. The role of school education is to provide the necessary tools for understanding our experience of the world and the dynamics of life, human and natural. It provides a conceptual and historical perspective in terms of which we apply this understanding in making sound judgments in concrete situations. The purpose of education is the cultivation of the art of human living, not stuffing the mind with abstract, useless ideas."

"What does it mean to grow in humanity?"

"It means to actualize the potentialities that constitute the human essence: the capacities of knowing, feeling, and willing. We become our human selves inasmuch as we grow in the actualization of these capacities. The first aims at wisdom, the second, at love, and the third at life. I discovered early on in my life that wisdom is a necessary condition for appreciating beauty, holiness, and love, and for celebrating the rite of human living. It is the light that illuminates our way in our endeavor to love and live. I do not exaggerate if I say that wisdom is pure light; it is the light that emanates from the mind that fills it."

"Well, what do you mean by wisdom?" Father Sergios asked with a provocative tone in his voice. His question crashed upon my ears with a scream! I fell silent; I became immobile for a few seconds. A whiff of perplexity hovered on my face. He must have felt my perplexity, for he added: "Vocationally, you are a student of philosophy, which implies that philosophy is a way of life. You do not only teach philosophy, you also seek it as a way of life. But philosophy is the love of wisdom. So in your life you aim at wisdom, and at living wisely. Am I correct in this line of reasoning?"

"Yes, you are."

"Let me, then, ask my question again. What do you mean by wisdom? Am I justified in asking this question?" The perplexity that was hovering on my face earlier was by this time transfixed in my eyes and on my lips. I felt as if an arrow was rising from the depth of my being and darting into the center of my consciousness. It was an urgent call to focus my heart and mind on the most important question of my life, the same question that prompted me to pay a visit to the Syrian Desert.

"Yes, of course," I mumbled. I knew what he was aiming at, so I added: "It seems to me we should distinguish between two types of wisdom: human and universal."

"Interesting. What do you mean by human wisdom?"

"Human wisdom is the art of sound judgment, the kind that leads to good or right action in a particular situation. The domains of action are many: politics, business, religion, family, profession, law, morality, aesthetics, medicine, interpersonal relationships, personal life, and so forth. In trying to make a wise judgment, in anyone of these and similar domains we normally evaluate the situation that creates a need for a judgment in terms of a valid principle or in terms of some knowledge of right or good. The judgment is sound inasmuch as it is an adequate application of the principle or knowledge. Generally speaking, we can say that, from the standpoint of human wisdom, a judgment is sound inasmuch as acting on it leads to desired or useful consequences. But what works in one situation is invariably different from what works in other situations. The soundness of the judgment depends on the cultural and the personal conditions under which it is made. Change the conditions, you necessarily change the basis of the judgment. But these conditions are continually changing, and they change from one culture to another, so are the principles on which they are made. People learn the art of making sound judgment from experience: trial and error, observation, past experience, intelligent deliberation. They are expected to heed the values, customs, traditions, norms, and rules society upholds. The more they understand the social and cultural context they live in, and the more they undergo different types of experiences in that context, the more skillful they become in making sound judgments. Accordingly, what works in this or that situation, or in the life of this or that person, may not necessarily work in any other situation or in the life of any other person. In practical life, there are no universal principles or knowledge for making sound judgments.

"Can we infer from what you have just said that human wisdom is a kind of knowledge, that this knowledge is practical in the sense that it is derived from experience, that it is valid because it is instrumental, and that it is instrumental within a sociocultural context at a certain time and in a certain place?"

"What a string of inferences! Yes, I follow you."

"Can we also infer that this kind of knowledge is human because it originates from a particular context? By the way, this inference is based on the assumption that human beings are its source and that they are the judges of whether it works. Culture is, after all, a human creation."

"Yes, I agree."

"You indicated earlier that, as a student of philosophy, you are not interested in human but in universal wisdom. Can you please shed a ray of understanding on universal wisdom?"

"I shall try; but what I shall say will be tentative, at least hypothetical."

"Why?"

"Because students are, by definition, seekers, and students of philosophy are seekers of wisdom. If they are in possession of wisdom, they would not be students or seekers."

"But," the monk interjected, "if you are a seeker, you should know what you are seeking, and if you know what you are seeking, there is no need for you to seek it."

"Yes, I am aware that my quest for universal wisdom is formally paradoxical; but in fact it is not. Please, in order to avoid the possible charge of being a prey to an irresolvable paradox, let me explain my position in some detail, only because my quest is not merely conceptual but existential in character; and it is existential, because the object of my quest is not an ordinary object, and we can say it is a supra-object. It is the kind of object that transcends everything that the human mind can think, or sense, or feel under the ordinary conditions of human experience. And yet, I can experience it. But I do not experience it the way we ordinarily experience anything that is a part of nature. I experience it as an infinite presence, as a presence that is immanent in my life and the life of the world. I experience it as the foundation of my being and the universe. What is amazing is that the more I open my mind and my heart to it, the deeper I delve into its infinite depth, the more my mind and sensibilities penetrate this depth, the more I can see, feel, and testify to its absolute presence, sublime radiance, and boundless power. This testimony is a window to its wisdom. Even the words I am now using are inadequate descriptions of what I experience in this infinite depth. They denote concepts constructed by the human mind. But they point to the way I experienced this infinite being, the way I felt and understood it. This experience is the basis of my earlier claim that I am a seeker of wisdom."

"But not of human wisdom?"

"Of universal wisdom," I rejoined.

"I appreciate your attempt to explain why your quest for universal wisdom is not paradoxical. It may seem unfair, but, what is it that prompted you to seek universal wisdom? The greatest majority of human beings are comfortable with human wisdom. It is, as you said, instrumental in leading to desirable results in the sphere of individual and social life. Actually, they adhere to it tenaciously and would strongly frown upon universal wisdom. They would even wonder if someone were to offer them another kind of wisdom! 'We love our way of life; it is the surest path to happiness,' they would say, and happiness is what they want. They are not naïve, as some might think, for they clearly understand the facts of human existence: its strengths, weaknesses, possibilities, and promises. They understand what it takes to survive, to discover their inner capacities, their needs, and what makes them happy. And if you question them about the adequacy of their understanding, they would ask you with a puzzled face: 'What more should we desire?'"

"Yes, I desire more, and what I want is not an expression of greed or selfishness, but a response to a demand that arises from the core of my heart."

"Your heart?"

"Yes, the heart that gives rise to my humanity, the powers that constitute the essence of every human being."

"What exactly do you want and seek?"

"I seek universal wisdom, and I want it with all my mind and all my will. I am not unaware of the value and fruits of human wisdom; I have experienced and enjoyed its fruits. I am not opposed to it, not because it leads to satisfaction, for it does, at least partially so, but because it embodies a good slice of rational insight. However, I seek universal wisdom because I have a wild appetite for truth, not this or that truth, but the universal truth that underlies any and every claim to truth. I seek this truth because I want to live from my real essence and because I have a burning desire to be true to myself, true without a shred of doubt. This desire comes from the depth of my being. It stands on the edge of my consciousness and, like a rooster, calls me every dawn to listen to the call of this desire every day. And the call does not reach my ears as a request or as a command but as a song, a song of longing. Yes, of longing for something supremely dear, supremely precious to me. I know that human wisdom can guarantee a reasonable measure of satisfaction, enough to keep me content to the end of my life, but the truth it has so far articulated is limited and does not express the richness of the longing of the human heart. Living according to it has always left emptiness in my heart; it has left a nagging desire for something more important, whose fulfillment would bring peace to my mind."

"Longing of the human heart? A song of longing?" Father Sergios broke in: "What makes you think that there is such a thing as universal truth, especially when the sciences and philosophy are dominated by relativism rather than universalism—statistical, not universal truth—not to mention the fact that the concept of universal truth is vague?"

"Please, Father, I have not been speaking as a philosopher or as a scientist but only as a student of philosophy, as a person who has adopted wisdom as a way of life. Nevertheless, I have not been unmindful of the findings of science and philosophy."

"Do you think that universal knowledge is within reach now or in the future?"

"Yes."

"I am impressed by your optimism."

"To confess, it is not optimism. What I have just admitted is not so much based on how far the human mind has progressed in its attempt to know the world or as we experience it in this attempt."

"What do you mean? An inkling of an explanation would be helpful," the good father said. I knew he was not trying to test me, or even to challenge me, but to be acquainted with the logic of my thinking.

"Well, we may distinguish two ways of experiencing nature: as a composite of particular objects and as a whole. In their endeavor to know nature, human beings included, scientists and philosophers assume a disinterested attitude; they view the object of experience as a datum, as an object, to which they are superior. There is a distance between them and the object. What the object is is determined by the way they perceive it. They, not the object, determine our knowledge of the object. To be an object is to be powerless, silent, in the presence of the subject that perceives and knows it. This is, to my mind, a main reason why philosophical, and to a great extent scientific, views are formulated from the standpoint of a particular human mind, or in terms of the conceptual equipment of that mind. But there is another way of experiencing nature as a composite of objects, according to which we undertake a quasi-dialogical posture with the object, in which the object is neither silent nor impotent but speaks with a voice, albeit shy, that originates from its inner constitution, or being."

"How?" Father Sergios asked with a flame of enthusiasm darting from his eyes.

"The natural object we experience is not merely a bundle of qualities; it is an integrated system of meanings. Every quality we perceive in it is an event of meaning. When I perceive it, it does not exist for me as an objective quality but as an event of meaning in my mind; its essence as the quality it is comes to life in my mind as a drop of meaning. The redness I see when I look at the rose is not in the rose but in my mind as an event, or experience, not as an object hanging on the wall of my mind or out there in the garden. During this experience, my mind is the redness it experiences, because it fills its domain of consciousness during this event. But when this experience ends, when my mind reflects on this experience, which is still fresh, it forms an idea of it, which is an abstraction of some of its essential qualities. The idea is then stored in a proper place in my memory. But once the original experience of the red color of the rose ends, it ceases to exist; what exists is my idea of it. Now the redness I experience when I look at the red rose would not come into my mind if it were not amenable, docile, and I would say willing, to enter my mind, because it does not enter as a physical quality but as an event of meaning. I am able to perceive it only because it speaks, and it speaks by being the essence it is, by being a possible meaning that can come to life as meaning in my mind, which is itself a flame of life. You see, it announces itself for such a possibility by being shared with some mind; and how can it make such announcement if it is not of interest to my mind? The language it speaks is the language of essence: meaning.

"The quality I perceive in the rose points beyond itself; it points to the meaning potential in it. It asks to be experienced as the meaning which constitutes its essence. How many a person walks in the garden without even noticing the tapestry of colors that makes the garden a garden? The red that is a quality of the rose shows forth its shade of color only if we are interested, if we are willing to rise in our minds to the meaning present in it, if we come to terms with it as a particular kind of meaning, otherwise it would remain silent. In effect, it says you can know what I am only if you are willing to experience me as an event of meaning, the kind that constitutes my essence as this particular shade of red. But the quality of red I perceive in the rose does not exist discretely; it exists as a part of a whole. It exists jointly with the other qualities that make up the formal structure of the rose—the visual and tactile qualities, and the qualities that emerge from the sort of organization that gives the rose its unity. The kind of quality it is, and the kind of meaning implicit in it, is what it is in virtue of the relation it has to the other elements and to the rose as a whole. Its identity is determined by this relation, by the role it plays in this organization. But it also contributes to the purpose, or function, of the rose. The rose becomes a rose because of the presence and contribution of the different qualities to the mode of organization peculiar to it. On the other hand, the rose itself is an object. And as an object, it is a mode of organization, or formation. This organization produces in it other non-sensuous emergent qualities that are potential in it. They are emergent, because they are not given to our senses the way red, smoothness, or shape are given; for example, the quality of order, or beauty, or existence. They emerge in our experience when we perceive it, not as this or that particular quality, singly, but when we perceive the rose as a whole, as a rose. Like my experience of red as a particular shade of color, the non-perceptual qualities announce themselves for perception, but refuse to give themselves to my perception as ready-made qualities. I have to make a special effort to perceive them; they offer themselves for perception by the kind of formal organization the rose is. I must meet the rose on its own terms, that is, I must contemplate this organization and seek it. In order for me to succeed in this effort I should seek it as a potentiality for meaning: I should speak its language, the language of meaning, of course, in virtue of the qualities that belong to it actually and potentially. The rose performs a number of functions. Displaying beauty is one of them. However, the basic meaning that is a necessary condition for experiencing every other meaning, actual or potential in it, is its being a rose. The experience of the rose as a rose, in contrast to any other object around it, entails the experience of a particular object. The way its elements are organized gives it its particular identity and individuality.

"But as a cluster of meanings, actual and potential, and as a particular object, the rose points beyond itself. To generalize, every object that is a part of the scheme of nature, be it a grain of sand or a galaxy, is a cluster of meanings that point beyond itself, primarily because it is a particular kind of formal organization. The infinite diversity of the objects that constitute the structure of the universe is grounded in the fact that each one of them is a unique formal organization. But, the universe itself is an object: It is a cosmos, a harmoniously organized order. If we contemplate the inner structure and the infinite mosaic of its qualities, which would take us more than several lifetimes, we can discern that it, too, is an infinite cluster of meanings, actual and potential.

"Now, let me revert to the rose for a moment. Let us call upon the most comprehensive, the deepest, and the sharpest contemplative mind, the mind that has penetrated the wisdom of the sciences, arts, and philosophy, and let us ask this mind to dwell upon this rose, not only as an object named 'rose,' but also on its constitution, on its relation to the soil, the garden, the sun, the atmosphere, in short, everything of which it is a part. If we respond to this call, we can certainly find ourselves standing before a world of being, before a wonder!

"And now let us have a dialogue with it in which it can speak, since, as we already saw, it can speak, and the language it has already spoken is the language of meaning. Let us flatter it at first and acknowledge to it that it exists and that it is a wonder, of which fact it should be proud; it may smile, and it has a right to smile! Let us next ask it: 'Why do you exist, and why do you exist as a wonder to the human mind?' It would accept our flattery, because it can certainly experience its existence and the wonder that shines from its essence. But when it comes to our twofold question, it would at first feel puzzled, but then, after reflecting on what the question asks, on both its existence and its being a wonder, and especially on the fact that, as meanings, both existence and wonder point beyond themselves, yes, having reflected on its existence and its being, it, the rose, would certainly admit ignorance, not because it is dumb, but because it does not have a basis for an answer. Its eyes would stare us in the face, saying: 'Ask the one who created me: my source! The meaning you experienced when you perceived me points beyond my being. I am not its author. You can have answers to your questions by having a discourse with my author. Please, be assured that you can have such a discourse, because I exist. If I exist, my author exists. Let me remind you, it would add, that if you have a similar dialogue with every object that is a part of the universe, you would receive the same answer.' Then, after a moment's silence, this wonderful rose would add that the universe itself as an object, which is the wonder of all wonders, would, if you were to have a similar dialogue with it, give you the same answer. It would not stop here, oh, no! It would say to you, with a joyful smile on its lips, that the secret of the wonder that permeates the universe and gives rise to its being is only a ray of the True Wonder that gives rise to it."

"What you say," the monk interrupted, "is inspiring. But would you please explain a small point before expounding your view?"

"Yes, if I can," I responded without hesitation.

"What do you mean when you say that the meaning of everything that exists—quality, object, the universe itself—points beyond itself?"

"What I mean," I continued after a moment's reflection, "is that the meaning that infuses everything that exists is, by its very essence, relational; it is an expression of purpose. It expresses a purpose implicit in an object. To experience something as meaningful is to experience it as having a purpose, a kind of aim or goal. Meaning arises from the realization of purpose. Everything that exists is purposeful, therefore, meaningful, not because it is merely a form or a design of some kind, but because it is purposeful. Its form signifies the kind of purpose or meaning it has. The experience of meaning potential in the purpose is what enables the object to point beyond itself. When I contemplate the scheme of nature, or any part of it, I do not experience it as an abstract, insipid form, but as a dynamic, vibrant reality. Meaning is, as I mentioned earlier, an event. This event has a direction and points beyond itself. This clearly implies that it is not the source of its own purpose but exists as a purposeful object. What is interesting is that the purpose of every object is harmonious with the purpose of the whole to which it belongs. It is this feature that entitles me to say that the universe is the wonder of all wonders. But if the universe is purposeful, if the meaning potential in it points beyond itself, then I should feel some confidence in my quest for its source.

"It became clear to me as I have been opening my soul, heart, and mind to the desert during the past several days, and I made similar attempts elsewhere earlier, that acknowledging this source can never be the result of logical arguments, no matter how sound they might be, but of an existential quest, the kind that begins in a direct contemplative encounter with the world as a purposeful order. There is a big difference between thinking it and experiencing it. The attempt to establish its existence by reasoning alone assumes, erroneously, that it is an object of some kind. But it is not! How can we prove the existence of the fire that is burning in our being and in the being of the universe? How can we establish the existence of the light that enables us to see and without which we cannot ask our question? But what became clearer to me is the fact that my experience of this source in the rays that emanate from it arouses a feeling of longing for it, and the more I progress in this experience, the more intense the feeling gets. My experience of this emanation in the world and the longing for its source is the basis of my confidence in my quest for universal wisdom. I am now certain that the source is not a source but The Source, the eternal source I have been seeking ever since I made my decision to become a student of philosophy. My quest for it cannot be paradoxical, not only because paradox is a function of formal logical reasoning, not of reality, but also because of the depth and richness of its being in the world."

Kamal, who was absorbed in our conversation and did not stir a bit during that time, gently reminded us that dusk was spreading its cloak over the mountain, and recommended that we take a break and ready ourselves for the evening. The radiance of his caring and thoughtfulness shone brightly in the center of this cloak. Even though I suddenly realized that I dominated both the time and the conversation, I did not feel guilty, because I knew in the depth of my heart that genuine love does not understand the language of guilt or thankfulness. More loving is the only language it understands. And since I was a stranger to the ways of Amana Mountain I remained silent. Father Sergios slowly rose to his feet and embraced Kamal with his warm arms: "I am so happy for this unexpected visit, dear Kamal, and especially for giving me the opportunity to share some insights with Dimitri on the nature of his visit to the desert." Turning to me, he said: "I really hope you can stay with us for a few days; though a solitary spot, I think you will find this mountain interesting. Besides," he added with a smile, "we should continue our conversation. What you said this afternoon has stimulated my intellectual appetite for reflection and stirred serious questions in my mind, and, I am sure, in Kamal's." Then he looked at us and said: "How about some rice and beans for supper!" Both of us accepted his proposal with a deep sense of appreciation. Kamal, who must have been acquainted with the monk's way of life, offered to help in preparing our supper. The first thing he did was to reach for his rucksack and pull two bags out of it. They contained lentil and fava beans. Without saying a word to our host, who was building a fire on the southern side of the hut, he placed them in one of the drawers. Then he removed some cooking pots from the box and followed the monk. I was left alone, alone with a storm of feelings and ideas in my mind.

Frankly, I do not to this day fully comprehend why I felt at home with that hermit, but I did. I remained seated on the cot enfolded by the soft rays of the dusk trying to recover my self-composure. The storm of feelings and ideas that filled the sky of my mind a little while ago slowly passed away, leaving behind a state of critical reflection. Father Sergios did not say much during the conversation, but the effulgence of the grace, and of the kindness, that radiated from his face communicated acceptance and trust. I am certain he understood every word I said and grasped every feeling that pulsated in my heart as I was trying to answer his questions. He did not act as a teacher or as a disputant, for every question he asked arose from the logic of my answers. His aim was to help me revisit my own ideas and see with my own eyes their potential relations and implications. He wanted me to answer my own questions, and he wanted our conversation also to be a self-conversation. He knew that any quest, whether it is for knowledge, beauty, happiness, or God, is a solitary undertaking. It cannot be given, sold, imposed, offered as a gift, or taken by anyone. We must individually plan it, will it, and strive for it. The only help we need is the understanding and love of those who appear to us. Why? Because any quest, insofar as it is human, is an activity of growth from within. Our being consists of growth, not of having or consuming knowledge, food, pleasure, power, or fame!

The silver light of the moon was shining in the hut when my host appeared at the door. "I hope we have not left you alone for a long time! Our supper should be ready shortly."

"I have never been alone ever since I set foot on this desert. There is something magical in the air, in the sky, in the moonlight, in everything around me, Father Sergios. I feel the power of this magic, I feel its fire."

Amana Mountain

"You must be extra careful, Dimitri. This fire is addictive, and as it is the case with any kind of excess, it can be harmful."

"Even with virtue?" I asked. He did not answer me. He only smiled.

"How about a glass of wine? Kamal brought a special bottle with him."

"That is a splendid idea," I said. Within a few seconds Kamal came in. He announced that our meal should be ready in about one hour, and then fetched the bottle of wine from his rucksack. In the meantime, our gracious host fished for three tin cups from the drawer. Very gently Kamal poured wine in our cups. Raising his cup a little, he said with a celebrative tone: "Wine gladdens the heart. May the light of gladness illumine our hearts?" The three cups of wine met in a twinkle. The twinkle summoned forth a warm feeling of intimacy in my heart. It was a pure, precious moment. Its purity was matched only by the purity of the moonlight that filled the space around us. We left the hut and went into that wide-open space. The moon was surrounded by a tapestry of shimmering stars. The desert was quiet, peaceful; so was my mind. I contemplated this tapestry—the way the stars shimmered, the way they formed a chorus and sang for the moon, Queen of the Night—and I contemplated the light that was dancing joyfully to the song of the choir. There was a mild flurry of exuberance in my mind. The focus of my contemplation went beyond this magnificent spectacle to the depth from which it arose. I felt like I was standing next to the choir. I had a great desire to leap into the bosom of that infinite Beyond, but I did not. The moon, who was watching me with her tender eyes, motioned to me as if to say, "Sing! Celebrate the glory of The Night!" When I regained my ordinary consciousness I discovered that I was not in a reverie, not at all; I was with a real choir celebrating silently the glory of The Night. Kamal and the monk were swept by that magnificent spectacle. It was clear to me that we were united by the song of the choir. How could it be otherwise if the same song was gracing our hearts at the same time? When the song stopped I sipped some wine.

It was delicious, gratifying. "Our meal should be ready," Father Sergios announced. Then he went to the fire to fetch the pots, while Kamal went directly to the hut. "How about supper under the starry sky?" suggested Kamal. "Most appropriate," I said. Feeling at home, I went into the hut and offered my help to Kamal. He understood, as he always did. He gave me a mat and some plates; he brought the rest of the things we needed. Father Sergios was waiting for us with two pots, one containing rice, and, the other, beans.

"I propose a toast to Dimitri," Father Sergios said after we were seated on the ground around the food. It was hard for me to sit on the ground, but I tried without crossing my legs! Both of them smiled without making any remark. "It is a good moment," I said, "it shall remain a ray of life in my heart." It was a simple but nourishing meal. Neither Kamal nor the monk spoke a word during this celebration of human presence. We were together sharing a life-enhancing experience. We did not eat as solitary individuals but as a community. The silence we shared was not a silence of indifference but of mutual appreciation. In our society today, eating has been reduced to a necessary function. People eat their daily meals to keep their bodies healthy, so they can perform other functions. But I have always thought that sharing a meal, especially supper, since it represents the conclusion of a productive day, is an event of celebration, of communication, in which we do not only share the means of survival but also of our spiritual life, of the love that unites friends, lovers, or families. Such an event is an implicit affirmation and appreciation of the value of life and the sacredness of humanity. I realized, as I was eating, that I was becoming more proficient in the art of silent conversation. I know this idea may seem strange to many people today, but it should not be, because it is not enough to understand what other people say; it is equally important to understand them as individuals. There is a basic impetus in human nature to share not only our ideas and experiences but also ourselves with the ones we love: "I want you to understand what I say, but, more importantly, I want you to understand me." In this kind of understanding, I go beyond the verbal or written message to its source. I feel the humanity from which the ideas or experiences originate, and I feel with it. I feel with it when I respect it and when I make my own feeling common between us. This kind of communication is a moment of human growth. The message we share should illumine this source; and this illumination should be an occasion for communion, in which I feel, recognize, and uphold the other as she is in herself. The ideas and experiences we share can be treated as instruments, and most of the time they are treated this way, but we cannot treat a human being merely as an instrument, merely as a means to an end. However, what is especially exciting about human communion is the fact that it is an event in which we feel the humanity of the other and the divine that glows from its center. This is why true love between friends and family members is an intimate relation, one we cherish dearly, and this is why we feel an urge to celebrate it on certain occasions: Who wants to share a meal or have sexual union with her husband if he hides from her behind a wall of estrangement, or hypocrisy? Who wants to be at a Christmas party in which the guests are mainly interested in drinking, eating, and gossiping? Who wants to be in a church service where the members of the congregation are mostly interested in watching who is present or absent, in what the others are wearing, and in planning gossip sessions in the church hall after the service is over? The spirit that dominates these and similar occasions have unfortunately become social functions, means of social and professional encounters and ways of numbing the feeling of social loneliness and boredom in their hearts. I am not opposed to such occasions; no, they were created as a response to the cry for human communication and solidarity. I am only lamenting the fact that they have in many cases become increasingly soulless, lifeless.

A mild breeze, furtively gliding on my cheeks, woke me from my train of reflection. I did not know how long I was lost to my meditation; but I felt like I was emerging from a good dream. My comrades were gazing at the stars when I opened my eyes to the starry heaven. When he noted that I was in full command of my waking consciousness, Father Sergios announced that it was time for him to go to bed. With a feeling of embarrassment he added: "I shall miss you tomorrow, but I shall see you after tomorrow morning as early as possible. I am sure you will have a good day together. Do not be bashful, Dimitri; be at home. Explore the ways of the mountain; they are interesting and sometimes provocative!" This announcement came as a surprise to both of us, especially to me. I had not realized until then that the evening was giving way to the night. We gathered the utensils of our evening meal and returned to the hut; then we washed the pots and plates and restored every utensil we used to its place. The monk offered me his cot for the night. I tried to offer it to Kamal, but he was adamantly opposed to my offer. His smiling but firm look was overpowering. I had no choice. Father Sergios removed a knapsack from his storage box and swung it over his shoulder with a warm look on his face. He bid us a good night and then disappeared into the night.

The cot I slept on that night was made of two wood boards covered with a thin cotton mattress. A pillow was placed on one end and a folded blanket on the other. Kamal helped himself to a sleeping bag from the storage box. He decided to sleep in the chapel. Both of us were tired and fulfilled. The ascent to the monk's hut, which was challenging, in addition to the afternoon visit, which was spiritually demanding, created in me, and, I am certain, in Kamal, a strong inclination to sleep. After he spread his sleeping bag on the southern side of the chapel, he approached me with grateful eyes: "It has been a good day," he said. "I wish you a peaceful sleep, Dimitri. If you need anything during the night, please do not hesitate to wake me up, and do not neglect to use the blanket, because it gets cold at this time of day here." I was deeply touched by the grace of his spirit. "I, too, wish you a peaceful sleep. I look forward to another good day tomorrow," I said. Tears quivered in the corners of my eyes. They were warm. I did not know why they made their appearance. I wanted to communicate the message these tears conveyed, but it remained in my mind. I stood there in front of him speechless and motionless for a few seconds. He did not see my tears, or even my eyes, for he bashfully looked at the ground when he wished me a peaceful night. When the tears that come from the depth of the human heart speak, the words that come from the depth of the human mind speak the language of silence. But then, was there a need to speak? The heart that overflows with love cannot speak or even hear. I lingered in the midst of this consciousness for some time and then left my bedroom. There was a mild chill in the air. I sat on a rock near the hut for about one hour admiring the starry heaven above and reflecting on my conversation with Father Sergios. I felt a strong urge to be with the stars for the rest of the night, but I could not, because Hypnos rang his bell with a whisper: "It is time to sleep!" Within minutes, I slumbered under his protective eyes.

Kamal was up and around when my eyes welcomed the golden rays of the sun. He was sitting where I sat the night before, but he was watching a different spectacle. I stood at the door of the hut and looked into the distance that absorbed his vision. It was a gorgeous display of luminosity flowing, as though endlessly, from the vibrant flames of the sun. He must be communing with The Light! He did not feel my presence, at least not immediately. I sat quietly at the threshold of the hut and for a few minutes gaped at the sun scene. "This is how Kamal prays

Amana Mountain

at dawn and I am sure at dusk. Prayer is, for him, a ritual in which he drinks a cup of life from The Fountain twice a day." But my rumination did not last long, because he slowly turned his face toward me and said: "Good morning! I hope you slept well!"

"Yes, I slept very well, indeed."

"It seems we are going to have another hot day. Would like to have breakfast?"

"Yes, I feel rather hungry."

"I too feel hungry. Let us build a fire first. How about fava beans? I know the Pythagoreans avoided them with a vengeance, but I think they are very nutritious. I hope you like them?"

"I am not a Pythagorean, Kamal. As a matter fact, I like beans and eat them once a week. I shy away from meat as much as I can." It did not take much effort to prepare and eat our breakfast, thanks to Kamal's skillful hands. But it was a good meal! Kamal suggested that we pay a visit to the area adjacent to the hut. It was an agreeable idea, I thought. Our stroll was interesting, because we found ourselves walking between mazes of rocks. Our walk was invigorating. Pointing to a shaded area that overlooked the desert, Kamal asked: "Would you like to sit here for a few minutes?"

"Yes, Kamal, finding our way through this maze of rocks was not easy. It might be a good idea to take a short break." We sat on the ground and leaned our backs against a big rock. I soon discovered that the spot he chose for our short recess was mainly to show me one more beautiful face of the desert. The vista that extended before my eyes was an aesthetically pleasing sight. Its form must have been designed by the hands of an exceptionally creative volcano. It was a harmonious formation of mounds, dunes, ridges, punctuated by craters. The medium of this formation was sand. It glittered exuberantly under the golden rays of the sun. I could not refrain from saying: "This is an exquisite sight!" Kamal responded to my spontaneous reaction approvingly. But I felt, from the way he expressed himself, that there was something on his mind. He was a little restless, hesitant in his demeanor. I was concerned. "I hope nothing is wrong!" I said. "There is a slight change in our schedule," he said. "It is not serious. Father Sergios had for some years been in the habit of meditating on the western side of the mountain. This practice has become an integral part of his life. He must have an irresistible urge to meditate in a cave there. I think there is some kind of magic in that spot. He did not know that we were going to visit him at this time. He very much enjoyed his conversation with you yesterday and would like to provoke you again if you allow him. He insisted that we spend at least two more days with him. Would this arrangement be agreeable to you?"

"Yes, by all means!" I said, relieved; for I had thought the cause of his awkward restlessness was more serious than this. "On the contrary," I added, "I am enjoying every minute of my visit to the Syrian Desert. Believe me, Kamal, I lost my sense of ordinary time the moment the bus on which I traveled approached Tadmur. I beg you not to admit any feeling of anxiety to your mind concerning this matter."

"It is, I think, prudent to pay a visit to the pond," he suggested. I endorsed his suggestion. He went to the hut and in a few minutes returned with his empty rucksack.

Our descent was much easier than our ascent. We were at the pond in about fifteen minutes. "We need to replenish some of our provisions," Kamal pointed out. "So I need to go to the van and will be back in no more than one hour. In the meantime, feel free to take a bath, or a swim, and explore this part of the mountain." His proposal was judicious. I looked at him appreciatively. Our eyes met silently. The first thing I did when he left me was to take a bath. I felt refreshed. I sat on the edge of the pond and watched the ripples floating on the water; they seemed to be coming from nowhere and going to nowhere leisurely, indifferent to their destiny. "Water in the heart of the desert!" I exclaimed silently. "There is water here and near the hut, but there is no sign of life anywhere, except in the vicinity of Father Sergio's small garden." This struck me as a strange phenomenon. My mind groped for an explanation, but it could not stumble on any kind of clue or clarification. The only idea that suggested itself for consideration was the distance of the mountain from civilization and perhaps the shortness of the winter and spring seasons. How else can we account for the absence of animal and vegetative life? I did not let this thought delay me from wandering among the thicket of rocks around me. My first attempt was to draw a mental sketch of my route in order to avoid getting lost. I tried to coordinate the motion of the sun with the course of my path. The deeper I went into this thicket, the more interesting it got. The rocks were not always smooth and curvy; they were also geometrical and in some cases perforated. A number of the perforations were large enough to be classified as mini-caves. I even climbed into one and sat there for a few minutes. It provided a beautiful perspective of the desert. "Does Father Sergios meditate in a similar cave?" I wondered. "Here one can see without being seen; and here one's eyes can contemplate The Eternal without any kind of disturbance. If The Eternal is absolute silence, it should be loved in silence." But I did not tarry long in any spot. In one path, the rocks were so close to each other that I had to walk sideways to go through. My cheek touched the rock. Lo and behold, it was cold and damp! When I freed myself from that tight spot, I examined it with both hands. Yes, it was damp. "This must be the area that stores the winter water which leads to the pond. There must be a similar system near the monk's hut. I sat there for a short time. Luckily, the rocks of that side of the mountain degenerated into a flat, rough stretch. I walked around and took a view of the desert. It was impressive, intriguing. I could not ignore it, so I sat on a small boulder and watched the scene. It certainly was beautiful, but not in the ordinary sense of the word. It was a furtive, alluring, captivating beauty, the kind that awakens the vital powers of your being; that makes you stand on your feet and cry for the sun, for the light that gives rise to every luminous reality in the world; that transports you to The Edge where you can take a peek into The Infinite! When you open your heart and mind to it, and let your imagination fly in the sky of its elegance, you do not know whether you are in heaven or on earth; you simply float in pure light. You do not see beauty, because you are enfolded by it; you do not feel it, because you are one with it; you do not desire it, because you are filled of it; and you do not think it, because you live it. Its allure comes from the bosom of the infinite, from the light that illuminates your experience of the beautiful. It would not be too much amiss if I state that the beauty my eyes fell in love with that morning was sublime. I do not here mean the sublime in contradistinction to the beautiful; I mean the beautiful that is itself sublime. The sublime in art or nature is overpowering, awe-ful. It creates in us a feeling of fear and respect. It repulses and attracts at the same time. Its overpowering effect is simultaneously threatening and safe. But, although sublime beauty is overpowering, it is not repulsive, because it does not create in us a feeling of fear but a feeling of absolute respect: How can you be afraid when you feel the safety of its gentle, yet strong, arms around you? It is absolutely attractive, because it is infinitely charming. In its presence that day, I felt overwhelmed by the depth of its beauty. I felt like one of those children of Hamlin who were enchanted by the magical music of the Pied Piper, but, in my case, I was not led to the arms of death but to the arms of The Eternal.

I do not remember how long I sat on that small boulder. It must have been long, because when my eyes left that scene of sublime beauty I noted that the sun had already moved closer to the western rim of the horizon. My heart was filled with the beautiful radiance of The Eternal. I suddenly realized that I had a promise to keep with Kamal. But, he was standing a few paces away with a loaded rucksack on his back! I did not at first notice him, because he was waiting behind me. But when I made a stir, in an attempt to return to the pond he moved forward. "It is a beautiful landscape," he remarked. "It smiles at you lovingly, especially at dawn when the choir of heaven glorifies the creation of a new day."

"Yes, Kamal, I believe what you say."

"I hope you did not have any difficulty finding this spot?"

"I did not, for I was just rambling among the rocks; I stumbled upon it. There is something mysterious about these rocks. They seem to form a shield that protects the interior of the mountain from hostile forces." Kamal listened to my observation silently. A little later he said: "Yes, this mountain is the supreme enigma of the desert. No one has, so far as I know, given an adequate explanation for how it is covered with these rocks. It is lamentable that scientists do not show sufficient interest in it." Then, looking into the distance for a few seconds, he added: "It is getting hot, and will get hotter very soon. It would be prudent to return to the hut."

"Of course! To tell the truth, I already feel the heat penetrating through my flesh." Kamal led the way upward through a different route. We were climbing on the western side of the mountain in order to avoid the sunlight. We reached our destination in a rather short time. Kamal went directly to the hut and placed his rucksack in the corner. His face exuded contentment. "How about a short stroll?" he suggested. I did not speak; I looked at him with appreciative and approving eyes. I am now convinced that when there is mutual understanding between two human beings silent language prevails. Their actions flow from a deep sense of respect. This kind of relation generates trust, confidence, and the impetus to care. As we walked side by side in the opening that surrounded the hut, I wondered: "What can two human beings smitten by the fire of The Eternal do on the top of a rocky, almost bare, mountain in the middle of the desert?" The only answer I could muster to this question was to try to move closer to the source of this fire. How? I was unable to ponder this question in any detail, because Kamal abruptly pointed to an interesting rock configuration and asked: "Would you like to sit here?"

"Yes," I said instantly.

"We can watch the sunset this evening," Kamal said after he found a comfortable spot.

"Or, how day and night meet?" I rejoined whimsically. Kamal smiled: "But, then, do they meet?" And After a short silence, he added: "Do they exist?"

"They must, otherwise, we would not be here wondering about their existence."

"Yes, I see what you mean. But I am thinking about where they meet, whether they at all met, and whether they are one and the same." In his subtle way, he was directing my attention to the phenomenon of change and the question of its possibility. This question has always vexed my mind. I did not think that Kamal was interested in a discussion of the paradoxes of change and permanence but in the experience of that which gives rise to both of them. He wanted to think about day and night, not from the human standpoint but from the standpoint of The Eternal. Any horizon, be it physical or intellectual, cannot be viewed as a final limit but as a peak, as a lighthouse, in our quest for The Eternal.

We sat on that rock for some time silently watching the sun slowly as it was gathering its golden rays from the desert. An unusual feeling of peace swept through my mind and body. I felt at home with myself, with Kamal, and with the desert. It was a moment of total self-consciousness. "After we complete our visit to Amana Mountain," Kamal said, shattering that precious moment, "we shall travel back to Tadmur. We can, if you want, visit some historical sites. A few of them are interesting."

"At the present," I broke in, "I am not interested in historical sites; in fact, I am not interested in anything that relates to time. I am paying a visit to the Syrian Desert only because I have a profound, unyielding desire to pay a visit to The Eternal, to the source from which time and all being flow."

"I hope that your visit has so far being rewarding?"

"Yes, it has, but not..."

Yes, it had, but until that point, it had not been completely rewarding. Something essential was missing. I was able to feel the presence of the divine in the world, of the eternal in the temporal, of the infinite in the finite, in the light of The Eternal in the world, but I had not yet been able to stand in its presence, gaze at it directly, and allow its arms to hold me with their infinite warmth. I wanted to know what it is like to stand in the fullness of its light, of its truth, of its power. I wanted to drink from the nectar that flows from its fountain of life and be forever intoxicated by its effect.

I could not complete my sentence when Kamal asked me about whether my visit had so far been rewarding, because I was unable to communicate this profound and urgent desire. I felt checked for fear that I might be unrealistic in my expectations. Kamal, my gentle friend, did not insist on an answer to his question. And yet, I was certain that he felt the craving that was gnawing at my heart from the beginning to that juncture of my visit. I am equally certain that he wanted to help me in this endeavor. He exemplified the noblest qualities of friendship, the true spirit of giving and sharing, not from a selfish motive but from good will. He was a rock I could lean on. Although my situation did not show it, he was confident that I was a similar rock for him.

"Let us inspect Father Sergios's garden, he said, changing the subject of our conversation. There should be some good vegetables at this time of summer. I thought I noticed some eggplants in one of the patches. Do you like eggplants?"

"Oh, yes! It is one of my favorite vegetables. It was served at our home at least once a week when I was growing up."

"Good, then." Sparks of fervor flew from his eyes as he jumped down from the rock and showed the way to the garden. I followed him. There were more types of vegetable than I expected. "How does Father Sergios gain access to all these plants and to the means of cultivating them?" I asked. "Seeds and friends. A number of his friends and students visit him frequently and always make sure that he has what he needs."

"Students?" I inquired.

"Yes," Kamal replied as he was looking for the vegetables we were going to cook that evening. "Father Sergios was and remains a teacher, not the academic sort. Academicians aim at the mind; he aims at the heart. He teaches by conversation. He is a kind of magician. He does not converse with his mind but with his heart. The words he uses are infused with love. You cannot resist listening to him when he speaks. There is something in his voice, and in his words, that makes you know that he is serious, that he cares, and that what he says is important, even though you may not understand him or agree with him. The ideas that reach your mind are droplets of life. They come directly from his heart. For him, a conversation is an occasion for giving from one's self; it is a context in which two hearts connect. Conversing with a loving heart is a necessary condition for growing in understanding. The idea that is supposed to be transmitted to you becomes an invitation to witness the heart that reveals it. Although concepts are the medium of a conversation, human connectedness is its aim. What makes Father Sergios a remarkable teacher is that he does not teach from a certain religious or philosophical point of view, or from any particular point of view. He teaches, and converses, from the standpoint of The One.

"The One?" I interrupted him and stood in my place motionless. Our eyes met.

"Oh, yes, not in the sense that he knows, or claims to know, him, for he always taught against the possibility of such knowledge. He is a very humble and self-denying human being. He never said or pretended to know, or even hint, that he was conversant with The One. Everyone who has had a conversation with him, and I am one of them, would testify that he speaks from the standpoint of his vision of The One. It is clear that he is an authority on what he says, but the authority with which he speaks derives its power from a superior source. When he speaks, his eyes are most of the time droopy or unfocused, not because he is disrespectful or because he suffers from some kind of psychological imbalance, but because his mind is focused on something distant from which he receives the power and the wisdom to speak. And when he consciously looks at you his eyes dart fire. They glow as two bright stars. I have frequently mused about this striking aspect. How can the human eye sparkle in such an extraordinary manner?"

I was listening to Kamal with an intense and subdued feeling of curiosity, and I was trying to review in my mind the scene of the conversation we had the day before. I was unable to remember the details of that scene, primarily because his contribution consisted of raising questions and mine of trying hard to answer them. The remarks Kamal made about the monk intensified my interest in him. I made a resolution there and then to seek some spiritual enlightenment from him. We picked some tomatoes, eggplants, peppers, and onions. "You will become a vegetarian by the time you return to the U.S.A.," Kamal remarked as we were returning to the hut. "Yes, I wish!" I said. I feel lighter and healthier this way.

We sat on a nearby rock under the evening sky silently for more than one hour after supper. The desert was quiet, still. Life crawled into the bosom of its stillness. "I have read that the desert is the scene of violent, destructive storms. When does the storm season start?" I asked shattering the stillness that enveloped us.

"It should start fairly soon. It is hard to predict their arrival or their course, though. Sometimes they rage in this region rather early."

"Do they reach Tadmur?"

"Now and then they approach Tadmur. We have always to be on our guard, for they sometimes wreak havoc in every place they touch. The same desert that can be quiet and dreamy one day can be violent and destructive the next. Or could it be that we human beings are the ones who attribute to it such qualities? What is it like to view nature in itself, not from the standpoint of human beings? But this stream of reflection was interrupted when Kamal said: "it is hard to foretell when Father Sergios will return tomorrow morning. It might be prudent to be ready for him when he comes back."

"Will he eat breakfast with us?"

"I do not know. But let us be on the safe side. We shall prepare breakfast for three and wait for him."

"A most agreeable idea!"

"And let me tell you, Dimitri," Kamal said with a touch of humor in his voice, "this has been a most agreeable day for me!"

"And the evening?"

"Yes, and the evening!" he added. "I wish both lingered a little longer, but I am afraid that we have a promise to keep. "Yes, I agreed silently. His face illumined a pensive look, but it did not last long, because he suddenly sprang to the ground and waited for me to do the same. I realized when I stood next to him that it was late. We strolled back to the hut and were sound asleep soon afterward.

The soft rays of dawn were still shimmering in the hut when I left the world of Hypnos. Nature was quiet, peacefully quiet. A waft of this peace flowed into my heart. It was not an ordinary peace; it was the kind that empowers your mind and warms your soul, the kind that makes you feel the divine presence on earth. I sat on the edge of the cot embraced by this presence, and by its tenderness. I did not move, because I could not resist its seduction. I wished I could remain there within the arms of that embrace, but my wish was not fulfilled, because I heard voices coming from a nearby source. Slowly I abandoned my cot and moved toward the door. Kamal and Father Sergios were talking. They must have woken up early. A good morning wish reached my ears before I had a chance to greet them. Both of them welcomed me with the most joyful smiles. "It is a good morning," I said silently as I stood with them.

"I hope you slept well," Father Sergios inquired.

"I slept very well, indeed."

"And yesterday?"

"There was not a yesterday," I answered paradoxically.

"What do you mean, Dimitri?"

"I have discovered that in this desert time flows. What we call yesterday, or an hour ago, or a second ago does not vanish into non-being but flows into and gives substance and life to what we call now, not to mention the next second, or the next hour, or the next day. The past is the time that lives in the present."

"And the future?"

"It is the continuous unfolding of the present. Neither the past nor the future exists, for it is inconceivable for them to come from nothing. What we call past or future are ways of organizing our life experiences."

"Interesting!"

"I do not experience something called past or future the way I experience this rock or that plant," I added. "There is nothing in nature called past or future, or even time. These words are human constructs; they refer to the order of my experiences of the world, myself included.

Kamal, who was listening to this unexpected interchange, cleared his throat, as if to remind us that it was time to eat breakfast. Father Sergios understood Kamal's reminder, because both of them must have awakened early and together prepared our morning meal. "May we continue our conversation later on, because Kamal wants us to eat now? The question of the nature of time has been nagging my curiosity ever since I was a young man. I am still keenly interested in it and would very much like to hear your thoughts about it," he said as we proceeded toward the rock where Kamal and I communed with nature last evening.

"Frankly, it is I," Father Sergios rejoined, "who would like to hear your thoughts about the subject. What I said were spontaneous reflections that began to gather in my consciousness during the past few days. I do not know whether they are cogent or even significant."

"They strike me as insightful and worthy of serious consideration."

"Here we are!" Kamal said. He graciously requested us to climb to our breakfast table. Father Sergios and I smiled when he made his request. We gladly complied. It was a modest but fulfilling meal. We ate in reverent silence. Eating was a ritual for the citizens of the desert. "Why?" I wondered. "Food is the source of life, and life is sacred. Eating for them is an occasion for celebrating the sacrament of life. The language of this celebration is silence: communion with the source of life." The eyes of my comrades conveyed an expression of gratitude when they finished eating. I was watching them, and I was trying to learn their ways, their language. Father Sergios suggested that we climb the mountain up to the summit. Looking at me, he remarked: "You would enjoy being at the summit. We should make this excursion as early as we can in order to avoid the heat of the sun." I nodded with a smile of appreciation on my lips. We gathered our tin plates and spoons within a few minutes, cleaned them, restored them to the drawer, and moved upward following Father Sergios's footsteps. The size of the rocks decreased, the higher we climbed. I felt as if I was climbing a pyramid. However, the tip was, in fact, neither round nor pointed. It was an irregular expanse of land. The sun was slowly gliding toward the center of the Dome when we reached the summit.

The scene that welcomed my eyes when I stood on that small patch of land was fabulous. I had been on mountaintops before, but I had never seen such a dazzling sight. The mountain stood as a point in the midst of infinity. The desert that spread around us as an ocean was encircled by the infinite; and the infinite horizon stared us in the face everywhere we turned! This ocean was an image of splendor, the splendor of infinity in its boundless depth. It is difficult for me now to estimate how long I stood there, unaware of my comrades or the ground on which I stood, flirting with the infinite, delighting in its splendor, and feeling the warmth of its charm. "The infinite is the image of The Eternal, a radiance of its effulgence. Why did the good Father lead me to this summit? Did he want me to have one more cup of the nectar of The Infinite? Did he intend to give me one more lesson in silent dialogue?" These and similar questions coursed through my mind as I was trying to drink my cup of nectar. I could not stand still, because I was trying to comprehend the incomprehensible horizon that encircled me and the whole scene around me. I was not used to this kind of nectar. I must have drunk a large cup of it, because I felt delirious; and a delirious vertigo buzzed throughout my consciousness. I wanted to remain within the grip of that vertigo, for I wanted to climb on its back and slide as far as possible so I could have a peek into its source. When I was able to collect the threads of my consciousness into some kind of focus I entertained the thought that Father Sergios brought me to this peak for one single reason: to inflame my longing for The Eternal. But I dismissed this thought faster than I entertained it, not only because the fire of my passion for The Eternal had been crackling in my mind for a long time but also because I had a vivid intuition that it reveals itself in every element of nature, even in a grain of sand. Although I cherished every moment of my visit to the mountaintop and would repeat it again and again, I aver that I could not then muster an adequate explanation for it, and I did not insist on one—why should I? Who would not prize an encounter with The Infinite in the radiance of its splendor?

 Well, I was delivered from the grip of my vertigo by the heat of the sun, which was sitting on its throne in the apex of the heavenly dome. Neither Kamal nor Father Sergios was in sight. I walked around the ridge of the ground on which I was standing. They were sitting on a small rock on the western side of the mountaintop just under the ridge in the mode of conversation. But they were not looking at each other nor were they making bodily gestures of any kind. Their eyes were focused on the infinite that dwelled in the ocean of sand that spread around them as a limitless vista! I stood there watching them without being watched, not with the motive of a snooper but with the curiosity of a loving heart. A wild realization flashed through the walls of my mind. "A conversation in the lap of the infinite?" I exclaimed silently. "To commune in the lap of the divine is to celebrate the glory of The One." But the light of inspiration that was flowing into my mind did not last, because Father Sergios, who must have felt my presence, suddenly turned his face in my direction and said: "Dimitri, we missed you! Would you like to join us?"

"Yes, I would like to visit with you and Kamal. I am sorry I abandoned you!"

"No, you did not abandon us. Why do you not sit here next to me?" I slid slowly over the ridge and sat beside him. "Kamal and I were appreciating the tranquil spirit of the desert," he added.

"I hope I have not disturbed your conversation!"

"Not at all!" he rejoined kindly. "Our conversation would be richer and more meaningful with you, in your presence. A heap of gratitude rushed into my heart, but it did not leave it. I had forgotten, ever since I met Kamal, how to say thank you; this phrase became an irrelevant, meaningless expression. I sat next to him in silence, contemplating the divine presence in the desert. A strange urge emerged from the midst of this silence: Why not resume my earlier conversation with Father Sergios? I had a nagging desire to seek enlightenment on the dynamics of the leap that leads from the light that illumines the way to its source, on what it takes to stand before The Light, if it is at all possible. I do not recall how long it took this urge to crystallize and become articulate, because human silence is atemporal. You cannot measure it; it resists measurement or temporal quantification of any kind. But when it took hold of my attention I could not resist it. I had to shatter that sacred silence; I had to speak; but how?

"I am curious, Father Sergios. . ." I started. "In a conversation with Kamal last evening he mentioned in passing that you are a philosopher of clothes. Frankly, I have never heard or read that thinkers have seriously reflected on the nature of clothes. Much is written in the fashion industry about clothes, and many people are preoccupied with the kind of clothes they wear. But I have not heard anyone analyze them from a philosophical point of view, much less construct a philosophy about them. Can you please shed some light on this subject?" When he heard my question and then my remarks, Father Sergios looked at me with astonished eyes. He was somewhat perplexed, and the source of his perplexity was the surprise element of my question. He looked at Kamal and let a soft smile shine on the corner of his lips. Kamal retuned the smile with a similar smile. There are no secrets, no scandals, and no recriminations between friends. Their hearts are connected with the light of truth and the fire of love. Kamal's smile was an implicit request for an answer to my question. Confined as he was between the two of us, he could not escape. He gaped at the infinity that stretched before us for a few moments, then he fixed a serious look at me.

"I am not a philosopher of any kind. In fact, I abandoned philosophy and the philosophical way of thinking long time ago. In truth, I deny any relation to philosophy. There is nothing philosophical about me."

"But. . ." Kamal broke in.

"Yes, dear Kamal," he said, interrupting him, "I know that there is a rumor about me that I am a philosopher of clothes. This rumor must have originated from a discussion I once had on the philosophical implications of clothes as such, specifically, on what it means for something, any of the things that make up the furniture of nature, to wear clothes."

"Clothes as such?" I asked, interjecting.

"And things wearing clothes?" Kamal said immediately following my question.

"Yes, clothes as such, and things wearing clothes," he asserted.

"What do you mean?" Kamal, whose eyes were facing the desert, directed the totality of his attention toward Father Sergios: "What you say is unfamiliar, intriguing. Would you please explain what you mean when you say that things wear clothes?"

"Only if you do not treat me as a philosopher of clothes, but as one who has some thoughts on the nature of clothes."

"Yes," Kamal said. A gleam of appreciation shined from his face.

"The notion that a thing wears clothes implies two types of reality: the thing itself and the garment it wears. Would you agree?"

"Readily."

"Let us begin with the nature of clothes. The nature we see around us and every element of it, be it a mountain or a tree, or nature as an ordered whole, is a garment. The cloth, and we my say the texture, of this garment is made of two ingredients: space and time. They are the stuff from which the garment is weaved. There is no need for us to discuss the nature of space and time or how they are related to each other at the present, but we can in general say that everything that exists is an object that endures in time in a certain place or that it is a spatiotemporal object: It is extended in space and time. All the qualities an object may have hang, in some way, on these two structural ingredients. If space and time were, for some reason, to vanish, nature and everything in it would simultaneously vanish. The amazing spectacle we ordinarily call nature, which presents itself to our eyes as a canvas of colors, shapes and a multitude of sensuous qualities, is a garment, and the garment is weaved out of space and time. We call this canvas, which is a particular design, 'nature,' and we view it as a unified whole, because it is made of one continuous stuff: space and time. There are no gaps in nature. To say that there are gaps is to assert that nothing exists, since we have to view a gap as a quantum of nothing, but nothing, or nothingness, does not exist. We would commit a gross contradiction if we say that such gaps exist. Besides, we do not know of any human being who has encountered or experienced a reality called nothing, for the moment she reports her experience, she posits nothing as something, a concrete reality, thus denying that it is nothing. The unity of space and time is what enables us to call nature a 'garment.'

"Ordinarily, a garment is an object a human being wears. We identify or name it a garment in contradistinction to any other kind of object in virtue of the functions it performs. We wear clothes to protect our bodies from the injurious effects of natural forces or influences, to decorate our bodies, to signify a social status, to make a social or political statement, or to express a certain cultural value. I urge you to view the idea of garment generally, not from the standpoint of its human functions, but primarily as a dress someone wears, a cover that envelopes, or enfolds, something within it. A house, a box, or a suitcase envelopes a certain space. When we paint an object with a certain color, the paint envelopes the object. In both cases, the envelope can serve the functions of protection and decoration. The point to stress is that a garment is an object that covers something."

"But," Kamal interjected, "it seems that there is a major difference between nature as a garment and the garments human beings wear. Human clothes are made of different stuffs such as wool, cotton, or some synthetic material, while in the case of nature there is only one kind of stuff."

"Yes, of course, the monk rejoined. "We should keep in sight that these different types of clothes are objects of nature, and, as such, made from its stuff. We can view them as spatiotemporal formations, as natural creations. They are elements of the design that makes up the general structure of nature."

"Now," Kamal asked "in the case of the human dress, the garment covers the human body. The garment is the cover, and the body is the covered. But when we come to nature, we seem to have a cover without a covered. Should we not ask: What does nature cover, or of what is it a garment?"

"Your question logically follows from the distinction I made. Before we move on to an account of what it is that wears nature as a garment, it would be interesting to point out an analogy between nature as a cover and nature as a covered object. Yes, we can view nature as a covered object, where the object is the underlying spatiotemporal stuff and the mosaic that makes its sensible forms is its garment, or cover. Here the spatiotemporal stuff is not directly sensible; neither time nor space, nor their intersection or unity into a higher reality, exists as a direct object of sense experience. What is perceptible sensuously is nature as it appears to our senses. In the sphere of ordinary life, we live in the world of Euclidian geometry. Thus, nature as it appears to us is the garment, while the stuff that underlies it is the object that is dressed, or covered, by the garment.

"But given the distinction between nature as it appears to us and nature as it is in itself, the idea I am proposing to you now is that nature itself is a garment."

"The claim that nature is an object that wears a garment," Kamal, pointed out, "that the object is the spatiotemporal stuff and the garment is the appearance we experience by the senses, is so far as we know, a hypothesis based on scientific and philosophical reasoning. It is reasonable to hold that what we intend when we speak of nature is not merely the appearance we perceive by the senses but also what underlies and constitutes the foundation of the appearance we perceive. But if we turn our attention to the claim that nature itself is a garment we have to assume an object of which it is a garment. As far as I know, such an object is not given to us in sense experience. Can you explain the sense in which it is a garment, if it is one? Is it meaningful to characterize it in this manner if there is not an object of which it is a garment?"

"Let me reiterate," Father Sergios insisted, "that I am neither a philosopher nor a scientist. Thus, I cannot offer a scientific or philosophical demonstration for the view I am expounding. And yet, I can assure you that the proposition I shall advance is not inconsistent with scientific and philosophical findings, and that, on the contrary, it stems from a critical and patient reflection on the meaning and implications of these findings. Scientists and the majority of contemporary philosophers do not concern themselves with the foundation and destiny of the world and especially of human life. But it is an essential desire of human nature. There is no need for me to justify this claim, but an examination of the way people live, the way they conceive their life projects and the way they set their priorities, confirms the validity of this claim. I am one of those strange human beings who was born with a craving, the kind you cannot stop or silence, to explore the source, the ultimate secret, of this amazing world. Ever since I opened my eyes to the world, I have been impressed, and, most of the time, mesmerized, by its mysterious dynamics, its order, and the way it works. There is a profound mystery in the way it works. I recognized that we may be able to discover the laws and relations that hold its fabric together. and perhaps the nature of this or that phenomenon, but what has baffled my mind is the why of these relations and phenomena: Why do they exist at all? My bewilderment was intensified beyond measure when my mind dwelled upon the mystery of human nature, upon the mode of its existence and the kind of elements that make up its constitution. I climbed on the back of this mystery in the course of an inquiry into my inner self as well as that of the history of civilization trying my hardest to unlock one of its doors, but I failed. I wanted to delve as far as I could into its depths and work my way into its source, into the wonder of this source that underlies it. At first, I sought to understand it. My eyes were always covered with a thin veil; I could not see or think clearly, and my mind could not comprehend what it saw adequately. I felt I was living in some kind of darkness groping for something that can never be found. Now, in retrospect, I can say that this darkness obstructed my vision in my search for that door! But it is not easy to live in the dark, not for a long time, but I did, and I confess I suffered painful bouts of frustration and sometimes of consternation. My mind was always seeking a way to remove the veil of darkness from my eyes, but to no avail. One night, the pain of frustration was so acute, so depressing, I wept. The tears that rolled over my cheeks were hot, burning hot. They originated from a soul in agony. In the turmoil of this agony, I heard a voice from within asking: 'Why are you so anxious to know the secret of the world, of its reason for being?' Once it conveyed its message the voice faded. I was left alone with this question in the sphere of my consciousness, as if it was insisting on an answer from me. At first, I thought that the answer will be easy, and clear, but then when the vibration of its buzz became irritating I cast a critical, searching look at it. The more my mind lingered on it, the more I realized that it was not an ordinary but an oracular question. So I began to scrutinize it from all sides trying to discover its thrust. The same veil that clouded my vision in the earlier quest seemed to cover my eyes in this next quest. I sat in bed in a fetal position with my arms bracing my two legs and my head dangling between them listening to the storm of ideas that were raging within my mind. My heart was throbbing loud and fast. I was desperate for a resolution, if not a solution, but neither was forthcoming. In the thick of that mental state, I heard the same voice asking a question, but this time tenderly: Why? It seemed to me then that the voice whispered from my heart, not from my mind. You see, the calling of the heart is different from the calling of the mind. The mind aims at knowledge, the heart aims at life. When the voice faded I cast another look at the 'why' the voice left behind. It was an innocent why, free from all the conceptual intricacies and logical shrewdness of the scholar. A tremulous stir, a kind of jerk, was reverberating in my mind when the noise of this stir quieted down. I began to see in a brighter, clearer light. It seemed as though the veil that covered my eyes was dissolving. I realized that the question I was asking was not meant to sate a thirst of intellectual curiosity but of life. The whisper of the voice was a gentle request to go beyond the academic ramifications of the question and consider its practical implications. What if I had within the grasp of my hand all the knowledge of nature and the origin of the world, of the secret of all secrets, so what? What then? I saw there and then, in the light of the darkness that enfolded me that night, the truth of my question: I do not seek to live in order to know, I seek to know in order to live. It was this insight that propelled me to ask my original question about the impulse to seek life. For some reason, my desire to know had overshadowed my desire to live! Yes, the primary impulse in human nature is to live, not to know—to live a life becoming of our humanity. But then, when I focused my attention on my supreme priority I asked myself: "How should I live? How can I gratify my thirst for life?"

Kamal, who was listening to this moving confession, suddenly made a rather intrusive stir that attracted Father Sergios's attention and disturbed the flow of his narrative. He looked at me and then at Kamal questioningly. "I am afraid," he said apologetically, "it is getting very hot for all of us, especially for Dimitri. The sun is already approaching the western horizon. May I suggest that we continue our conversation in a shaded area near the chapel?"

"Oh, yes!" I responded.

"I forgot myself. Kamal is my guardian angel." As usual, Kamal did not respond, at least not verbally, but instead, simply paved the way for our descent. The air was mild when we arrived at the hut. He pointed to a niche created by two large rocks adjacent to each other. It overlooked the eastern side of the mountain. It impressed me as a good place for a social visit. As before, our host sat in the middle and faced the east. He remained silent in that position for several minutes. We did the same. Was he communing with The Infinite? Was he trying to collect his thoughts on the nature of clothes? I was strongly interested in his view on this subject. I felt that what he had to say about it might help me find my way to The Eternal; and even if it did not, it would be useful to seek such help directly. Fortunately, he looked at Kamal and then at me: "Yes," he said recapturing the thread of his narrative, "the greatest challenge human beings face in this short life is how to live, not how to survive. It is easier to survive than to live. The more I reflected on the request implied by this question, the more I realized that seeking an answer to how we should lead a good life should proceed from an understanding of the essential nature of our humanity. The inner thrust of the impulse to life is to be one's self, to be true to one's self. How can I lead a good life, if I were false to myself? In contemplating the meaning, assumptions, and consequences of this question I saw that knowledge of the basis and purpose of human life is a necessary condition of good action and, consequently, of the best life. Not to live from the essence of my humanity would certainly entail that I live in bad faith; it entails that I live from an external source, not from myself. Such a life is not worth living, and I wanted to live a life worth living, one that originates from my mind, soul, and heart. But, then, I asked myself again: How do I know how to live such a life?

"I first looked at how people live and how they understand the question of the good life. I discovered that they understand it in terms of happiness; but they interpret the meaning of happiness in terms of pleasure, wealth, health, power, fame, or knowledge. They think that living according to anyone of these values guarantees happiness. Although, as goals, these values are important, and, I can say, conditions of the good life, their attainment does not gratify the impulse to lead a good life. The gratification they produce in us is shallow, short-lived. They do not meet the essential demands of the impulse to life. In pursuing any one of them, no matter how much you maximize its realization in your life, there will always remain a painful emptiness in your soul; you will always want more and more of the same. No one of them is fulfilling at the human level. They dominate your mind and heart, and you lose control of your life. You become a hostage to them.

"Then, I turned my attention to philosophical wisdom and reflected on their ideas of the good life. They were enlightening, instructive. Like the majority of human beings, they generally argue that the good life consists in the pursuit of happiness, but they interpret happiness differently. They think that it consists in perfection, and they characterize perfection in terms of self-realization, self-fulfillment, self-determination, pleasure, growth, or self-completion. They proceed in this sort of interpretation from the assumption that, in their natural state, human beings are born to the world as possibilities, or potentialities, for being or becoming perfect. Their destiny lies in the realization of this possibility. But, then, when I examined the principle and the method one should adopt in fulfilling one's destiny I faced a recalcitrant problem, one that leads to a dead end: No two philosophers agreed on the nature of the principle and method we should adopt in leading a good life. All of them appealed to reason in establishing the validity of their views, but apparently the voice of reason they heard was different in each case. 'Can reason speak in different voices or languages?' I asked myself. An uncontrollable consciousness said 'No.' But why did these wise people hear different voices from the mouth of reason? Under what cultural, ideological, religious, idiosyncratic, political or scientific conditions did they listen to this voice? Did they listen with healthy ears free from any type of bias or prejudice? Were they fully competent in listening to this somewhat enigmatic voice? And, most importantly, where did they listen to this voice? Again, most, if not all, of the philosophers viewed human beings as natural beings, as parts of nature, but they were not clear on the sense in which they are natural. Am I nothing but a rational animal? What is this power in me that craves to love, to appreciate beauty, to seek the truth of what I know, to ask about the ultimate cause of the world, or to desire to live permanently? I could not find either a uniform or a comprehensive account of this power.

"When I analyzed these and related questions, when I dwelt on their presuppositions and the direction to which they necessarily lead, I felt like a man who, in the course of his life, inattentively bumps into a hard, formidable wall. He feels the shock of the bump; he stands still next to it bewildered, lost. The shock he feels is a wake-up call. It is a call for knowing why, for re-evaluation, for an urgent desire to discover the right way that leads to the good life."

Father Sergios stopped for a few seconds, looked into the distance contemplatively, and then he continued: "Yes, I sat next to that wall and leaned against it for a long time trying to find my way into the good life. It gradually became clear to me that I could not rely in my quest on hearsay, regardless of its source or the degree of its wisdom. This did not mean I should ignore the wisdom of the learned or refuse to learn from them. It simply meant that I should not borrow, plagiarize, or paraphrase the ideas or ways of others. My life cannot be a series of quotations adapted from this or that mind or way of life. The beliefs and values I live by should originate from my own mind and will. The life I live should originate from my own heart. If I acquire an idea or view that relates to my life, I can adopt it or act on it only if it is baptized by the hands of my mind and the spirit of my will. I understood that in achieving my objective I should read three books: the book of nature, the book of civilization, and the book of my heart. In reading the first, I sought help from the physicists, biologists, and cosmologists. They enabled me to acquire knowledge of the scheme of nature at the macroscopic and microscopic levels. I was able to form a conceptual framework of the basic structure of the world, of its general nature and the laws that govern its activities. In reading the second book, I sought help from the anthropologists, artists, historians, and philosophers. The works of these scholars provided an account of the life of the human mind in the course of history, of its capacities, functions, and limits. I was especially interested in this book, because it is a mirror in which I could see myself. The deeper I delved in the history of human civilization the more I grew in self-understanding.

"Reading the first two books, the book of nature and the book of civilization, paved the way for reading the book of my heart. They provided the conceptual equipment for exploring the territory of my own mind, of its capacities of knowing, feeling, and willing, not as an abstract entity, nor as a member of some species, but as the particular individual who lives in the world. I was anxious to see myself not in the mirror of the history of human civilization but in the mirror of my own consciousness. One does not become a physician merely by reading a prescribed set of medical books but also by dissecting and knowing the parts of the body in the laboratory with his hands and eyes, by relating the abstract knowledge he learned to the actual anatomy and physiology of the human body. Similarly, I wanted to see and feel myself with my own eyes; I wanted to see the heart that gives rise to the structure of my human self and makes me who I am. Here in this living laboratory I can stand face to face with this heart and examine its texture: its impulses, capacities, desires, needs, powers, and limitations. Only by examining this texture can I discover the nature of my inner self, and, consequently, the nature of my destiny.

"I cannot report to you what I actually saw and felt when I looked into the mirror of my own consciousness. How can anyone capture conceptually the subtlety, richness, and depth of a profound aesthetic experience, a tragic experience, or the experience of one's love for the woman he loves and adores? We may use general or metaphorical words or symbolic expressions to communicate the kind of experience we have in these and similar experiences, but not the details of the experience. Knowledge of the inner world of the human self is always, and in principle, a solitary undertaking, because it is an individual and subjective reality. I can, however, report to you an outline of the most striking findings and conclusions I reached in reading the book of my heart. I shall emphasize the discoveries that are relevant to my quest for the good life."

My eyes brightened when Father Sergios reached this point of his confessional narrative, because I was almost certain that the account of these discoveries would help in leading to a direct encounter with The Eternal. But I remained silent. Kamal, on the other hand, who noticed the glow of my eyes, cleared his throat and gently urged: "Both Dimitri and I would very much like to hear your report, Father Sergios."

"On one condition, Kamal."

"Whatever condition you set."

"Only if you do not ridicule what I shall report, because some of the ideas and the way I shall present them may seem strange, if not outlandish."

"Not at all, Father!" Kamal responded with the most loving smile in his eyes.

The good Father turned his eyes away from us and fixed them on the eastern horizon. He remained in that position for a short while and then continued:

"The first fact that impressed my eyes when I left all the concerns of my conscious life and moved into my inner self is that I was in the midst of a world of ideas, emotions, habits, moods, impulses, desires, feelings—yes, a world, because, although this content was in constant motion, the way actors usually move on stage, it was, to some extent, organized in a certain way. Their mode of organization resists accurate description. Whether it is an idea, an image, or an emotion, every detail is related to other details, actually or potentially, in the strangest manner. One stir in one detail can open up a marvelous network of relations that connect it with other details. For example, the moment you focus your attention on an idea such as cause, or pleasure, a large number of ideas that are related or can be related to it loom in the perspective of your perception. It was difficult for me to comprehend in one synoptic vision the details of this whole content, because it was unusually rich, variable. What is amazing is that the way these ideas are related or can be related is always a possibility for a new mode of relatedness. I could have spent a very long time inspecting the relations that existed between them, or the different possible ways they can be related to each other. Again, some of the ideas seemed vivid and important, others, faint and unimportant. This world presented itself as a kind of spatiotemporal order. Everything I experienced there was perceived at a certain place and time. If, for example, you suddenly mentioned a name, such as Alexander the Great, I would immediately think of a particular human being with a large number of attributes and features who lived in Macedonia in the fourth century BC, who conquered a large part of the civilized world at that time, and who died prematurely, in short, I would present to myself a slice of history whose elements are weaved from the many parts of my mind, some of which can be used in constructing another slice. When this representation engages my attention, the rest of my inner world waits around its fringe as a potential object of interest or perception. I discovered that my inner world is an intersection of two sequential maps, the first, temporal, historical, and the second spatial, geographical. Every detail is located in these two maps simultaneously. Could it be that the world that throbs in my heart reflects in its structure and logical dynamics the outer world of nature and human life? After all, every detail that exists in the inner world is derived from my experience of the external world. Whenever I perceived anything, I felt myself in it; I felt it as mine. How could I experience it as mine if I was not in it or if it was not in me? There was nothing there in which I could not feel myself, primarily because the subject, the 'I,' that thinks, feels, and wills in me was present in each one of these details. It was immanent in the totality of that sanctuary I called myself.

"It is not my intention this evening to describe the wonder I discovered in the exploration of the world of my inner self. I made the preceding remarks only to emphasize two prominent features. I noticed in the process of self-inspection that my inner self has the characteristic of world, mainly because it emanates from one source. The unity of this source gives rise to the feeling that it is my world, that I am one with it and that it is one with me: I am this source and I am this world. I become actual in this world and my world reveals my true essence. This source is the power that thinks, feels, and wills in me. These three types of activity give rise to every type of detail I may encounter in my inner self. The first aims at knowledge and truth, the second aims at beauty and love, and the third aims at life, at actualizing myself as a human being, at fulfilling the destiny for which I exist in this world. No one of these activities is at all possible without the source that underlies them and is immanent in them. I become alive, I shine in these activities. If the activity happens to be an act of knowledge, or love, or appreciation of a beautiful object, it is I, as a source, which knows, loves, and appreciates the beauty of the object. I feel the oneness of myself every time I perform a certain kind of action, and, without this feeling, freedom, responsibility, or consciousness is not possible.

"The second prominent feature I would like to relay to you is the discovery, and I should say experience, of a new kind of light unlike any I have ever seen in the natural world. As I was examining the territory of my inner self I inadvertently noticed that my examination was made possible by this special light and that this light originated from the same source that gave rise to my inner world. How could I have perceived, recognized, and identified any item of my inner self or performed any act of thinking, feeling, and willing in the dark? I felt, when this realization loomed in the field of my consciousness, a warm thrill reverberating throughout my being. Instantly, I directed my attention from the light under which I was examining my inner self to its source. At first, I felt it was the source of my being, but now I experienced it as a luminous source, a spark. I gazed at it and reflected on the world it illuminated and then on the condition of my gaze: I could not see myself as a luminous source if I did not have eyes that see, for, without such eyes, I could see neither my inner world nor its source. The more I gazed at the spark, the more I saw that this special light was the source of my inner life, my spiritual life, for, without it, I could not perform any kind of activity. If life on the face of the earth collapses when the physical light of the sun fades away, life in my inner world would likewise collapse if the spark that illuminates it were to fade away. Do we not describe an ignorant human being as one who lives in the dark, in the netherworld? A strong desire to know the nature of this light surfaced into my mind: I wanted to know the nature of this illumination. What kind of light is it and how does it shape my spiritual life? My eyes reverted to its origin."

Father Sergios stopped for a few seconds, then he looked at me and said: "Do not think that this is a digression; I am not trying to avoid an answer to the question of the good life."

"Not at all!" I answered. "In fact, I am beginning to see the purpose of your remarks on the inner self. It would be crucially important to continue the thread of your narrative."

"And you, Kamal?"

"Yes, of course, only if we can have a supper recess. It is getting dark. Would you allow us a short recess, Father?"

"It is indeed a most welcome idea."

Our meal, whose ingredients were potatoes, onions, squash, and chickpeas, was ready within one hour. All of us participated in preparing it. It seemed to me that the achievement of that small task was a kind of ritual, a celebration of life and friendship.

Throughout this small ritual I noticed that Kamal was anxious for us to resume our conversation. He had never shown, since I first met him in Tadmur, any kind of haste or perturbation, until that evening. I saw, by the way he acted during our forthcoming conversation, that he was deeply interested in Father Sergios's confession just as I was.

I surmised, whether correctly or not, that his passion for The Eternal was insatiable and that he wanted to take a peek into the monk's heart, perhaps to see the kind of light that glowed there. Can a lover of The One afford not to be a lover of knowledge, of beauty, and of the other human being? My respect and admiration for that son of the desert were infinite and indelible.

Soon after we ate our meal, Kamal fetched a box of matches, went to the chapel, and lit the candle that was placed at the altar. Father Sergios and I were watching him with sympathetic eyes. "It would," he began, "be appropriate to resume our conversation in the light of The Night." I thought it was an excellent idea, because I felt that an event of communication in which human beings share the warmth and radiance of their presence is an event of divine worship, but Father Sergios was silent. I threw a look in his direction; tears were quivering in his eyes. "He must have been moved into the core!" I thought. A few seconds later, he said: "Truly, Kamal!" But Kamal remained silent. His eyes shied away from the monk. We sat around the candle and assumed a position of waiting, as if to say that we were ready for the remainder of his confession. Father Sergios understood our gesture.

"Yes," he said. "I sat in front of that spark for a long time contemplating it. Contrary to my expectation, it was a substantial round reality, but it did not have a boundary. It had a circumference and a center from which an indefinable plentitude of rays flowed the way a river flows from its spring. It was light, but it was not offensive to my eyes. It was elegant, attractive. I tried to penetrate its essence with my gaze. The longer I gazed at it the more glamorous it became to my eyes. When I was young I used to gaze at the sun, because I felt some attraction to the magic of its radiance. My eyes would hurt from the sharpness of the light, and I could not keep them on it for a long time, because of the acute pain. But in the presence of this radiance, I did not feel any pain; on the contrary, it was soothing and alluring. It was a simple quality but unusually rich in its simplicity. It seemed as if it were a garden of simplicity. I felt an urge to visit it. I did. I strolled in its lanes without any awareness of space and time. I stood in its midst and looked around: My eyes were graced by a delightful scene. Then, I looked in the distance, into the world of my inner self. I reflected on the conceptual framework derived from my study of the book of nature under the light of my inner sun. It was an icon of splendor. For the first time, I was able to see it in the complexity of its design: It was a joyful dance! My gaze lingered on this icon for a while. Then I turned my attention to the conceptual framework derived from my study of the book of civilization. I contemplated its tapestry. Alas! It appeared to my gaze as a wondrous design, as the most magnificent icon of beauty my eyes had ever witnessed. For a moment, I thought that the structure of this tapestry sprang out of the book of nature. I sat on a bench in the garden of my inner sun and contemplated the synergetic interplay between the two icons for a long, long time. In the course of my contemplation, I recognized that the two icons formed a realm. The relation between them was organic, and they existed in and through each other. You see, during my visit to the garden of my sun, I discovered, and for the first time, that the realms of nature and civilization were books, that, as books, they were written by an author and that the spirit of their author is revealed in them. And, during that visit I also discovered that the two icons that constituted the structure of my inner world were made possible by the spark that shone in my heart as a sun. They were fashioned out of its light and they revealed the grandeur and beauty of its garden."

When he uttered this last sentence, Father Sergios fell silent. His eyes were glued to the flame of the candle. His face was a canvas of serenity. Both Kamal and I were mesmerized by the light that flowed from his empyrean eyes. I was stupefied, not only by his poetic, yet enigmatic, description of his experience, but also by the translucent light that beamed from his eyes. It was not an ordinary light. Although I could not understand, at least not adequately, the words, I understood him. He was believable. Any intelligent person who could have listened to him would have readily testified that he spoke with authority: He spoke from the heart, and he spoke from a direct vision.

Father Sergios noticed our solemn silence. He cast a gentle look at Kamal, then at me, and said: "I realized that the sun, which shone as a sun in my inner world, was only a spark, a flame that derives its being from a higher source! This discovery fell upon my mind as a thunderbolt. It widened the scope of my vision and intensified the power of my understanding. Before my visit to that garden, I had thought that I understood myself, hoping to use my understanding in pursuing the good life. But after I finished my visit, and regained my ordinary consciousness, I realized that my understanding was deficient, perhaps fragmentary. I tenaciously held on to the belief that I could not articulate the principle that illuminates the way to the good life unless this principle is founded on an adequate knowledge of myself; and I could not attain this knowledge unless I gazed at the source of the world and my inner self.

"But, then," I asked myself. "What is the way to The Sun that gave rise to me and everything that exists?" In raising this question I proceeded from a conviction, whose validity I saw with my mind and felt with my being, that my quest for The Sun, whose radiance shone in and through the books of nature and civilization, was the ultimate object of love and desire, because it is the source of my being and of my knowledge of the good life."

Father Sergios stopped, gaped at the candle for some time as if he were having a dialogue with it, and then continued: "You might think that the last sentence I uttered was out of the ordinary, perhaps outrageous, but let me assure you that it is not. Please, let me explain. Do we love our parents? Of course, yes. But why? If we reflect on this question carefully with the aim of discovering the reason that justifies this respect, we are bound to say that we love them because they are the source of our life, both biologically and culturally. Being a source entails that there is continuity between the parents and offspring; both share one essence. But more importantly, it entails that the parents are the reason for being of the offspring. The relation that connects them and arises from the exercise of being a parent is love. In receiving its life and being from its parent, the greatest gift the offspring receives is the gift of love. Love arises from the bosom of this relation. The parent loves its offspring in the act of giving, and the offspring loves its parent in the act of receiving. The presence of love in their hearts is what creates the desire to be with and to respect each other. And when, for some reason, they are separated from each other, a feeling of longing is generated in their hearts. Now, if we love our parents because they are the source of our lives, not in the sense of creation but of reproduction, can you imagine the magnitude of our love for the being that is the source, not only of our parents' lives but also of the universe? Yes, dear friends, The Source is good and therefore lovable, because it is a giver. The creation of the universe is the greatest act of love we can imagine. Since this source is infinite, it is reasonable to say that it can command our infinite love. This general understanding, which grew and matured under the light of the spark that shone in my heart, created in me a burning passion to stand before The Source: to feel its warmth, tap into its wisdom, purify my eyes with its light, drink a cup of the nectar that flows from its loving breast, delight in its majesty, in short, to find my way to The One, the only source, because it is my supreme passion in life.

"Yes, The One, the source of my being and the being of the universe, became the object of my ultimate concern. I realized, when I dwelt on this new enlightenment, when I examined its meaning and the truth of it implications, that this concern was the highest good, and that it is most appropriate for me to see it with all my heart, mind, and soul. In time, this realization became a firm belief. Who said that ideas do not change the course of history? No, ideas, true ideas, are the vehicle of change and progress in history, socially and individually. They act as instigators, as lighthouses that illumine our way in the near and distant future, and they create the urge to seek the good life. This is the kind of urge I felt when my realization changed into firm belief. I felt a sharp itch in my mind to have an audience with The One, to embrace and, more importantly, to be embraced by it. Divine love is the eternal embrace of the Beloved. The One was my heart's ultimate preoccupation. It became the passion of my life."

My heart palpitated with expectation when the monk reached this point of his confession. I was anxious to hear what he had to say about the way to The One, not because I was a conformist or a follower, but because I was in search of insight, or some understanding of its logic. I had, until that point of my quest, felt The Sun in the world; I experienced its presence in the books of nature and civilization and derived deep gratification from this experience, and I stood on the edge of being, trying to make a leap into the bosom of The One. How can one make such a leap, into the unknown, into The Source? How can the finite expand its being into the infinite? How can it sit in its lap and listen to the pulse of eternal creation? How can it gaze into its eyes and relish the beauty of its garden?

I felt an irresistible impulse to interrupt the monk: "Did you have an audience with The One? Did you. . ."

"Renounce the world?" he interjected, anticipating my second question.

"Can we really renounce the world, Father, if we are integral parts of it, if we live in it, and if our destiny seems to be enmeshed in its destiny?"

"Yes, we can. The act of renunciation is not an act of rejecting or repudiating the world but of renouncing the misguided ways of the human world, of the view that its beliefs and values are, or can be, the basis of the good life. We may ask: What are these beliefs and values? The answer is obvious: pleasure, power, health, wealth, fame, knowledge. These values reflect important human needs, and we should not reject them blindly but meet them according to the demands of reason. We move closer to The One when we recognize that the pursuit of these values, taken singly or jointly with others, cannot lead to the good life, not completely, and closer still when we comprehend the truth that we should plan and live from the standpoint of The One, from the standpoint of the understanding we attain from our union with it, from that luminous vision we have of it! We renounce the world when we read the books of nature and civilization as emanations from its light, when we see nature as a rational order and the human race as a human community."

"How did you manage to renounce the world and proceed into a union with The One?" I asked, since the possibility of this kind of union was uppermost on my mind. He turned his eyes away and fixed them on my forehead, as if he was reading the script of my desire on its furrows. Solemnity hovered around my face.

"Let me remind you that I cannot, no matter how much I may try, give you an exact account of how I proceeded to a union with The One, not only because it defies description of any kind of human language, but also because it is a personal, solitary, endeavor. All I can do is try to communicate to you, so far as I can, the structure of my adventure. And let me stress that it is an adventure."

"I understand."

"My quest for The One began with a visit to the world of my inner self. I am convinced that I could not look upward toward The One because I was not armed with self-understanding, an understanding of what I truly am and whether my quest expresses the supreme desire of my heart. It was not enough for me to know that I should renounce the world but also how. How could I realize this purpose if I was not absolutely certain of what I am? I sat again in the light of the spark and again read the books of nature and civilization. Something extraordinary happened as I was reading them. I heard a voice coming from the depth of my mind: 'Reading the books of nature and civilization is not enough. Try to comprehend what you read. Extract the meaning implicit in what you read. Look into yourself.' Alas! 'I am within myself' was my immediate reaction. I fell silent, bewildered for a while. I gazed at the spark again and again. The request of the voice to comprehend what I was reading was flashing in my mind throughout these gazes. What did the voice mean by its request? After a painful yet solemn process of reflection, I discerned that my inner self was heavily dressed."

"Dressed?" I broke in impulsively. We were about to be initiated into the philosophy of clothes! My eyes sparkled with curiosity. The monk looked at me sympathetically.

"Yes, I thought that the self I thought I had seen with my eyes and known with my mind was clothed and that my real self was covered with four layers of garment. The moment I discovered this truth the voice spoke again: 'Undress yourself; but first look into the mirror of your consciousness!' The logic of this instruction was evident. In order to have a clear idea of my inner self, I should undress myself; in order to undress myself, I should understand the kind of clothes I was wearing; and in order to attain this understanding, I should read again the books of nature and civilization. I was what I was, the individual I was, in and through nature and culture. The structure of my real self was derived from these two books.

"The first garment was social in character; it was weaved out of the general norms, customs, symbols, beliefs, values, in short, the general worldview of my society. My character, the one I presented to the world, was an interpenetration of the beliefs and values that make up the structure of this worldview. I felt, thought, acted, and you can say lived from its standpoint. My self was, to some extent, a social self. It was an extension of the larger social self, so to speak. This dimension of me was acquired in and through the institutions within which I grew up and lived. No matter how the members of a society tinker with the way they think, feel, and behave, they remain alike, too alike! They are related to the members of the larger whole the way sheep are related to the herd. When the idea of this garment became clear to my mind, the voice spoke again: 'Be a-social!'

"Hidden underneath the social garment was a second: religion. The texture of this garment was weaved out of the religious beliefs and values that relate to the meaning and destiny of human life. They are usually applied in the web of rites, ceremonies, symbols, and practices of the religious community. Their interpenetration results in what we may call the religious garment. It is usually tailored by the religious community in and through the family and the religious institution to which one belongs. When people want to present themselves to society as religious, they wear this garment. In some cases, wearing this garment reflects a genuine religious nature, in others, it does not. Broadly speaking, it is complete and ready to wear in society when people leave their adolescence behind. The moment I was able to identify this garment in my mind, the voice spoke again: 'Be a-religious!'

"A rather opaque but substantial garment rose to view when I looked deeper into myself: fantasy. This garment was weaved out of my inner desires and wishes, of the kind of life I wish to live but for some reason cannot realize, because it was impossible to realize these desires and wishes under the prevalent personal, material, and cultural conditions. Nevertheless, although I could not fulfill them, I could not get rid of them. It is really difficult to get rid of deep-seated desires and wishes. In fact, they color and underlie much of what we plan and do in our lives. When I discovered the boundary and terrain of this fantastical garment, the voice spoke again: 'Be real!'

"When I took off this garment I felt cold. I looked into the mirror of my consciousness to see the source of this feeling. The only thing I saw in that mirror was my body. My body, a garment? Yes, of course! How could it be otherwise if I had already discovered that the essence of my being was the spark that illuminated my rational and material life? I cast a critical, investigative look at this biped, at this lump of flesh, in the mirror. Alas! It was a garment weaved out of space and time. Its purpose was to provide a home for the spark. As I stood before the mirror gazing at this newly discovered garment, the voice spoke one more time: 'Be true to yourself!'

"Yes, to be true to myself meant to be true to this spark, to live from it and in its light. I could remove the garments myself, but I could not remove the light from the spark, which is the source of my life, because the spark cannot exist without its light. I kept my eyes fixed on that mirror. The more I contemplated my inner self, on the way it was clothed, and on the way these garments were related to each other, the more I understood what it means to live from the standpoint of the world. But could I live from the standpoint of The One? And how could I know what it means to live from its standpoint if I could not see myself in the fullness of its truth? The purpose of distinguishing and understanding the function of the garments I wear is to liberate my will from external influence, my eyes from the dust that accumulated on them during my shallow pursuit of worldly happiness, and my emotions from erroneous interests. The point is to live from my inner self.

"The voice was wise: Self-understanding, which comes from reading the books of nature and civilization, not to mention the book I composed in the course of my own life, is a necessary condition for renouncing the world. How do I abandon the way of the world and adopt the way of The One? How can my life flow from the spark that shines in my heart? Ironically, the voice spoke again, this time gently: 'Love the world!'

"We renounce the world by loving it, by caring for it, by nourishing it. The way to The One is the way of love. The rays that emanate from the inner spark are rays of love, and the light that spreads in the world of the self is the light of love. Love is the beginning and the end, and it is the destiny of human beings. If you choose, and you should, then choose to love!

"Listening to the last commandment of the voice instigated a peculiar episode of thinking on the nature of love, for if it is the way to The One, I should understand it adequately. I sat again in the garden of my heart and gazed at the light that illumined the books of nature and civilization, but this time the focus of my attention was the light itself. I sat there for a rather long time. In the middle of that gaze, I caught myself smiling as I was trying to penetrate its texture. The light that existed earlier as a transparent medium in which the furniture of my inner world became visible to my eyes appeared to me in that contemplative posture as a vibrant dance of passion. It was gliding upward in its movement. It appeared as an ongoing procession originating from the center of the stage of my heart. It was not the kind of dance that presents a show and aims at arousing a certain feeling in the audience but the kind that seeks to engage the audience in the dance. It was beautiful, and its beauty was alluring. I gave myself to its charm; for how I could I fully understand it, if I did not participate in it, see it, and feel it for what it was?

"I was not mistaken in my adventure, for as my feet moved effortlessly on that stage, I felt the upward surge of the dance and the infinite source from which the dance was proceeding. That dance, Dimitri, was the dance of love. It derives its power of giving from the spark and it derives its longing for The One from loving. Love is the eternal longing for The One. And it is such longing because it emanates from the spark, but the spark longs for its source. When this insight found its way into my mind, I saw as clearly as possible that in whatever I thought, felt, and did, I should proceed from this insight, regardless of what people might think or feel about me, even of how they might treat me. I became indifferent to their ways, but not to them: The impetus of my inmost passion was to love.

"A life-enhancing surprise was waiting for me as I followed the way of love: The more love flowed from my heart abundantly, the stronger, the more resourceful, the more determined I became in my quest for The One. This quest does not consist of a leap of faith, cogent arguments, prayer, or doctrinal commitment. Its birthplace and thrust is love. I knew that, in spite of growth in my ability to love, I was weak. But the knowledge and recognition of this fact always inflamed my passion for The One, for I was convinced that this weakness would be improved once I stood before its majesty, strolled in its garden, felt the warmth of its presence, and especially when I had a vision of its radiance. This vision will be the basis of my life, for I will be the source of the knowledge I shall need in leading a good life.

"I cannot relay to you the rest of the details of my quest, for this is impossible, but I can say to you that the life I led after my audience with The One centered on social action, in which I tried to serve society; inquiry, in which I read as thoroughly as I could the books of nature and civilization; and aesthetic adventures, in which I listened to serious music and read as many literary works as I could. Knowledge is a necessary condition for wise judgment; productive activity is a necessary condition for growing up as a human being; and aesthetic experience is a necessary condition for appreciating the mystery and beauty in nature and human works. I tried to lead a productive, meaningful life, avoiding idleness and trivial activity as much as possible. In whatever I did, I sought to keep the light of the spark in my heart as the impetus and aim of my action. I do not know if or how much I succeeded, but I tried my best."

"What about your audience with The One? What was it like? I know you try to avoid this subject, but, if possible, can you describe this encounter?" Kamal asked with a soft smile on his face.

"I cannot."

"Why?"

Father Sergios looked at him with an astonished, solemn look. "Because The One is Silence, perfect silence."

"I understand," Kamal said, "but is it at all possible to describe how you felt, and perhaps thought, after that encounter?"

"It is very difficult, but I can make general remarks."

This admission evoked my curiosity. My eyes beamed with interest. I could hear Father Sergios's chest heaving. He must have been either tired or looking for the right words he needed to express himself. After a short silence, he resumed his confession.

"The feeling that permeated every fiber of my being after that encounter, enduring until the present moment, was one of renewal. I became a different person after the audience was over. A new wave of life swept through my body, a new light shone in my mind, a new flame of enthusiasm burnt in passion for life, and a new power energized my will. I began to see myself and the world with new eyes. In the past the world existed as a fast-moving show, as something unimportant, irrelevant to my life, but now I see it as real, as significant, as a meaningful extension of my own being. I see myself in it, and I see it in myself. I used to make a special effort to meet the demands of my daily life, as if what I had to do was an imposition on my will, a kind of drudgery, but now my life flows from me the way water flows from its fountain. What I think, feel, or do is no longer a response to an external stimulus, social or natural, but emanates from myself, from the standpoint of my vision of The One, that is, from the standpoint of the insight, the light, and the inspiration I received during my audience with The One. For example, I used to appreciate beauty in works of art, natural scenes, and human beings; the outcome was a deep feeling of pleasure, or gratification. Now, I appreciate the same beautiful objects from the standpoint of my vision of the supreme beauty I witnessed during my encounter with The One; the result is not only a feeling of pleasure, but also a feeling of divine presence in my heart. I used to act on the principle of the right and the good; the result was a feeling of satisfaction, of human growth. Now, I act on the same principles, but from the standpoint of my understanding the supreme principles of the right and the good; the result is longing for the One. Now, I know that the beliefs and values I live by are valid and that their validity is grounded in my vision of The One. I do not exaggerate if I admit that now my life flows from that vision. This kind of flow banishes one of the worst evils in our life: doubt, hesitation. How can you doubt when you ground your action in direct vision of the source of goodness and wisdom? I still recall how one of the ancient sages gladly and peacefully faced death and accepted it on the firm belief that the principle of the decision he made was absolutely valid. He was indifferent to death and to public opinion. Yes, I feel inner peace and freedom, not only because I am indifferent to the worldly pursuits such as fame, power, pleasure, knowledge, wealth, and health but especially because my life flows from the eternal fountain: The One. What is puzzling about this feeling is that the more the stream of my life flows from my heart, the more I love the world, the more I want to be a part of it. How can my life flow from me if its world does not flow into it? I feel the pulse of the world in my heart and the pulse of my heart in the world. A strange but delicious feeling took hold of my consciousness recently: I want to live in order to be able to kindle the love of life in the hearts of human beings; I want to open their eyes to the significance of love in their lives; and I want them to enjoy the meaning of true joy in their lives. This is the only thing that justifies my existence on this earth.

"I know I am boring you with this narrative, but I shall reveal to you one secret: A powerful, irresistible longing for The One has germinated in my heart. It grows in intensity every day I live! I want to spend every moment of my existence close to my source; I want to live on The Edge so I can be ready for a union with it. I examined this feeling to ascertain whether it arose from a selfish motive or from a kind of weakness or from fear of death. I discovered that it did not, but that it is a strong desire to grow in being, in perfection. The seams of my sense of being have been bursting in my heart. I want to empty myself in The One, and I want to return to the world, again and again, a richer person, so I can spread the light of truth and love in the hearts of my fellow human beings. This is my destiny; I cannot change it."

Father Sergios ended his confession with a frown on his forehead. He looked at us for a moment and then remarked: "I hope you accept the confession of a silly old man compassionately."

"Oh, no!" I said apologetically; but Kamal rose to his feet, moved closer to the monk, and kissed him on the forehead. Tears glittered in the monk's eyes under the light of the candle. "I wish I could have explained myself in more detail, but I know, Kamal, that you are constrained by a tight schedule."

"Yes, Father; it is getting late. I am, afraid we have to leave at dawn tomorrow."

"Yes, I understand. Are you prepared for the second part of your journey? The southern wind might blow in this direction any time now."

"Yes, so far as I know."

chapter 8

The Storm

When the rays of dawn greeted us the following morning, our breakfast was waiting for us. Father Sergios must have risen early and prepared a kind of farewell meal. It was delicious and wholesome. Soon after we ate, Kamal and the monk visited alone in the chapel for about twenty minutes. I took advantage of this lull, sat on a rock nearby, and watched the sun rising from the east. The earth was waiting for its graceful rays, for its warm embrace. A feeling of peace filled my heart. I wanted to expand it to its farthest possible limits and dwell in it forever, but unfortunately it did not last, because I heard Kamal's footsteps approaching. I left the rock and moved toward the monk, who was waiting for us. We stood face to face, smiled, and then embraced. Tears rushed to my eyes, but I did not let them see the light of day. Why should they speak when love united us with its flame?

    The van was parked in the same place when we reached the bottom of the mountain. The morning was still young. Soon after we started the engine, Kamal remarked that our trip back to Tadmur should be short and smooth. Then he wondered whether there was a particular historical or religious landmark I wanted to see before I returned to the U.S.A. "No," I answered, "not now; perhaps one day. I would like to explore the old cities, both dead and alive, in this whole region, but before I embark on this project, I should master the language of history and religion. I had learned to read the history of human civilization as a narrative, but I have discovered in this short adventure that I should learn to read the language of The Spirit in this history. I have a strong desire to feel it and see it with the eyes of my mind, if possible. And to confess, I would very much welcome the opportunity to pay a second visit to Father Sergios. His heart is a fountain of wisdom. I hope to be able to drink from it again. I want to explore in greater depth the philosophy of clothes. I know time is coursing against us!"

Kamal, whose eyes were glued to the road, remained silent. A few minutes later he said: "I hope you plan a second trip in the near future." The voice with which he conveyed this response was tense. It was not the confident, solemn voice I was used to. "Something must be wrong," I thought. I too directed the totality of my attention at the road. My concern was confirmed when we moved to the main road that led to Saada.

"The southern wind is moving in our direction. I think its arrival is imminent. From now on, I shall drive full speed. My plan is to avoid it, if possible. It is a most destructive wind, not only because it gusts like lightening and like a tsunami that sweeps everything in its way, but also because it carries with it tons upon tons of sand. It usually sweeps through the Syrian Desert in early autumn, but Father Sergios, who is proficient in the ways of the desert, warned me about its impending arrival." Kamal's fear was confirmed sooner than he or I thought. Within seconds, he was driving fast, very fast. Unfortunately the storm was racing with time! The sun was gradually fading and the van was hard to control. We were under the mercy of the wind. However, Kamal's strong hands kept the vehicle under control, but not for long, because clouds of sand were flying over in all directions. He tried to drive faster, but without success. Very soon, the road was covered with sand, and it was impossible to see the road or to drive on it. We were stuck, grounded. He looked at me with frightened eyes. He pulled his phone out of the glove compartment and spoke with someone in Arabic. Then he opened his door, with some difficulty, and left the van. I did the same. I looked around. The desert was transformed into an infinite ocean of sand. The scene my eyes grasped was alarming. The storm that had already subjugated the desert to its will was dumping heaps of sand everywhere. "We should remain inside the van," Kamal shouted. He was right, because the level of the accumulating sand was rising faster and faster. It was extremely difficult to open our doors again, but Kamal somehow managed to do so. We sat looking at each other and at the rising sand around the car. "Please, do not be afraid!" he said. "We shall be fine." He crawled to the back seat and brought some dates, peanuts, and walnuts. That was a small but nourishing lunch. I never dreamed that I would be imprisoned in a box, and I never thought or imagined what it is like for a prisoner to be locked up in a prison cell until that afternoon. The atmosphere in the van was becoming increasingly oppressive, because the heat was rising slowly. Kamal, who must have had a similar experience before, kept a cheerful face. Neither he nor I could speak. The level of the sand kept rising. It seemed that we were dug in and that there was no way to escape from this predicament. Frankly, I did not know what to say or even feel; I had never been in a situation like that ever! We remained watching our fate unfolding before our own eyes. "If you feel drowsy, allow yourself to doze off. This might help," Kamal said. Later on I discovered the wisdom of his advice. The factor that I overlooked was the possibility of suffocation. The amount of air in the van was limited and slowly shrinking; this fact escaped my attention. I cannot remember how long we stayed in that position, for we were enfolded by darkness sooner than I expected. I must have dozed off. Lack of oxygen and excessive heat put me to sleep.

When I opened my eyes again, Kamal was sitting next to my bed watching me. With him were a woman and two children, a boy and a girl. I was surprised, and I was mystified! I never expected to be in a family setting. I looked around me with blank eyes. My immediate reaction was: "Where am I? What happened? Who are these people?" Kamal's face evoked in me a feeling of safety, of warmth, of hope. I could not help myself, but my eyes looked at him inquiringly.

"I want you to meet my wife, Jamilé, my oldest son, Tareq, and my oldest daughter, Jasmine," he said. They greeted me with smiling faces.

"I am very pleased to meet you," my faint voice communicated. Before I asked about where I was or what happened to us, Jamilé said in English: "You must be famished!" Then she went to the kitchen and returned with a meal she had prepared. "Please, try the soup first!" They watched me with eager curiosity as I ate. When I finished eating, Kamal described to me how I fainted that afternoon and how we were rescued by the desert police that evening. Our van was drowned in a sea of sand. Luckily the outline of its top was visible. Kamal had already alerted his family about our general location and the state we were in. He was very weak and I was almost dead. Jamilé and her children were waiting for us when the ambulance brought us home. A son of the desert, Kamal recovered quickly; it took me a whole day to recover my rational faculty. Apparently, the suffocation episode I went through was severe. I stayed two days at Kamal's house in Tadmur. I was embraced by the warmest family I have ever met in my life. We visited the Tadmur Oasis and discussed a number of philosophical and religious questions; they were enlightening and life-enhancing discussions. But the most precious treasure I brought with me to Antioch was the spiritual light I received from the desert and its sons and daughters.

When I was in full command of my physical and mental faculties, I declared my interest in returning to the U.S.A. I wanted to take a taxi to Latakia, but Kamal insisted on driving me to Damascus airport. Jamilé and her children said good-bye to me; they kissed me on both cheeks. Tareq gave me a box that contained a beautiful statue of Queen Zenobia saying: "Please come back!" I embraced each one of them and said: "My home is yours. Tareq, think seriously about my proposal. It would be a good idea to continue your university education in the U.S.A." He smiled and said: "Yes, sir!"

They were waiving to me as the van was leaving their driveway. A breeze of warmth streamed through my heart. I felt the joy of inner peace. Both Kamal and I spoke very little on the way to Damascus. "We should pay a second visit to Father Sergios," he said as we embraced at the entrance of the airport.

"Yes, I hope so!"

Bibliography

Al-Ghazzali. *The Alchemy of Happiness*. Translated by Nabih Amin Faris. Lahore: Sh. Mohammad Ashraf, 1966.
Alexander, Samuel. *Space, Time, and Deity*. London: McMillan, 1920.
Applebaum, David. *Disruption*. Albany: SUNY Press, 1996.
Attar, Farid ud-Din. *Conference of the Birds*. Translated by C. S. Nott. London: Routledge and Kegan Paul, 1961.
Augustine, St. *Confessions*. Translated by Rex Warner. New York: The American Library, 1963.
Bamford, Christopher. *An Endless Trace: The Passionate Pursuit of Wisdom in the West*. Albany: SUNY Press, 2003.
Batchelor, Martine. *The Spirit of the Buddha*. New Haven: Yale University Press, 2010.
Bokenkamp, Stephen R. *Early Buddhist Scriptures*. Berkeley: University of California Press, 1999.
Brainard, F. Samuel. *Reality and Mystical Experience*. University Park: Pennsylvania State University, 2000.
Carter, John R. *In the Company of Friends*. Albany: SUNY Press, 2012.
Ch'en, Kenneth Kuan Sheng. *Buddhism in China*. Princeton: Princeton University Press, 1972.
Chisti, Amatullah Armstrong. *The Lamp of Love*. Oxford: Oxford University Press, 2006.
Chittick, William. *In Search of the Lost Heart*. Albany: SUNY Press, 2012.
Chodkiewicz, Michel. *An Ocean Without Shore*. Albany: SUNY Press, 1993.
Consolmagno, Guy. *Way to the Light*. Notre Dame: Notre Dame University Press, 1998.
Corbin, Henry. *Alone with the Alone*. Translated by Ralph Manheim. Princeton: Princeton University Press, 1998.
Danielou, Alain. *Yoga, the Method of Re-Integration*. London: Christopher Johnson, 1949.
Davies, Oliver, and Denys Turner, editors. *Silence and the World: Negative Theology and Incarnation*. Cambridge: Cambridge University Press, 2002.
De Bary, William Theodore, Wing-Tsit Chan, and Burton Watson. *Sources of Chinese Tradition*. New York: Columbia University Press, 1960.
De Unamuno, Miguel. *Treatise on Love of God*. Translated by Nelson R. Orringer. Urbana: University of Illinois Press, 2007.
Dunne, John S. *A Search for God in Time and Memory*. Notre Dame: Notre Dame University Press, 1977.
Eckhart, Meister. *Works of Meister Eckhart*. Translated by C. de B. Evans. London: John M. Watkins, 1924.
Eliade, Mercea. *The Quest*. Chicago: University of Chicago Press, 1969.

Bibliography

Esposito, John. *World Religions Today*. Oxford: Oxford University Press, 2011.
Fadiman, James, and Robert Frager, editors. *Sufism*. New York: Harper One, 1997.
Ferry, Luc. *Man Made God: The Meaning of Life*. Chicago: University of Chicago Press, 2002.
Franke, William, editor. *On What Cannot be Said: Apophatic Discourses in Philosophy, Religion, Literature, and the Arts*. Two volumes. Notre Dame: University of Notre Dame Press, 2007.
Gilson, Etienne. *God and Philosophy*. Second edition. New Haven: Yale University Press, 2002. Originally published in 1941 by the same publisher.
Glucklich, Ariel. *Sacred Pain: Hurting the Body for the Sake of the Soul*. Oxford: Oxford University Press, 2001.
Hafiz. *The Gift: Poems by Hafiz*. Translated by Daniel Ladinsky. New York: Penguin Books, 1999.
Hamilton, Edith, and Huntington Cairns. *The Collected Dialogues of Plato*. Bollingen Series 71 Princeton: Princeton University Press, 1961.
Happold, Frederick Crossfield. *Mysticism: A Study and an Anthology*. New York: Penguin Books, 1963.
Hartshorne, Charles, and William L. Reese, editors. *Philosophers Speak of God*. Chicago: University of Chicago Press, 1953.
Heine, Steven, and Dale S. Wright, editors. *The Zen Canon: Understanding the Classic Texts*. Oxford: Oxford University Press, 2004.
Helm, Paul. *Eternal God: A Study of God without Time*. Oxford: Oxford University Press, 2011.
Hollywood, Amy. *Sensible Ecstasy: Mysticism, Sexual Difference, and the Demands of History*. Chicago: University of Chicago Press, 2002.
Ibn Arabi, Muhyiddin. *What the Seeker Needs: Essays on Spiritual Practice, Oneness, Majesty and Beauty*. Translated by Tosun Bayrak and Rabia T. Harris. Putney: Threshold Books, 1992.
James, William. *The Varieties of Religious Experience*. New York: Barnes and Noble, 2004. Originally published in London: Longmans, Green & Co., 1902.
Kessler, Michael. *Mystics: Presence and Aporia*. Chicago: University of Chicago Press, 2003.
King, Sallie B. *Journey in Search of the Way*. Albany: SUNY Press, 1993.
Laozi. *Dao De Jing: The Book of the Way*. Translation and commentary by Moss Roberts. Berkeley: University of California Press, 2001.
Lorenzen, David N. *Praises to a Formless God*. Albany: SUNY Press, 1996.
Lubac, Henri Cardinal de. *Corpus Mysticum: The Eucharist and the Church in the Middle Ages*. Translated by Gemma Simmonds, Richard Price, and Christopher Stephens. Edited by Laurence Paul Hemming and Susan Frank Parsons. Notre Dame: University of Notre Dame Press, 2007.
Maimonides, Moses. *The Guide for the Perplexed*. Translated by Michael Friedländer. New York: Trubner and Co., 1885.
Massignon, Louis. *Hallaj: Mystic and Martyr*. Abridged edition. Edited and translated by Herbert Mason. Princeton: Princeton University Press, 1994.
McGinn, Bernard. *The Essential Writings of Chinese Mysticism*. New York: The Modern Library, 2006.
Netton, Ian Richard. *Islam, Christianity and the Mystic Journey: A Comparative Exploration*. Edinburgh: Edinburgh University Press, 2011.

Neville, Robert Cummings, editor. *Religious Truth*. Albany: SUNY Press, 2000.
Nugent, Christopher. *Mysticism, Death, and Dying*. Albany: SUNY Press, 1994.
Olson, Carl. *The Different Paths of Buddhism: A Narrative-Historical Introduction*. New Jersey: Rutgers University Press, 2005.
Otto, Rudolph. *West-östliche Mystik: Vergleich und Unterscheidung zur Wesensdeutung*. Gotha: Leopold Klotz Verlag, 1926. Translated into English by Bertha L. Bracey and Richenda C. Payne as *Mysticism East and West: A Comparative Analysis of the Nature of Mysticism*. New York: The Macmillan Company, 1932.
Papanikolaou, Aristotle. *Being With God: Trinity, Apophaticism, and Divine-Human Communion*. Notre Dame: University of Notre Dame Press, 2006.
Paper, Jordan D. *The Mystic Experience: A Descriptive and Comparative Analysis*. Albany: SUNY Press, 2004.
Peters, Francis Edward. *A Reader on Classical Islam*. Princeton: Princeton University Press, 1993.
Plotinus. *The Essential Plotinus*. Translated by Elmer O'Brien. Indianapolis: Hackett Publishing Company, 1964.
Prebisch, Charles S, editor. *Buddhism: A Modern Perspective*. University Park: Pennsylvania State University Press, 1975.
Proudfoot, Wayne. *Religious Experience*. Berkeley: University of California Press, 1985.
Pseudo-Dionysius. *The Divine Names; The Mystical Theology*. Translated by John D. Jones. Milwaukee: Marquette University Press, 1999.
Reinhold, Hans Ansgar, editor. *The Soul Afire: Revelations of the Mystics*. New York: Image Books, 1973.
Roy, Louis. *Mystical Consciousness: Western Perspectives and Dialogue with Japanese Thinkers*. Albany: SUNY Press, 2003.
Rue, Loyal. *Nature Is Enough: Religious Naturalism and the Meaning of Life*. Albany: SUNY Press, 2011.
Rumi, Jalal ad-Din Muhammad. *The Essential Rumi*. Translated by Coleman Barks. New York: Harper One, 1995.
Ruysbroeck, Jan van. *The Life of Contemplation of God*. Translated by Eric Colledge. London: Faber and Faber, 1953.
Sa'di. *The Gulistan, or, Rose Garden*. Translated by Edward Rehastek. London, Allen & Unwin, 1964.
Schweig, Graham M. *Dance of Divine Love: India's Classic Sacred Love Story: The Rasa Lila of Krishna*. Princeton: Princeton University Press, 2005.
Schweitzer, Albert. *Christianity and the Religions of the World*. Translated by Johanna Powers. New York: The Macmillan Company, 1923.
Shihadeh, Ayman, editor. *Sufism and Theology*. Edinburgh: Edinburgh University Press, 2007.
Silvers, Laury. *A Soaring Minaret: Abu Bakr al-Wasiti and the Rise of Baghdadi Sufism*. Albany: SUNY Press, 2010.
Smith, Huston. *The World's Religions*. New York: Harper One, 1991.
Smith, Margaret. *Rabi'a the Mystic and Her Fellow-Saints in Islam*. Cambridge: Cambridge University Press, 1928.
Smith, Richard J. *The I Ching: A Biography*. Princeton: Princeton University Press, 2012.
Staal, Frits. *Exploring Mysticism: A Methodological Essay*. Berkeley: University of California Press, 1975.
Stace, Walter Terence. *Mysticism and Philosophy*. Philadelphia: Lippincott, 1960.

Bibliography

Stepaniants, Marietta T. *Sufi Wisdom*. Albany: SUNY Press, 1994.
Streng, Frederick J. *Emptiness: A Study in Religious Meaning*. Nashville: Abingdon Press, 1967.
Taves, Ann. *Religious Experience Reconsidered: A Building-Block Approach to the Study of Religion and Other Special Things*. Princeton: Princeton University Press, 2010.
Taylor, Mark C. *Mystic Bones*. Chicago: University of Chicago Press, 2007.
Underhill, Evelyn. *Mysticism: A Study in the Nature and Development of Man's Spiritual Consciousness*. London: Methuen, 1911.
Wainwright, William J. *Mysticism: A Study of Its Nature, Cognitive Value, and Moral Implications*. Madison: University of Wisconsin Press, 1981.
Wildman, Wesley J. *Religious Philosophy as a Multidisciplinary Comparative Inquiry*. Albany: SUNY Press, 2010.
Wolfson, Elliot R. *Through a Speculum That Shines: Vision and Imagination in Medieval Jewish Mysticism*. Princeton: Princeton University Press, 1995.
Woods, Richard, editor. *Understanding Mysticism*. Garden City, N.Y.: Image Books, 1969.

www.ingramcontent.com/pod-product-compliance
Lightning Source LLC
Chambersburg PA
CBHW071442150426
43191CB00008B/1213